Matthew Phipps Shiel

The Yellow Danger

The Story of the World's Greatest War

Matthew Phipps Shiel

The Yellow Danger
The Story of the World's Greatest War

ISBN/EAN: 9783744711364

Printed in Europe, USA, Canada, Australia, Japan

Cover: Foto ©ninafisch / pixelio.de

More available books at **www.hansebooks.com**

THE YELLOW DANGER

THE STORY OF THE WORLD'S GREATEST WAR

BY

M. P. SHIEL

AUTHOR OF "THE MAN-STEALERS," "PRINCE ZALESKI," ETC.

BREVIS ESSE LABORO!
Messrs. Horace and Gibbon.

R. F. FENNO & COMPANY, 9 AND 11 EAST
SIXTEENTH STREET : NEW YORK CITY
LONDON — GRANT RICHARDS
1899

CHAPTER I

THE NATIONS AND A MAN

As all the world knows, the Children's Ball of the Lady Mayoress takes place yearly on the night of "Twelfth Day," 6th January. In the year '98 the function was even more successful than usual, owing to Sir Henry Burdett's fine idea that the children should be photographed in support of the Prince of Wales' Hospital Fund. The little Walter Raleighs, Amy Robsarts, flocked in throngs to the photographer's studio adjoining the grand *salon* of the Mansion House; while all that space outside between the Mansion House, the Bank, and the Stock Exchange was a mere mass of waiting, arriving, and departing vehicles.

If anything tended to take a little of their exuberance from this and other New Year jubilations, it was a certain cloudiness in the political sky; nothing very terrifying; yet something so real, that nearly every one felt it with disquiet. An Irish member, celebrated for his "bulls," was heard to say: "Take my word for it, there's going to be a sunset in the East." Men strolled into their clubs, and, with or without a yawn, said: "Is there going to be a row, then?" Some one might answer: "Not a bit of it; it'll pass off presently, you'll see." But another would be sure to add: "Things are looking black enough, all the same."

It was just as when, on a clear day at sea, low and jagged edges of disconnected clouds appear inkily on the horizon-edge, and no one is quite certain whether or not they will meet, and whelm the sky, and sink the ship.

But the horizon had hardly darkened, when again, it cleared. The principal cause of fear had been what had looked uncommonly like a conspiracy of the three great Continental Powers to oust England from predominance in the East. First there was the seizure of Kiao-Chau, the bombastic farewells of the German Royal brothers; then immediately, the aggressive attitude of Russia at Port Arthur; then immediately the rumor that France had seized Hainan, was sending an expedition to Yun-nan, and had ships in Hoi-How harbor.

All this had the look of concert; for within the last few years it had got to be more and more recognized by the British public that centuries of neighborhood had fostered among the Continental nations a certain spirit of kinship, in which the Island-Kingdom was no sharer.

In the course of years the Straits of Dover had widened into an ocean. Europe had receded from Britain, and Britain, in her pride, had drawn back from Europe. From the curl of the mustache, to the color and cut of the evening-dress, to the manner in which women held up their skirts, there was similarity between French and German, between German and Russian and Austrian, and dissimilarity between all these and English.

It is true that the Russian hated the German, and the German the Russian and the French; but their hatred was the hatred of brothers, always ready to combine against the outsider. This had been begun to be suspected, then recognized, by the British nation. Alone and friendless must England tread the winepress of modern history, solitary in her majesty; and if ever an attempt were made to stop her stately progress, she was prepared to find that her foe was the rest of Europe.

But very soon after the unrest had arisen, it began to subside. France denied the annexation of Hainan; the semi-official *Nord-deutsche Allgemeine Zeitung*, inspired by Wilhelm, painted Germany as the patron of commerce, with an amiable weakness for theatrical displays; Russia was defeated in the matter of the removal of Mr. MacLeavy Brown, and seemed sufficiently limp after it; while spirits were raised by the probable guarantee of a Chinese loan by the British Government.

But meanwhile, at the children's ball at the Mansion House, events were working in a quite different direction from that of peaceful settlement.

Ada Seward was the presiding deity in the nursery of Mrs. Pattison of Fulham. On the night of the 6th, Dr. and Mrs. Pattison had to be present at a ball in the West End, and Ada on that night was busy; for it was necessary for her, first of all, to convey Master Johnnie Pattison, costumed as Francis I., to the Mansion House; and then to hurry homeward again to take Miss Nellie Pattison to a children's evening with charades in South Kensington.

The fact that it was wet when she reached the Mansion House may have had something to do with her troubles. The landing-place was occupied by some other carriages, and dismounting with her charge, an umbrella over him, she cried to the coachman in a hurried manner through the drizzle:

"Wait till I come back."

The man afterwards declared that he understood her to say:

"Go away, and come back."

At any rate, when Ada again came forth into the crush to look for the Pattison brougham, it was nowhere to be found.

And now her lips went up in a pout of vexation. "What on earth is any one to do now?" she said. She was pressed for time, and yet at a loss.

The throng of private carriages seemed to have banished all cabs from the region of the Mansion House. She looked and saw none; then into her pocket, and found only sixpence. These two circumstances decided her against the cab. Instead, she ran a few yards, dodging among the carriages, and at the entrance to Poultry, skipped into a moving 'bus.

She sat in a corner for five minutes, with agonized glances out of the door at the slowly receding clocks. Then some one—a man sitting nearly opposite, whom she had not noticed—addressed her:

"Why, Miss Ada, is that you?"
"Oh!" she cried, "Mr. Brabant, is that you? It's a long time since—how are you?"
"Well, I'm pretty fair, Miss Ada, as times go, you know. Hope you are the same."
"Still in the army?"
"Oh yes—the Duke of Cambridge's Own, you know. You living in London now?"
"Yes—at Fulham."

Here conversation flagged; and in that minute's interval, Brabant, with a sudden half-turn to his left, said:

"Just allow me to introduce you to my friend here —Miss Seward—Dr. Yen How."

In the light of the 'bus lamp Ada Seward saw a very small man, dressed in European clothes, yet a man whom she at once took to be Chinese. With a wrinkled grin, he put out his hand and shook hers.

He was a man of remarkable visage. When his hat was off, one saw that he was nearly bald, and that his expanse of brow was majestic. There was something brooding, meditative, in the meaning of his long eyes; and there was a brown, and dark, and specially dirty shade in the yellow tan of his skin.

He was not really a Chinaman—or rather, he was that, and more. He was the son of a Japanese father by a Chinese woman. He combined these antagonistic races in one man. In Dr. Yen How was the East.

He was of noble feudal descent, and at Tokio, but for his Chinese blood, would have been styled Count. Not that the admixture of blood was very visible in his appearance; in China he passed for a Chinese, and in Japan for a Jap.

If ever man was cosmopolitan, that man was Dr. Yen How. No European could be more familiar with the minutiæ of Western civilization. His degree of doctor he had obtained at the University of Heidelberg; for years he had practised as a specialist in the diseases of women and children at San Francisco.

He possessed an income of a thousand tael (about £300) from a tea-farm; but his life had been passed in the practise of the grinding industry of a slave. Nothing equaled his assiduity, his minuteness, his attention to detail. He had once written to the Royal Observatory at the Cape pointing out a trifling error in a long logarithmic calculation of the declension of one of the moons of Jupiter, originating from the observatory.

In the East he could have climbed at once to the very top of the tree—Even in the West, had he chosen. But he chose to lie low, remaining unnoticed, studying, observing, making of himself an epitome of the West, as he was an embodiment of the East.

In whatever country he happened to be—and he was never for many years in any one—he was most often to be found in the company of people of the lower classes; and of these he had a very intimate knowledge. So great was his mental breadth, that he was unable to sympathize with either Eastern or Western distinctions of class and rank. He often struck up chance friendships with soldiers and sailors about the capitals of Europe; and these patronized and exhibited him here and there.

Yen How knew that he was being patronized, and submitted to it—and smiled meekly. In reality, he cherished a secret and bitter aversion to the white race.

He had two defects—his shortness of sight, which caused him to wear spectacles; and his inability, in speaking without effort, to pronounce the word "little." He still called it "lillee."

On that date of 6th January, when he drove westward with Brabant and Ada Seward, he was perhaps forty years of age, but seemed anything between sixteen and sixty; a hard, omniscient, cosmopolitan little man, tough as oak, dry as chips.

Yet in that head were leavening some big thoughts; and his heart was capable of tremendous passions.

In reality, could one have known it, as he fared onward through the drizzle in the trundling 'bus, smiling behind his spectacles, he was the most important personage in London, or perhaps in the world.

Dr. Yen How was capable of anything. In him was

the Stoic, and the cynic, and the tiger; with a turn of the mind he could become a *savant*, or a statesman, or a crossing-sweeper, or a general. He possessed this excellence: a clear brain.

By one of those extraordinary freaks of nature for which there is no accounting, this man wanted to see Ada Seward a second time after parting with her that night.

Brabant, who had known her in her native town of Cheltenham, accompanied her to the gate of the Pattison villa, Yen How with them.

As he was leaving her, the little doctor put his mouth to her ear, and whispered hurriedly:

"I will wait here to-morrow night at eight for *one lillee kiss*."

The girl was astounded.

"Well, the idea!" she just gasped.

Before she could proclaim her indignation, the two men turned off.

Till he reached his home in Portland Street, Yen How was engaged in one long, continuous, secret smile—a smile at his own expense. This outburst of his in the rôle of lover was new to him, absolutely. His relations with women hitherto had consisted in the business of curing their sicknesses. By what subtle physiological or psychological affinity this one particular English girl had been able to evoke from this particular dry Chino-Japanese a request for "one lillee kiss," he was unable to divine. Such an affinity there undoubtedly was; but its origin lay among reasons far too abstruse for the unraveling of Yen.

Yen How smiled that first night, but he presently found that this was no smiling matter.

At eight the next evening he was duly at the Pattison gate; but, alas, no Ada was to be seen. Ada, however, was there, though invisible. She, with the Pattison cook, whom she had brought out to enjoy the fun, was hiding behind a shrubbery, and peering through, shaking with laughter at the futile waiting of the little doctor.

And now Yen How, for the first time in his life, began to suffer on account of a woman.

He loved; and in his love was the concentrated passion of many other men. Melted rock is lava—and he suffered.

He used at night to hang about the house, which was lonely at that hour, waiting. To his patience there was no end—to his resolution to possess her, by fair means or foul, no end.

Even in the matter of love the Eastern is essentially different from the Western. It is impossible for us, in anything, to understand them, so foreign are they. With us love is frequent, a powerful mood; with them the whole man is involved, and love becomes a passion having all the characteristics of ordinary flame.

One night, as he lurked about, he met her returning from some shopping. By this time Yen How had become a standing joke for Ada in the kitchen and the servants' bedroom. He walked to her.

"Ah," he said with sideward head, and a cajoling smile, "you are here, then? You will give poor Yen How one lillee kiss?"

The whole idea of courtship possessed by this clownish and unpractised lover consisted in asking for one little kiss. Ada Seward's views of the matter were more elaborate. She despised his strong simplicity.

"Perhaps you are not aware whom it is you are talking to," she said.

Yen was aware; he could have shut his eyes and drawn an exact picture of her face.

"Ah," he said, "not even one lillee——"

"I'll give you one lillee box of soap to wash your face, if you like!" she cried, running and looking back. The house was near; he could not overtake her.

Perhaps it would have been impossible for Miss Seward to utter words more calculated to drive Yen to madness than this reference to "soap." If his suit was hopeless, it was now borne in upon him that it was hopeless on account of his race. The girl did not listen to him, and reject him; she rejected him without taking him into consideration at all. It was as though a mule, or a cat, had asked her to be his.

But his persistence did not fail. He flung his other

pursuits to the wind, and the Pattison villa became for him the center of the world. Sometimes he caught bright glimpses of her. Once again he met her in the street, and once again she overwhelmed him with jeers. So passed January, February, and March.

To Yen How, the *bourgeois*, the thought never at all occurred that the girl was below *bourgeois* class. He was a great man, and merely saw in Ada the eternal woman. Dukes marry duchesses; but the Goethes, the Mahomets, wed cooks and water-carriers. On that very plan was built Yen How.

At the beginning of April he stood one night outside the Pattison gate, when he saw her. It was eleven o'clock; she was coming from the theater, leaning on the arm of Private Brabant. Brabant, since their meeting in the 'bus, had several times been "out" with her.

As the two approached, Ada saw the little doctor.

"There's that little Chinaman again, John," she said, pressing Brabant's arm. "It's getting too much of a good thing now, isn't it?"

"Confound the little rat," said Brabant; "he wants his nut cracked, I should think, doesn't he?"

The doctor tripped up to them, smiling nervously. Before he could speak, Brabant, who had had a glass, said:

"Come, come, Mr. Yen How, get out of this. Can't you see the young lady doesn't want you fooling round her?"

"Well—but—my soldier friend," said Yen, "there is no harm done——"

"Come, get out of it!" said Brabant more roughly.

"No, no, you go too fast, you see," began Yen apologetically.

"Are you going—yes or no!" said Brabrant, now flushing angrily.

"Go away, why don't you?" put in Ada.

"Ah! I—I am here to see my lillee girl," hazarded Yen.

"Oh, don't be a stupid little goose of a Chinaman! Just fancy!" she said.

This was the most unkindest cut of all for Yen. He winced, touched with anger.

"Are you going or not?" said Brabant, an ultimatum in his tone.

"No," said Yen; then, more decidedly, "no, no!"

Brabant put out his arm and pushed him on the shoulder.

It was not a violent push, but in an instant the doctor's face was almost black with rage. He had in his hand a stout bamboo stick, which he at once lifted and slashed with terrible force across the soldier's cheek, leaving a bruised weal which Brabant bore with him to the grave.

In retaliation the soldier lifted his large and bony fist, and sent it into the doctor's face. Yen How dropped.

The street was deserted. Not knowing what to do, the girl and the soldier bent over him for five minutes, when, to their surprise, Yen How raised himself slowly, placed his handkerchief against his red and dripping face, and slowly limped away without a single word.

Once he stopped deliberately as he moved off, turned, and looked at them; and in the moonlight they distinctly saw him twice shake his forefinger warningly in their direction.

Then he went on his way.

Between that night and the beginning of May he never once stepped outside the house in which he lived. He had resumed his close and far-reaching studies.

At the beginning of May he was on board the *Peninsular*, bound for the East.

By the end of September he was a member of the Japanese Parliament.

In December we find him a leading spirit in the Tsung-li-Yamen, or Chinese Foreign Office, and making voyages between Tokio and Pekin.

CHAPTER II

THE HEATHEN CHINEE

YEN HOW was nothing if not heathen. He was that first of all.

His intellect was like dry ice. Though often secretly engaged in making *The Guess*, on the whole, he despised all religions—the faiths of the West, the superstitions of the East, he despised them all alike. He was full of light, but without a hint of warmth; and so lacked the religious emotion.

It is not likely that ordinary ethical considerations would much influence the aims of such a man. He was like an avalanche, as cold, and as resistless.

What was Dr. Yen How's aim? Simply told, it was to possess one white woman, ultimately, and after all. He had also the subsidiary aim of doing an ill turn to all the other white women, and men, in the world.

If the earth had opened and swallowed him, then he would have renounced his hope; but for no lesser reason. He went coolly and patiently to work to secure his desire.

But no man, surely, ever employed means so huge to an end so small. A European, perhaps any other man, having once conceived the means, would quickly have forgotten the end in the tremendous interest of the means themselves. But in all that Yen did the face of Ada Seward was always consciously "before his eyes." The nature of this man was as simple as the elemental rock.

His career in the East, from the first hour of his return, was meteoric. He rose like a rocket. The order of the day in China, and especially in Japan, was Western modernity; and here was a man who simply breathed Western modernity, and who yet was an Eastern of the Easterns. His skin was more yellow than the yellow man's, and his brain was more white than the white man's. When the English Inspector-General of Roads and Bridges at Tokio asserted that the Imperial tax in Britain on railway passenger traffic was, he believed, £3 per cent, Yen How's face wrinkled into a chaos of smiles. "No—two," he said quietly; and no one doubted which was right. Yen introduced a new method of protecting bridges during the daily earthquakes of Japan, by means of articulated joists and sleepers. When the Naval Director at Pekin introduced a specification for a new battle-ship to be mounted with two 111-ton guns, Yen proved by statistics (which he quoted from memory) that the tendency of the most modern shipbuilding was rather in the direction of quick-firing guns than of heavy armaments. The 111-ton became 45-ton. He was soon invaluable.

At this time the people of Japan were strongly excited against the freebooting of Russia and Germany in China, and strongly animated in favor of England. England was, in fact, the beau-ideal, the Great Pattern, of Japan. It required no great force of imagination for her to call herself "the Britain of the East"; this notion at once occurred, of itself, to every one; and, of course, the copyist sympathized with her original rather than with others. With England predominant in China, moreover, there would be an assurance of free trade; and Japan was a trader. So strong was the enthusiasm in favor of England, that the nation was even willing to put its fleet at the disposal of its Big Model in case of need.

The ulterior purposes of Japan, of course, remained in doubt. She was even then building in various parts of the world an additional fleet, which, when finished, would make her a sea Power far in advance of any nation in the whole earth, with the exception of England herself. What in the hour of her manhood, when she had cast her leading-strings, she would do with this vast force was a disturbing question to many; but, meanwhile, it was clearly her intention to use England as an ally—till the years ripened.

Under the Marquis Ito's Ministry Yen How was offered a post of Under-Secretary, but he refused it. He suggested that he should become Secretary to the Minister as his private servant; and this was arranged. He knew that high public rank in Japan would exclude him from high public rank in China, if his double personality should become known—and China was the chief field of his labors. Meanwhile, he was drawing large revenues as a mandarin, and lived, for his own purposes, in a style nearly princely.

"Poh!" he said to the Marquis Ito, sipping tea among rugs, "there are no statesmen now. Statesmen!—there are no such things. Not here—not in Europe. An ordinary man is a man who thinks in days; a statesman proper thinks in thousands of years. The outlook and computations of a statesman should be as much vaster than those of a private person, as a country is vaster than a tea-house. Believe me, there are no statesmen."

"Come, doctor, why do you say that?" asked the Marquis.

"Look forward five hundred, a thousand years, Marquis, and what do you see?" answered Yen How. 'Is it not this?—the white man and the yellow man in their death-grip, contending for the earth. The white and the yellow—there are no others. The black is the slave of both; the brown does not count. But there are those two; and when the day comes that they stand face to face in dreadful hate, saying, 'One or other must quit this earth,' shall I tell you which side will win?"

"Which do you think?"

"The white will win, Marquis."

"Perhaps I differ from you," said the Marquis Ito.

"Ah! you differ from me. But I am right all the same; and I mean, sooner or later, to prove it to you abundantly, abundantly! The white will win, I tell you! You great men in Japan are trying to copy them, straining your poor necks to come up with them; but

I have passed my life in studying them—and I've got something to tell you ; listen to it : you cannot, Marquis, you cannot, you cannot !"

"Our Navy already——" began the Marquis.

"Poh ! your Navy ! Who built it for you ? It was they. Your Navy is like a razor in the hands of an ape which has seen its master use it. The brute may or may not cut its own throat with it. And as soon as they build a navy for you, they will build one twice as big for themselves, and twice as good. There is no reason why you should not follow them, and go on following them—only understand that *you cannot catch them !* And this is another thing that you should understand —that the longer you follow them, the farther they get away from you. Their *rate* of progress is continually increasing. Every day that passes over the world gives them an additional advantage over you. To-day their guns can mow you down by hundreds; in a hundred years they will mow you down by thousands; in five hundred years by millions. Can't you see ?—you are losing time !"

"What *do* you mean ? "

"Ah, I mean that there are no longer any statesmen, Marquis. The eye of the statesman ranges far, far into the tracts of the future, doesn't it ? But we ! Here are we now—we Japanese, we Chinese, we yellow men—playing about in little diplomatic mud-puddles with French, and Russian, and English and German, as if all that mattered two sen ! And all the time we know well, yet seem not to know, that French, and English, and the rest, are equally our foe, and tyrant, and vulture, one not more than the other ! That if we do not eat them all now, at once, they all will swallow us whole some day, soon—soon. And to see China fighting with Japan in such a case, and Japan banging into China—is it not childish enough to make a donkey, or even a Grand Lama, laugh ? There are no statesmen any longer, Marquis."

"Well, come, I see something in what you are driving at," said Ito. " We and China are like two birds pecking at each other on a bough, when suddenly they are both down the belly of a serpent, which has been calmly watching them. Well, but what are we to do? By your own showing, the birds can do nothing against the serpent."

"Did I say that?" asked Yen, lifting his eyebrows in innocent surprise. "Oh, I didn't mean it! There are many birds, you see, and few serpents. In the world to-day there are 408,000,000 Christians and—mark the figures—1,004,000,000 non-Christians. I can see that you are startled."

"You think that by sheer force of numbers——"

"Yes, if we had taken our opportunity in time—if we had struck two hundred—a hundred years ago. Even to-day I believe that it is hardly too late, if the yellow race can find a great leader. I am perfectly sure that in a hundred years' time it *will* be too late."

"Why so?"

"I have told you. By that time the white man will have something like a magician's power over all nature. He will say to the mountains and the seas: 'Be removed!'—and at his mere whisper they will obey him. We yellow men, too, will have advanced, but they will have vastly outstripped us. We *cannot* follow them, I tell you. The day will come when our mere numbers will no longer be of any importance in balking and overthrowing them."

"You talk of big things, my friend," said Ito. "Are you serious?"

"Yes, Marquis, I am serious."

"You advocate a League of the yellow races?"

"I do."

"He! he! the idea tickles me; it is so very far from realization—there are so many obstacles——"

"No, really—I think not. I believe it is very near to realization. Events are at this moment in progress at Pekin which will *force* it to accomplishment—soon. Suppose I tell you that I, personally, have laid those events in train?"

"You, doctor? What, are you going to lead us all, then, against Paris and London? He! he!"

"Perhaps, Marquis."

"What, to face the Nordenfeldts, and the Maxims, and the Krupps? The Chinese will run from the first twelve-pounder!"

"*There may not be any twelve-pounders there when they get to Paris and London,*" said Yen How with absolute coolness, yet with an emphasis and an intonation of solemnity in his voice which held the Marquis from answer for a minute.

"Really, I don't understand you," he said at last.

"Yet my meaning should be clear."

"No—do explain yourself."

Yen How rose to his feet before he answered.

"Marquis," he said, "is it possible you do not see that China has it in her power to turn Europe into an exhausted waste within, say, three months from to-night, without firing a single shot, or spending a single tael?"

CHAPTER III

RUMORS OF WAR

As the year wore on, some of the International difficulties centering round Kiao-Chau, Port Arthur, and Hainan reopened. In England more than all the old unrest revived.

What added to this unrest was the fact that some of the items of the rapidly-succeeding batches of news were quite inexplicable.

From the beginning of the year it had been known that Germany had not made so brilliant a bargain in the acquisition of Kiao-Chau as she had imagined. The territory placed under her "sovereign rights" had been strictly limited by China, and granted only as a "lease." When Prince Henry of Prussia arrived with the *Deutschland* and *Gefion,* he found that there were no "laurels" to win, and nobody at whom to strike out with his absurd mailed fist.

Moreover, on much the same terms as Germany obtained Kiao-Chau, and, later in the year, Russia obtained Port Arthur, Britain obtained Wei-hai-Wei and Mirs Bay.

What, then, was the surprise of the world, including the Germans themselves, when, in the middle of December, came the news that China had ceded a large additional region to the Kaiser, absolutely without conditions !

There was not a single brain in Europe which could divine the motive of this virtual gift.

At this time Li Hung Chang, recalled to power by the Emperor at the beginning of the year, was still at the head of affairs in Pekin. But in the short space of two months he had acquired the habit of taking no step without the suggestion of the new element in Chinese politics, the far-seeing Oriental-European, the much-toiling member of the Tsung-li-Yamen, the omniscient Yen How. Already Yen had swung himself into the position of the virtual ruler of China.

Yen How seemed to Li Hung Chang, haunted as the old statesman had always been by the vision of dismemberment and downfall which overhung China, something like an angel of light. Here was another brain which saw as his had all along seen—only far more clearly, and with powers of invention far vaster to avert the catastrophe.

"Let us be definite," Yen had said, in words which old Li long remembered, one night as they smoked together alone on a moonlit veranda. "Do let us be honest with ourselves, your Excellency! You agree with me that the yellow man is doomed—if the white man is not; in your heart you think it. Then let us say it in definite words; for as soon as ever we have *said* it, we have gone half-way toward grappling with our fate."

"Ah, I have said it often and often," answered Li, "but to what good?"

"If you believe that now is the time for action, as I do, you have the matter in your own hand."

"How so?"

"To me it is clearer than the moonlight there. The facts of the situation seem to stare me in the face."

"Speak, Yen How."

"I will speak, your Excellency. To me it seems that if we could supply a motive to the combined Japanese and Chinese nations to traverse Asia and the Caucasus, and then to overrun the Europe of to-day, there is no power on earth that could permanently check the overwhelming momentum of their progress."

"It is nonsense, my son," said Li, with a pull at his long pipe.

"Note this," replied Yen—"I only say that I *believe* —for who can be sure? The white man is strong and stern; his frown is dreadful. I only say that I *believe* —though a host of four hundred millions cannot be mown down in a day, your Excellency. The throats of the Maxims might grow hoarse and burst at this task. Still, perhaps you are right—perhaps I talk nonsense. I did not seriously mean to propose a march against the Maxim thunder. But I have a thought—a thought. Suppose China and Japan can take away the Maxims *first*, and then march afterwards."

"Speak your meaning, Yen How," said Li; "all is dark to me."

"We wish the white races killed," answered Yen; "well, there are two ways, are there not? We might kill them ourselves—that, you say, is nonsense. The other way is to get them to kill one another."

Li's pipe came from his mouth, and the outer corners of his eyes screwed up into an expression of the most exquisite enjoyment.

"What is left alive of them after their mutual slaughter," Yen How went on, "*we* can kill. Their lands will be weak with loss of blood, their treasures will be exhausted—there will be no Maxims there any more."

At these last words his own eyes, too, wrinkled up into delicious merriment.

"The trump card is in the hand of China," he said.

How the white races were to be made to destroy one another Li never asked, though the conversation lasted far into the night. He knew well. That, at least, was simple.

"England," said Yen as they parted, "she is the worst. All the others against *her*."

A few weeks afterwards the cession of large additional territories in China to Germany was rumored.

And now followed, in rapid succession, a series of the most startling, the most inexplicable reports.

It seemed as if China was not waiting for dismemberment from abroad, but was dismembering herself wilfully, with precipitate frenzy.

First came the intelligence that France had been besought by the Chinese Government to assume the Protectorate, without conditions, of Hainan and Yun-nan.

These few lines of telegram threw Europe into a state

of fever. It was decided by every one that, if the intelligence was true, no earthly consideration of risk would keep the rapacious hand of the Frenchman from grasping at this plum.

In a week or so it was definitely known that the news was true, and that France had accepted the offer. Rumors of war filled the air. The world was agog, and every spot was an arena for discussion. Only one man was silent—the British Foreign Secretary. The newspapers besought him for a word; he remained wrapped in taciturnity. A deputation of merchants waited upon the Under-Secretary; he answered only with a few strong words of hope.

At this time Yen How's name got into the papers. It was said that this mysterious man, whose dazzling rise in the Celestial Empire was sketched, had recently taken a fresh journey to Tokio. Then a vague telegram, printed in England in small nonpareil type, appeared, stating that the probable object of Yen How's renewed journey was to conclude a secret treaty between China and Japan. But the report was unsubstantiated.

The real bomb was yet to burst into the midst of Europe. It was hurled by the St. Petersburg correspondent of the *Daily News*.

China had offered to Russia the protectorate of the Yangtse Valley.

It was now, for the first time, that it entered two or three of the shrewdest heads in Europe that China was deliberately seeking to plunge the world into war by working upon the rapacity and selfish greed of the nations.

One gentleman, living at a country-house in Hampshire, wrote to the *Times* to this effect. But his letter attracted no attention.

Yet, looking back now, it seems strange that the idea did not occur to others. For it must be remembered that the Yangtse Valley had been regarded as peculiarly the sphere of English power. More than this, England had now partly guaranteed a Chinese loan of twelve millions sterling, and it was agreed that the security for this should consist of the land-tax and the unpledged part of the Customs dues. Now, the chief source of both land-tax and Customs dues was the Yangtse Valley.

Yet the next day the Russian *Novosti* published an inspired article, stating that on no account could Russia withdraw from the prominent place into which events had forced her in the East.

The feeling in England was one of horror at the blind and criminal cupidity of the Continental nations. The word "war" was on every tongue. Twice in one day there were hurried meetings of the Cabinet. Thousands of private letters poured in upon the Foreign Office, urging patience and firmness.

But the hand of the Government was forced in an unexpected manner.

Two items of news followed each other rapidly.

First, that on the 21st day of the 12th moon of the 24th year of Kuang Hsü—that is to say, on the 14th December 1898—the Yellow Jacket had once more been taken from Li Hung Chang ; and that the dominant talents of the man, Yen How, had triumphed over all obstacles, and raised him to the very head of affairs at the Court of Pekin.

The next day a telegram from Sir C. M. Macdonald, the British Minister in China, reached the Foreign Office. This was at once made public.

It stated that China professed herself unable to meet the next accruing interest-instalment on the loan, though the Minister had information from Sir Robert Hart, the Controller of the Imperial Maritime Customs, which led him to doubt the avowal of inability.

Whatever else this might mean, it certainly seemed to mean war. The security for China's default, real or pretended, which was due to England, had already been placed under the control of Russia.

In the House of Commons the Under-Secretary stated that there was still a hope of peace—a hope that "the Empire of Russia would act with that spirit of fairness and magnanimity in this crisis which alone could prove her worthy of her great traditions." These words were borne at a run by dozens of excited members to in-

Rumors of War

terested individuals among the crowd which surrounded the House from Westminster Bridge round to the Aquarium.

London went to sleep with some degree of quietude that night, Mr. Curzon's reply having been published in an eagerly bought-up 10 o'clock edition.

But the next morning, Mr. Goschen being abroad at an early hour, it was suddenly discovered that, by some extraordinary means, Malta was telegraphically isolated from England; and a hurried telegram was at once despatched from the Admiralty to Admiral Sir Michael Culme-Seymour, the Flag-Officer in Commission at Portsmouth.

CHAPTER IV

FIRST BLOOD

BEFORE eleven o'clock the *Majestic*, the flag-ship of the Channel Squadron, was leaving Portsmouth harbor behind her at the rate of ten knots. She was under the command of the senior officer in command of the squadron, Vice-Admiral Sir Henry Stephenson, and with her went the little gunboat *Halcyon*.

The mystery underlying the sudden journey of this couple was not difficult to unravel. The truth was, the Government was greatly startled by the event of the morning. The *Majestic* was, in reality, a convoy to the *Halcyon*; the smaller vessel was acting as a despatch-boat to Malta, and the battle-ship was seeing her on her journey till she was deemed to be out of danger of molestation.

It had come to that already.

At the Government offices the words "treachery" and "war" had risen to more than one agitated lip. Europe, it was felt, was drifting, drifting—whither?

The task of the *Halcyon* was to warn the Governor of Malta, and to order the mobilization of the Mediterranean Fleet near the Straits of Gibraltar. It might be necessary at a few hours' notice to block the entrance of the Mediterranean; it might even be necessary to hurl back a foreign invader from the shores of England, and the Channel Squadron was wofully limited in weight of metal.

During the day business in London came practically to a standstill. Wholesale withdrawals of foreign securities were reported from the City. By 3 P. M. it was generally known that a military *attaché* to the Embassy at Paris had arrived by private yacht with a sealed despatch from Sir E. J. Monson, and had hurried to the Foreign Office.

A day of almost breathless tension reached its climax when, at 9 P. M., Mr. Curzon made the announcement to a full House that peaceful negotiations were still in progress with Russia, but that, late in the afternoon, Germany had made demands of England and China with respect to the recently-ceded territories, with which England, as he might say at once, would certainly be unable to comply.

The next morning, before break of day, England found herself telegraphically disconnected with the Continent.

About this precise hour, the *Majestic*, having her small companion some half a mile or more away on her starboard quarter, was butting her way about S. by W. through a rough Biscay sea. It was a cold and squally morning, still dark, though a chill hint of day now mingled bleakly with the East. The sea was handling both ships rudely, and the *Majestic's* ponderous lurching through some six or seven degrees brought the acrid green sea washing about the base of her forward barbette, while from the bows of the *Halcyon* it went hissing aft in a continuous rain of spray.

It was just after five bells in the morning watch, at an hour when the gloomy gray of the morning had lightened a little, that the lookout man of the *Majestic* reported a big ship astern steaming leisurely south about seven miles away. The rate of the *Majestic* was ten knots, that of the stranger about six; but immediately after her coming into sight, a black cloud of redundant smoke revealed the stranger's will to improve her pace.

That she had been lurking about with some object of search was clear. That she was now getting up steam seemed to indicate, if anything, that she had found what she was looking for.

In a few minutes it was made out that she was *La Gloire*, a French battleship of about the weight and armature of the *Majestic*.

La Gloire's cloud of smoke was premature—it occasioned a suspicion of her motives. The first thing which Sir Henry Stephenson did was to order the *Halcyon* by trumpet-call to steam at full speed S. W. a distant of six miles. The *Halcyon*, at all events, had to be kept out of danger.

Yet he could hardly have expressed his reason for giving this order. Was any one at war with any one? He was ignorant of the fact, if so.

He was not long in doubt. *La Gloire*, even while getting up steam, had pricked off her course three points to starboard. It seemed as if she was about to give chase to the *Halcyon*.

"What! Are we in for a fight then, Captain?" said the Vice-Admiral with a smile of surprise, and a puckered brow.

"It almost looks like it, certainly," replied Fleet-Captain Hardy.

"Well, come now, we shall see," said the Vice-Admiral.

By this time *La Gloire* had not only hoisted her colors but had extra colors on masts and stays. The *Majestic* wore the ordinary single ensign.

Captain Hardy had ordered steam for full speed. The next moment the *Majestic* swung round to starboard about six points. She was still ahead of *La Gloire*. At her present course and speed she would interpose between the English gunboat and the French ship.

For quite half an hour the two ships continued to approach each other slowly and obliquely, having started from a separating interval of about five miles. On this course the sea was more aft, and the rolling and sullen plunging of the ships less marked.

On board the *Majestic*, meanwhile, all was bustling action. Decks were cleared, magazines were opened, ammunition and projectiles got out; water-tight doors were closed. The dawn lightened to a chill and drear twilight.

The real object of *La Gloire* was to intercept and capture any despatch-boat from the Channel, which might attempt to take intelligence through the Straits.

First Blood

The sending out of the battle-ship with such an object was, however, a breach of international law, and an act of treachery; for no one had declared war against England, though declarations of hostilities were already in the *bureaux* of more than one of the ambassadors at London.

That the despatch-boat should be convoyed, and by a first-class battle-ship, was unexpected. *La Gloire* found herself checkmated. There before her lay her prize; but between her and it was the thunder and lightning of England.

But, though checkmated, she showed no intention of being checked. She kept on her way with rising speed. The two ships, in malign silence, like two red-eyed planets rushing to jarring combat, drew nearer. When their speed had increased to thirteen knots, they were about two miles apart. Decks on both were cleared, collision-mats were ready, preparations were made for rigging torpedo-nets in an emergency. Nearer, in awful silence, they drew, two giants with limbs oiled for battle; and the bleak and raw sea-wind of the dawning made hoarse sounds above their funnels.

But one of the ships was still in doubt whether there was to be fighting, and, if so, why. There was a brief consultation on board the *Majestic*, and then she signaled:

"Are we combatants?"

There was no reply.

To this silence the *Majestic* sent aloft the answer: "Trafalgar."

And now the baleful silence recommenced. Both commanders had stationed themselves in their conning-towers. On either ship not a soul was to be made out by the glasses save the crews of the quick-firing guns on the hurricane decks, and of the machine-guns on the tops. By five minutes past seven the fleet-engineer of the *Majestic* announced that he had steam enough to drive the vessel at her utmost trial speed.

The strategy of the French commander in not answering the *Majestic's* question was soon apparent, for

Sir Henry Stephenson felt himself bound to wait for the first shot, being uncertain how matters stood on shore. And the first shot in modern naval warfare must often mean victory.

The two vessels slowly converged, *La Gloire* on the other's starboard side, steering S. by E. ; the *Majestic* on the other's port bows, heading S. by W. Suddenly *La Gloire* sharply altered her course by several points to the eastward, and impetuously bore down upon the *Majestic*.

"Well," said Sir Henry Stephenson to himself, "that is uncommonly like an act of hostility. Well, then, Mr. Frenchman——"

Immediately the *Majestic*, too, pricked off eastward, her after-pair of 67-ton guns being kept trained on the enemy as she maneuvered. The ships were now so well within effective range that the *Majestic's* thin smoke, blown into a wide hovering fog by the east wind, half concealed her movement from *La Gloire*.

For a time it seemed as if the British ship were in retreat, and the French giving chase ; then suddenly both ships were hidden from each other. Sir Henry, taking advantage of his windward position, had thrown overboard some twenty casks of smoke-producing tow and naphtha and tar, which at once separated the two ships with a blackness of thick brown reek, mingled near the water with bickering tongues of flame. The commander of *La Gloire*, fearing that in this fog of fume the *Majestic* might suddenly turn about and ram him, at once changed his course southwest, and was immediately the retreating ship. The English admiral had guessed his thought, and when the region of the smoke-making composition was passed, the beam of the *Majestic* was abreast of *La Gloire's* poop.

It was the lieutenant in charge of the fore-barbette of the *Majestic* who first woke the thunder of this winter-morning tragedy.

Simultaneously, with one bang of wrath that shook the *Majestic* herself from stem to stern, both the 67-tonners of this barbette went crashing into *La Gloire's* quarters.

First Blood 33

At this moment the ships were not much more than half a mile apart. When the smoke cleared it was at once seen that the whole stern armament of *La Gloire* was in ruins, her after-barbette shattered, the two heavy guns unshipped. One of the shells had penetrated abaft her after-armored tube and there burst, killing fifty men, and rending into a chaos of débris all it met. From the poop of the French ship rose a wide hurry of white smoke. At the same time a steady bombardment of quick-firing guns was opened from both vessels. In three minutes all unarmored or unsheltered spots in each ship were cleared of every living thing. Twelve-pounders, six-pounders, three-pounders mingled in swift-cracking uproar, punctuated by the *brut* growl of the Gardners and the more rasping detonation of the Nordenfeldts. All the air was war, and all the intervening sea a commotion of hissing foam.

But now the machine-guns in the tops were silent, their protecting shields had been shot away, and their crews annihilated. One of *La Gloire's* funnels was gone, and the other pierced, while three projectiles from her had burst their way through shields of six-inch nickel steel, and put three of the *Majestic's* central battery guns out of actions, striking them fairly on the chase. Within three minutes the two ships had belched forth a flaming hail of some twenty-two thousand rounds of shot, riddling all except the most heavily armored parts of each other, tearing to shreds all light gun-screens, and turning unarmored ends and box-batteries into shambles.

Already it seemed improbable that either ship, unless the other were at once destroyed, could come out of this anarchy of thunder and live.

The starboard side of the *Majestic* was still presented to the Port of *La Gloire* but *La Gloire's* speed had been greatly reduced, owing to injuries to her funnels, and the *Majestic* had forged forward abreast, then somewhat ahead of the other.

Vice-Admiral Stephenson was every moment awaiting the second crash of his after-barbette into the

French ship's beam, when *La Gloire's* two fore-barbette guns sent out their voices simultaneously.

One of the shots glanced against the center armor-belt of the *Majestic* at the water-line, leapt, struck her fore-armored tube, and went driving far forward into the sea, where it burst in a high water-lily of spouting foam.

The other wrought terrible havoc. It struck the *Majestic's* central battery at the height of the deck, burst inside, blew away the chief part of the hurricane deck, and turned all the guns in that battery into a mere heap of twisted and crumpled metal.

But as the British ship staggered at this blow, her blue-jackets sent up a cheer, for the next instant the after-barbette in their own ship was talking, too ; and a few seconds afterwards it was seen that *La Gloire's* forecastle was on fire, that she had gone down by the bows, and that her screws, half out of the water, were furiously revolving in a broad mound of wheeling spume.

Was she sinking, then ? The British Vice-Admiral expected now to see her strike her flag. But even as he looked, he was undeceived.

Yonder, a hundred yards astern, somewhat to his port side, he saw a sight which might have made even the heart of a Nelson leap. It was a small object, looking like a cubical box ; and even as he glanced at it, it disappeared utterly beneath the waves.

He knew this to be one of the ingenuities from the Forges et Chantiers de la Méditerranée. It was a submarine boat, and the object which he had seen for a moment was the top of her conning-tower as she rose for an observation of distances and directions.

The submarine boat had been secretly lowered into the water from *La Gloire's* starboard side. Her motor was electric, supplied from storage batteries, and her speed, even at some depth, considerable. Vice-Admiral Stephenson knew that her aim was to pass under his torpedo-nets, carrying an electrically-fired torpedo, to be attached to his already half-ruined ship.

At once he went circling at full speed to starboard,

First Blood

crossing the bows of the now slowly-progressive *La Gloire*, one of whose fore-barbette guns was useless, and the other unready to fire.

At the same time he had rapidly lowered from his port side a second-class torpedo boat which he then carried on deck. By means of hot water from the *Majestic's* boilers, she was already under steam, and with careful handling, in spite of the parent ship's now headlong, wheeling flight, she touched the water in safety, and at once went fretting fussily through the billows, a mere cloud of hurrying spray, at a speed of fourteen knots. Like some buzzing bee with deadly sting, she drove straight upon *La Gloire*.

The alarm on the French ship at this hasting ruin resembled panic. Disregarding the movements of the *Majestic*, her commander at once put his helm-a-port, and turning upon his small foe the comparatively uninjured armament of his starboard side, poured forth, in one continuous roll of artillery, a bombardment of some twelve thousand pounds per minute. *La Gloire* was now, however, well in the trough of the sea, which flowed in bulky swells from east to west; the greater portion of her huge outburst of fire failed to take effect; and still the puffing thing came near and yet nearer, overwhelmed, but steadfast, drowned, but headlong, tiny, but terrible.

The climax of the fight was near. It had lasted but a few minutes: it had seemed like an eternity in hell.

At about three hundred yards from *La Gloire* the little torpedo-boat launched a Whitehead.

As the oiled and gleaming needle of steel slid swiftly into the water, it passed straight through the body of a great swell, and came instantly out on the other side, making directly for *La Gloire's* quarter; but before it could reach her, the ship maneuvered slightly to starboard, and the projectile slipped hurriedly under her stern, and exploded harmlessly some distance away.

But even as it did so, another torpedo came shooting through the waves from the little boat.

At the same time the crew of the torpedo-boat were

seen to be wildly leaping at random over her sides into the waves. Seen—but dimly seen—for the whole craft from stem to stern, as well as all that region of the water into which she was now plunging on her last voyage, was enveloped in one hissing white cloud of stinging vapor. Two of her men instantly sank scalded to death. A twelve-pounder, shot upwards, had burst into her boiler.

It had not come from *La Gloire*. It had come from the unseen thing which was cruising darkly beneath the sea in search of the *Majestic*.

Immediately the submarine boat rose again, and the man in her conning-tower, looking a moment abroad, saw the *Majestic*—or rather he saw a vast mass of smoke which utterly concealed the *Majestic* and the direction of her bow. All he could note was that she was fearfully and wonderfully near to *La Gloire*; that she was approaching *La Gloire*—rapidly, rapidly—with horrid impetuosity.

He did not hesitate a moment, but, putting his fins into play, instantly sank, and made for a point at which he believed he would intercept the rushing ship.

The mass of smoke which he had seen around the *Majestic* had been intentionally caused by her commander. The Vice-Admiral had ordered every gun which still worked to be discharged, whether they bore upon the French ship or not, and enveloped in the mantle of ascending reek which poured from the hot weapons, he put his helm hard down, suddenly left the evolutionary curve of sixteen points through which he had been circling, and drove straight upon *La Gloire*. He was going to ram.

At that great moment expectation stood in horror. "Prepare to ram!" went forth the command from the conning-tower, and every man on the *Majestic* fell flat to his face, as though at the sound of the trump of doom. And now, while the clock might tick, and tick again, the men on *La Gloire* became aware of what was coming. Up out of her envelope of vapor suddenly loomed the *Majestic* upon them, near and

First Blood

huge, like a monster rising from the deep. Just then the remaining fore-barbette gun of *La Gloire* was being discharged, and the ships being nearly bow to bow, the shell went forth with disastrous havoc, shattering the thickly armored fore-barbette of the *Majestic*, battering the conning-tower, destroying the funnels, and shocking the Vice-Admiral into a state of insensibility.

But even as it did so, the crash came. The ram of the *Majestic* touched *La Gloire* on her starboard bow, glanced a little, then with a horrid "*z-z-zip-p*," "*z-z-zip-p*," then with a bursting and rending uproar like the cracking asunder of an arsenal, went tearing and smashing a shapeless hole 20 feet in length along her beam. The sea poured into the doomed ship; and at once she lurched bow-ward to starboard.

But the ram of the *Majestic* was not yet clear of *La Gloire*, when the most stupendous hubbub of the whole battle, drowning every other sound, rent the heavens. It was a double detonation, yet the two reports followed so closely one upon the other, that they seemed almost like one.

They were the sounds of two torpedoes.

The 28,000 tons of the two great ships half-leapt from the water, and started apart, shivering to their keels; and two immense pillars of white cloud, which soon were one, rose high, shutting them from each other.

One of these torpedoes had been affixed by the crew of the submarine boat beneath the bow of *La Gloire*, which they had mistaken for the *Majestic*; the other was the second of the two which had been despatched from the *Majestic's* torpedo-boat before she had sunk. It had caught on to the keel of *La Gloire* aft, and its explosion had been delayed, perhaps half a minute, till now.

When the smoke cleared a little, the commander of *La Gloire* was seen, with blood-soaked clothes, and haggard face, and eyes staring with horror, standing on the wreck of his after-barbette, frantically hauling down his colors. He sent forth to the wreck which he had made of the *Majestic* this cry of terror—

"*Au nom de Dieu!*—we are sinking! *for God's sake...*"

The captain of the *Majestic* at once lowered his only boat which was capable of floating, though half of her port-side, too, was smashed away. The whole crew of the British vessel had hurried to deck, ready, even as they cheered in victory, to aid in the work of rescue.

But as the boat pushed off, men were seen leaping hurriedly from *La Gloire*, in a vain attempt to escape her suction as she went down. She gave them little time. The bursting of the two torpedoes fore and aft had simply turned her into a skeleton of disconnected ruin. She lurched a little aft—up went her bows like two hands laid together in prayer—then her whole length settled evenly lower; she lurched aft again, obliquely, clumsily; then, as if with sudden resolve, she skipped forward, dived her nose briskly into the sea, and disappeared.

Three of her crew of six hundred were saved.

Meantime, the captain of the *Majestic* was signaling to the *Halcyon*, waiting, eager for fight, five miles away:

"We are sinking—make haste."

The great ship was settling slowly down by the bows; for the torpedo which had burst beneath the bows of *La Gloire* had wrought great havoc upon the other's forward bottom also; nor could the pumps produce much impression upon the inrushing waters.

The *Halcyon* succeeded in taking off the hundred and fifty-two that were left of her crew, taking also on board the crew of the French submarine boat, who had escaped injury. They hardly stopped to watch the *Majestic* settle slowly down, before the gunboat's bows were once more turned, to bear her momentous message, toward the Straits.

But if Dr. Yen How had been there to see that battle of the giants, and its result, the corners of his eyes would have wrinkled up into a very web of tickled merriment.

CHAPTER V

HOW ENGLAND TOOK THE NEWS

ON the morning of the duel between *La Gloire* and the *Majestic* it was rumored at an early hour in the neighborhood of Fleet Street that China had dismissed Sir Robert Hart from the Controllership of the Imperial Maritime Customs, and that a Russian was about to be appointed in his stead.

The announcement appeared in the morning papers, and its almost immediate consequence was a rise of threepence per quartern in the price of bread.

But though there were few who were not by this time in a state of excited expectancy, things on their outside wore much their usual appearance. In London the commonplace 'bus and cab went about the streets, and the occasional bicycle, with swift and silent feet, maneuvered among them. Perhaps from Holborn and the Strand to the City the 'buses were fuller than ordinary, perhaps the cabs moved at a slight increase of pace. The pavements were rather crowded, as much perhaps, as on a Christmas Eve night, not nearly so much as on a Lord Mayor's Day. In back streets the coalmen cried " Coal," and their faces were black with the grime of the ordinary workaday of life.

Yonder, the sun wore his usual broad-faced benignity. He seemed to have no suspicion that on this particular morning his old earth was in her death-throes, and a quite new earth in travail to be born.

It was a bright and sunshiny forenoon, the 16th of March 1899—eighteen days and nine months before the dawn of the twentieth century.

The *Evening News* it was which, in a premature eleven o'clock fourth edition, applied the match to the latent mind of excitement which smoldered in the minds of the people. It declared in a little thunder-bolt of breathless news, five lines of "pica" type, that the Stock Exchange had been suddenly closed, and that it was rumored that the Government was appointing private brokers for the transaction of only such business as might be essential.

A step so decisive, as every one saw, could only have for its object the prevention of a financial panic which might be disastrous. And for this prevention there must be a cause not as yet generally known.

Yet such a step should have been expected; for hardly any, except the peace-at-any-price party, any longer hoped that war could be averted—though with whom the war was to be, against what odds, it was not so easy to decide. At any rate, no one could suppose that the cessions of territory by China to the three Powers were spontaneous; it was shrewdly suspected that they were the result of a secret understanding arrived at between them and China at the time when the three had combined to save China from Japan, after the Chino-Japanese war. It had, therefore, the look of a conspiracy to oust England from her share in an empire four-fifths of whose commerce was being carried by British ships; and from end to end of the land the idea that England should submit to such a conspiracy was scouted with indignation.

The severance of telegraphic and telephonic communication, too, between the Continent and England looked like an act of war, whoever was responsible for it. It was reported, and then denied, that three army-corps of 120,000 men were being mobilized toward Brest. It was known that the War Office, the Admiralty, and the Foreign Office were in intensely active inter-communication; that there were frequent and hurried meetings of the Cabinet. But still, with that silence which precedes the storm, with that subdued excitement which a trifle will cause to burst into passion, England waited, still hoping against hope to be allowed to go on her way in peace.

The public were in blissful ignorance of the fact that

the *Majestic* and *La Gloire* had already been lying four or five hours at the bottom of the Atlantic.

Then came the announcement of the *Evening News*, and the pent-up emotion broke suddenly out. In the City, even before this, the streets had become a mere sea, with currents and eddies, of thronging heads. Here the facts of the case were sooner known; when the rumor spread westward, London was awake. All pretense at traffic quickly ceased.

The general tendency and main current of this weltering human ocean was westward in that part of it which was east of Charing Cross, and eastward in that part of it which was west of Charing Cross. The House of Commons, as in all supreme moments of stress and danger, had become the cynosure and the magnet of the nation. Thither the throng pressed.

What was it all about? No one was certain. Was there war—at last?—in very truth? And with whom? No one knew.

For twenty-six years Europe has been practically at peace. The Græco-Turkish war, the Spanish-American were not wars—they were the bickering of naughty children. The Franco-German had been grim enough, but it had long since got to be recognized that the next, when it actually came—at last—would hardly resemble it; for the French and German nations had fought, and each still existed an integral nation in spite of the squabble; but the struggle that was looked forward to when Europe, in the fulness of time, next brought forth her monstrous offspring of war, would as men knew, be stupendous, world-wide, and final; the combatants would consist of mankind; the whole future of the world would be determined by it; and in the greatness of that day, war, the destroyer, would itself be destroyed.

This was the logical outcome of the conditions under which Europe, groaning under her weight of armor, waiting, watching, eager to end her foul disease of hatred, had for many years been living.

And now—at last—she was in travail—pang on pang, and shriek on shriek; and her birth-hour was at hand.

But in the London streets the crowd was worthy of the occasion—a crowd without violence, perfectly self-controlled—the meeting of a nation. There was a poor old Chinaman with a sore and swollen foot, on the heel of which he used to limp, begging, about the City and Holborn. By some chance he became involved in the crowd opposite the New Law Courts, where it was very thick; and he was soon at a loss what to do with his big, bandaged foot without boot. At that moment the name of China stank. But the old Canton beggar was no sooner seen to be in difficulties than the press opened before him; he hobbled forward; a murmur spread round him—half jeer, half cheer—and a rain of five or six pennies made him blessed. He hobbled through a lane which instantly closed behind him, thanking the gods for war.

The bells of St. Clement Danes burst out, telling the notes of a slow hymn-tune.

Eastward, in a window of the *Daily News*, there was a big sheet of paper, written over in large, blue-pencil letters with the words: "War with Russia."

Westward, in the façade of the National Liberal Club, there was a square, white space exhibited to the public inscribed with the words in charcoal: "War with France and Germany."

"I s'y," said a work-girl to her lover, "there's a blooming Frenchman a-looking at the placard. Can't you tell by the squint of him!"

"Oh, don't show him to me, or I'll go straight for him," said Bill; "a Frenchman mykes me sick."

But the girl's remark was passed on; eyes were directed toward monsieur. He turned white, finding himself at the mercy of the crowd. But no harm was done to him; he was only quietly but persistently hustled, till he reached a comparatively empty by-street, dripping with the sweats of fear.

The exhibition of gratuitous notices in windows and at doors was the order of the day. Old habits of Stoic silence seemed for the moment to have disappeared—for the moment was ecstatic. Europe, it was felt, had drifted—drifted from the old moorings—into what new seas and latitudes? At Gatti's place in the Strand was written up in huge letters: "Italy to the Rescue!" In the shop window of some foreign faddist in Soho appeared these words: "Russia is the Natural Ally of England;" and in Holborn, at the First Avenue Hotel, which was richly decorated with British and American flags, these words: "One Blood, One Race, One Speech."

A little street arab in half an hour attained to sudden wealth; he was a newspaper boy, and had in his hand a bundle of three *Stars*. In a moment of inspiration, Harry Tibbles, jammed against one of the lions in Trafalgar Square, nimbly flung and twisted himself on to the pedestal, and held aloft his *Stars*. Thousands of eyes turned upon him. He took from his pocket a match, and deliberately applied the flame to the papers. Pointing to the smoke and flame, he cried in his shrillest Cockney:

"That's the *French*. So much for *them!*"

Thereupon he turned and pointed upward to the statue of Nelson. A shout of cheers at once filled the square, while the urchin was bombarded with a hail of pennies, sixpences, shillings, till he could no longer gather them up. When he had been lifted down, and coddled by the laughing crowd, an old gentleman got from him his address, and promised to remember him "if".... but at "if" he stopped.

Down by St. Stephen's some cheers were making themselves heard. It was three o'clock—a Thursday. The members were arriving in crawling carriages, one by one.

Mr. T. P. O'Connor stood up, leaning forward in his cab, bowing on each side, like Royalty. One man shouted: "Strike hard, Tay Pay!" And another: "Don't spare them!" Mr. O'Connor drove out his large fist, and shook it in fearful menace at the sun.

The round orb of Mr. Chamberlain's eyeglass was all that could be distinctly made out of him, but behind it, his face seemed Rhadamanthine in its sternness, ashen in its pallor. A profound silence fell upon the people as he passed.

Within the House itself the benches were soon crowded, all but the Treasury and front Opposition benches. Prayers were read. So far there was no sign of impatience or emotion. There were "Questions," though there was nobody to answer them; there was also a Light Railway Bill for somewhere to be reported, and the House calmly proceeded to the business in hand.

It was a place of stately traditions; the exhibition of emotion had always been foreign to it. Even when the elementary passions of humanity broke through, and swept like whirlwinds within its walls, it had known how to comport itself with a dignity impossible to the other senates of the world.

No one, observing its outward aspect during that half hour, could have dreamed that the nation it had led so long from greatness to greatness stood on the very brink of swift and final ruin.

The Speaker put the question whether the Railway Bill should be reported. Only two Labor members rose to oppose it. The Speaker said presently:

"I think the Ayes have it."

The thing was done. All eyes cast furtive glances in the direction of the spot behind the Speaker's chair. At that moment the form of Mr. Balfour was seen advancing slowly toward the Ministerial Bench.

Behind him, in a strange topsy-turveydom of party, came Sir William Harcourt talking to Mr. Chamberlain, and Mr. Asquith whispering to Mr. Curzon. Others followed. Then it was seen with a thrill, born of the certainty now of calamity, that the Prince of Wales had just quietly walked into the Peers' Gallery, immediately followed by Lords Salisbury, Rosebery, and the Duke of Devonshire. Peering through the gratings of the Ladies' Gallery were Mrs. Gladstone, the Duchess of York, and others, while the Italian and American ambassadors sat in the places reserved for diplomats.

Below, in the body of the Chamber, was not a sound, except a faint scratching of the pen of the Clerk to the House. Yonder, in the Press Gallery, the alert pressmen held pencil or pen ready, eager to record forever every word of the momentous utterance which was coming.

In the spirit of the House was deep commotion; on the surface calm.

Mr. Balfour rose to speak.

His face bore traces of some sort of suffering, like that of a man who has passed through the travail of a great ordeal. This was partly due to a want of sleep, occasioned by the stress of the last few days. Under his eyes were the semicircles of fatigue. But, apart from this, the face which he turned absently round the House before he spoke was changed: the *dilettante* politician, the charming literary *amateur*, the *ennuyé* lounger—these familiar phases of his personality were no longer in evidence. Care sat on his faded cheek, a gravity heavy as the world.

He made a half-turn toward the Speaker, and as he said "Sir," and paused, his neck stiffened with dignity.

"Sir," he repeated, "I need make no apology at the present time for interrupting the ordinary routine of the business of this House. Some adumbration of what I have to say must have already entered the mind of every one present. And yet, perhaps, not even the most far-seeing and the most prophetic of us may have been able to forecast the gravity of the announcement which it is now my duty to make to this House and to the people of Britain.

"The recent course of affairs in China is known to all of us, and to all the world. It has not been suggested, even by our enemies, that our policy in that country, either originally or recently, was an aggressive one. The enterprise of our citizens, indeed, in the ordinary course of commerce, secured for them the greater part of the foreign trade of the land; but with that strong and large bounty of our race, which resembles nothing so much as the free air of heaven and the breadths of the ocean which it inhabits, we have left it open to every man on the face of the earth to go and do likewise, by engaging in free competition with ourselves. Later on we secured the appointment of an Englishman to the Controllership of the Imperial

Maritime Customs in China; in view of the fact that our trade with China amounted to a sum of ten millions sterling annually, this was a step dictated by ordinary caution. But what has been the consequence to other nations? This: that our nominee has impartially distributed all subordinate posts in his gift to French, German, Russian, and Englishman alike, regardless of nationality, regardful only of merit. Such has been our action in the past. With regard to recent events, we know, and our enemies know, that the Government of this country has, in its holy passion for the maintenance of the peace of the world, submitted to affronts, to wrongs, to insults even, which would, weeks ago, have driven any of the less restrained Ministries of continental empires into a declaration of war.

"Even on the points where undoubtedly many an Englishman would have considered that concession was derogatory to honor, we made concessions. We asked only of Germany that Tientsin should be a free port; of France, that Yun-nan should be open to British enterprise; of Russia, that the valley of the Yangtse river should remain neutral country. Without threats, with no exhibition of heat, we claimed these rights.

"The reply of France, of Germany, and of Russia has been a declaration of hostilities.

"Two hours ago their respective Ambassadors placed a notice of war in the hands of the Government."

The House received this announcement with a perfect stillness, in which horror contended with indignation. Mr. Balfour continued:

"It is impossible to doubt that this vast combination of power is the result of a wilful and wicked conspiracy, aimed primarily at the British Empire, but aimed, in the end, against the progress and happiness of the human race. It comes upon us, like a bolt from unclouded skies, at an hour when the democracies of the world, recovering from centuries of mutual bloodshed, begin to catch glimpses of the dawn of a better day, and look forward to the yet fairer fruits of the peace which they enjoy. Sir, the declaration of this war is a blasphemy against mankind, and can proceed only

How England Took the News 47

from those mysterious powers of evil which seem ever to stand ready to mar the blessedness of the earth. Away now, for many a day, with the fair aspects of our modern life, the quietude of homes, and the untroubled flow of things. With one thought, at least, every Englishman may console himself, as he goes forth to bear his part in this stupendous struggle : 'Britain is not to blame.' Not to blame—and yet not all-unprepared, I think, sir, to comport herself with high valor, as of old, in this the greatest crisis of her august history. Nor is it probable that there lives a single Englishman, who, even in this hour of trial, can doubt that that same Providence which has led our race from small beginnings to the empire of half the earth, will, in its dark purposes, conduct it yet further upon its destiny of triumph and glory."

Mr. Balfour sat down in the midst of a cheer which burst from every member of the House—English, Scotch, Irish, and Welsh—in a very tempest of loyal passion. The assembly leapt to its feet, and volley on volley of enthusiasm filled the chamber with sound. Exultation, for the moment, took the place of dignity; and there ensued an exaggeration of one of those whirlwind "scenes" which have occurred at intervals. Members bounded across the breadth of the House ; in the midst of the tumult, Mr. Burns was seen at the Treasury Bench, shaking the hand of Mr. Chamberlain ; two Irish members were sobbing in a kind of hysteria to each other ; and Mr. Labouchere, forgetting, was shouting to Sir Michael Hicks-Beach, who happened to catch his eye : "Russia must be conquered first, and then France—Russia first!"

During this row and chaos, Sir William Harcourt rose, seeming to wish to speak. A Labor member, who had been talking at the Speaker's chair, rushed away. "Order ! Order !" cried the Speaker, rising. Almost instantly the House resumed its quiet, and sat once more stern and impressive. In five minutes it had spent its exuberance. Now it was the Parliament of Britain again.

It was noticed now, with wonder, that Sir William

was at the Treasury Bench instead of on the Opposition side. Mr. Balfour near him, was leaning his head on his hands, in a pose of absolute weariness. Sir William said:

"I am asked, sir, to say a few words by the Leader of the House. It was his intention to add a few brief words to what he has already said; but the mental strain put upon him during the last few days has left him in a state of practical collapse. The right hon. gentleman has asked me to supply his place. If it should seem strange to any honorable member that the Leader of the Opposition should be asked to supply the place of the Leader of the House, I can only reply that the Opposition now consists of the countries of Russia, France, and Germany; in this country, certainly, there is no longer an Opposition. (Loud cheers.) I believe it to be a fact, sir, that if the rulers of the Continental empires in question had had any kind of conception of the real temper of the nation which they have wantonly and cruelly attacked, they would have paused—they would have hesitated. It is a country hard to conquer, sir—a race hard to quell; at least, it will be a united race and country. Liberal and Radical and Tory shall henceforth lose their titles in the common appellation of Soldier; there shall be no more Orangeman, and no more Parnellite; these shall merge their names in the common name of Patriot. The moment is great; but England is great, too, and equal to the moment. (Prolonged cheering.) I have risen to announce, sir, that the chiefs of the former Opposition have this hour come from a meeting in Downing Street, which we were requested to attend by the Leader of the House with a view to the formation, between us, of a Permanent Committee of Public Safety. I wish also to state that an immediate reduction of the interest on Consols and Government Stock from two and three-quarters to one and a half per cent. is proposed; that a tax on non-professional incomes exceeding £1,000, considerably in excess of the present rate, has been agreed upon; and that the House will be asked to read three times and report

How England Took the News

to-day—for it is possible that hostilities have already commenced—a Bill granting to the Government a sum of seventy-five million pounds for war expenses."

After this, with perfectly business-like calm and grasp of details, the House proceeded to the matter in hand, getting through a mass of work with a celerity which astonished itself. Near six it rose.

An hour previously the Sergeant-at-Arms, attended by a mass of city functionaries, had declared war against the three countries from the steps of the Royal Exchange.

Meanwhile, the news had gone like wild-fire through the country; and everywhere it met with the same indignation, scorn, and hard-headed pride. It was not, as Sir William Harcourt had shrewdly said, a particularly easy task which the nations of Europe had undertaken.

England might break; but it was already clear that she was not fashioned of the kind of steel which could be made to bend.

CHAPTER VI.

HARDY.

"INVASION" was the word which more frequently than any other rose to the lips of Englishmen.

The muster of French, Russian, and German ships in the Northern Seas was eagerly criticised. It was found that their weight of metal was overpoweringly great compared with the small muster of the Channel Squadron. Away out in the China Seas the British fleet had been strengthened; it was cruising in force in the Mediterranean; it was at the Cape, at Australia, at North America, at the West Indies, in the Pacific; it was not in the English Channel.

Under these conditions the warlike activity in Britain itself went on with intensity. Even before the declarations of war the Adjutant-General had issued telegraphic orders all over the country for the calling out of the first-class army reserve, and the mobilization of the militia and volunteers. With wondrous celerity commercial England turned herself into military England. What conscription did for foreign countries, that the manly mood of the race did for us. The women of England, especially, exhibited a spirit as warlike as the peril of their country was immense; and banishing fears and tears, they put on the sternly-proud brows of those heroic Roman matrons, who laughed when their sons were borne home dead with wounds in front. "Go along, boy, and give it 'em 'ot this time!" said a Clerkenwell mother, handing his musket to her son. "And don't be a-sparing o' thot sword o' thoine, Jock," was the admonition of a Lancashire wife as her husband, in premature haste, set out, like many another, to flock to the regimental center, before receiving the intimation that his presence was requisitioned. "And you'll give them a good taste of what old Devon men are like, won't you, Steve?" was the exhortation of a Bideford lass. This was the mood—heroic, nothing less. Night and day the regimental districts and all military centers were hard at work, calling rolls, drafting troops to their regiments, and making all necessary preparations. A sound of trumpets re-echoed through the land.

On the night of the announcement in the House of Commons, at about ten o'clock,—suddenly, on the east balcony of Buckingham Palace, the Queen appeared.

It had been supposed that she was still at Windsor, and by what contrivance she came here without attracting attention was unknown; to the crowds, thirsting, as they were, for some outward symbol of the might of England to which they could vent their intolerable emotions of love and loyalty, she appeared like a godsend dropped from Heaven.

One involuntary far-reaching shout of joy, spreading by contagion far up Piccadilly, far along Pall Mall, and re-echoed in thousandfold acclamations, even by those who could not see her, burst instantly forth. A strong lime-light or electric light arrangement had been contrived, which focussed a powerful beam of white concentrated luminosity around her, and shot in shimmering rays far out and down through the night. Grouped around her was a party of the Royal family. On the right, the Prince of Wales; on her left, Lord Salisbury. In her hand she held aloft an object, the significance of which the crowd for a moment failed to grasp. When it did, the enthusiasm intensified beyond all bounds. It was one of the faded and ragged old flags, brought that afternoon from St. Paul's, which had served as ensigns in Wellington's Peninsular campaign.

A scene similarly striking was being witnessed on the esplanade at Southsea at the same hour, where some seven thousand blue-jackets, and the marines from Gosport, were on parade, and were being reviewed by the Princess May. Hither she had hurried after witnessing the scene in the House, and by the side of her sailor-husband, and Sir Michael Culme-Seymour, rode from end to end of the improvised ranks. Prince George addressed the men with a message of confidence from the Queen, and hinted at the awful odds which they would probably soon be called upon to face. He and every one was conscious that he was talking to doomed men.

The Princess dismounted. She had a basket, which she opened, and from it took a strip of blue ribbon. A high flush of ardor mantled her face as she attached it to the bosom of a staff-captain near her. A touch of pathos was added to the ceremony through which she now deftly went by the fact that she wore a loose velvet mantle, the reason for which could not be concealed. To every officer, from fleet-captain and commodore to sub-lieutenant and cadet, she attached the little symbol of affection. So solemn was the rite that even the crowd was silent. It was her salute to the dying.

But even during the progress of this scene, one of a number of picket-boats which had been sent out from Portsmouth during the day was steaming into the harbor, fussy with news.

She and two companions, smart little steam-pinnaces which flitted through water like fish, had, earlier in the day, spied a fleet of *cuirassés, canonnières, croiseurs,* and *bâtiments de transport* about S. by E. from Newhaven, fifty miles out. They were mostly French, but there were some German also.

The three boats, at intervals of a few minutes, came panting into Portsmouth harbor, like fluttered birds. Each contained five men, and the fifteen, almost at the same time, stood grouped round the Commander-in-Chief on the Hard.

"Could you make out what ships they were?" he asked.

"We were rather too far off for that, sir," answered a sub, near him.

There was silence for half a minute.

It was broken by a voice, which said:

"The *Amiral Baudin* is among them, sir, the *Hoche*, the *Masséna*, the *Kaiser* and the *Deutschland*."

Sir Michael Culme-Seymour turned; he looked at the speaker; his eyebrows lifted a little. He did not know him.

Then, after a minute's deliberation, the Admiral said: "How many ships all told?"

"There are about seventeen battleships, sir," answered a middy eagerly, "about twenty to twenty-three cruisers, and a large fleet of liners—Messageries Maritimes and Norddeutscher Lloyd—with an indefinite number of gun and torpedo boats, tenders and composite small craft. They are making for Bognor, Littlehampton, or perhaps Worthing in a quadruple line of a good twenty or thirty cables' interval."

"There can hardly be *seventeen* battleships," said the Admiral musingly. "Do *you* confirm that?"

He turned suddenly to the unknown person who had addressed him before—a mere stripling with a face highly flushed with excitement.

"Well—not quite, sir," the young man replied; "I decided that there were fourteen battleships, twenty-four cruisers, thirty-eight troopships and liners, and a flotilla of 104 small fry."

"You seem pretty certain of your figures?" the Admiral said, with a smile.

"Middlingly certain, sir."

"May I ask—who are you?"

"My name is John Hardy, sir."

"And your ship?"

"The *Powerful*, sir."

"Then, what on earth are you doing here?"

(The *Powerful* was away out in the Yellow Sea, whither she had been commissioned since the previous year.)

"Looking about, sir," replied the young man, dropping his light-blue eyes.

"But why are you not in China?"

"I fell ill just as my ship was going to sail, sir, and as he said it, he gave one of those peculiar half-secret coughs, so indicative of the consumptive chest,

"I see. Well—but how came you to be in the *Jupiter's* picket-boat?"

"I was on the *Jupiter* as a middy before joining the *Powerful*, sir. Captain MacLeod knows me, and has been kindly pleased to notice me. I am a bird without a roost. I came down from London, hoping for some of the trouble down here. Captain MacLeod allowed me to take——"

"Ah, that explains it, then. Well, he seems to have done well."

The Commander-in-Chief bestowed upon him a smile of passing approval, and turned away. In a moment he had forgotten the young seaman; but when, a little later, he was reading a telegram from the chief coast-guardsman at Worthing, giving the sighted ships of the enemy, number for number as Hardy had given them, then he thought once more of John Hardy.

"Extraordinary genius for facts," he murmured.

The Admiral knew that the picket-boats must, in order to avoid being blown out of the water, have reconnoitered the advancing fleet at such a distance as to be themselves invisible, or nearly so, to the enemy. There could be no doubt that John Hardy's long-lashed, azure-blue eyes possessed the faculty of *seeing*.

It often happened that people who came into contact with this young sailor thought of him a second time at unexpected moments, as the Admiral now did.

In a previous chapter we said that Dr. Yen How, sitting in a London 'bus on a certain night, was "*perhaps*" the most important person in the world. We should have stated the fact with quite absolute decision, if it were not that we were thinking of this particular sub-lieutenant, John Hardy.

They two—the little Chinese doctor, and this consumptive English lad—held in their hands the destinies of the world.

Each had his own idea of the shape which the future of the human race should take; each was determined that it should take the shape which *he* chose, and no other; and each was immensely strong.

It was fated that these two should meet—soon—and more than once.

It was now six o'clock, and the blue-jackets had already passed in a swarm of hurrying boats to their respective ships. As the telegrams arrived from the coatsguardsmen on the southeast coast they were transmitted by semaphore to the fleet. The *Magnificent*, under Rear-Admiral John Fellowes, was the flagship of the second-in-command of the Channel Squadron, and now, in the absence of the *Majestic*, became the flagship of the fleet.

At the Horse Guards, meanwhile, Lord Wolseley was receiving and sending message after message, both telephonic and telegraphic, relating to the despatch of troops from Aldershot, Victoria, London Bridge, and Clapham Junction to the South. Every ten minutes a Brighton and South Coast train, packed with over a thousand regulars and volunteers carrying a day's cooked rations, dashed forth from each of these stations. Away in hasty flight swept the long strings of bristling carriages, the throttle-valves shrieking the dragon-cry of defiance and challenge which England sent out in answer to her foes.

By seven o'clock fifteen thousand men were massed upon Brighton, and an unaccustomed rattle of some ninety limbers sent thrills of very unusual dismay through the placid *bourgeoisie* of London-by-the-Sea. War, so long a word and a myth, had suddenly become a thing, real enough, near enough. Long files of private carriages, taking away mostly women and children, wended northward upon the Brighton road, while a crowd filled the steep street leading to the station, to watch the ever-new batch of arrivals which debarked at all the platforms, up and down alike, and at sidings, the empties being returned along the up and down lines according to convenience. By eight o'clock thirty thousand troops with one hundred and ten guns, under Sir Evelyn Wood, were concentrated, and waiting for the enemy; and all through the night the number was being rapidly increased.

But they waited in vain.

England had been several times invaded by foreigners. The last occasion was in the year 1066, and that occasion Providence designed to be the last forever. This land had since then nursed a race as superb and firm as the foot with which she spurned the breakers raving round her inviolate shores.

At one bell in the second dog-watch the signal was given from the flag-ship; the Channel Squadron, in a double line ahead, at intervals of six cables, some under forced draught, was to steam down Spithead for the Channel, the *Magnificent*, like the bell-wether, of a flock, leading one line, the *Prince George* the other.

At that moment John Hardy climbed from the look-out pinnace which he had been permitted to command, on to the deck of the *Jupiter*.

His heart misgave him, he shrank within himself, he slunk guiltily. He knew that he had only to be noticed to be turned peremptorily away. He was merely a visitor, a guest—a privileged one, it is true—but an outsider. That he should dream of taking part in the coming fight was preposterous, the more so as every man knew beforehand that all were going to certain death. And he had no shadow of status in any ship present.

But he wanted desperately to see the row, and his mind was one of those dominant ones not very subject to considerations of routine.

Once, when a "chief-captain" of cadets on the *Britannia*, with no further temptation to dissoluteness than his weekly two-and-sixpence of pocket-money, he had been reported to the Admiralty for "unsatisfactory conduct"; another such report, and he would have bidden farewell to the British Navy forever. It was that same gipsy attitude of mind, that sort of devil-may-care lawlessness characteristic of him, which was working in him now, as he stood sulkily there, abaft the after-funnel. He felt like being shut out and banished—and he wanted to see the row. He thought of skedaddling and hiding till the ship was well out from land.

But there was a suspicion of meanness in this contrivance, and even while he hesitated, Captain Angus MacLeod sighted him.

The captain had been an intimate friend of Hardy's father, and was an executor of the very large real and personal fortune of which the boy was the heir. Hardy now, at the age of nearly nineteen, was an orphan. The family was Hampshire. The country-house in which he had passed his earlier boyhood lies fifteen miles south of Andover.

The captain beckoned. Hardy ran and stood before him on the hurricane-deck with downcast eyes, and cheeks blushing like a girl's. By nature he was extremely bashful.

"You here?" said the captain, with a deep seriousness in his tone.

"As you see, sir," answered John, with a faint attempt at a smile, and a nervous shifting of a leg.

"You know as well as I do, John," said the captain sternly, "that this is only a piece of insolence on your part!"

"If it strikes you in that light, sir—of course: but I should take it very kindly of you if you could see your way to let me be in for the trouble."

"In for the trouble? This is a most unprecedented piece of cheek, John Hardy! Be good enough to get ashore, sir. Do you imagine that I am going to have your blood on my hands, then?"

"Whose blood, sir?"

"*Your* blood, sir!"

"My blood is all right, sir," said John sulkily.

"Come, come, are you sane? Can't you see that we are all going to pretty certain death, boy?"

"I can't think that, sir."

"Not?. Aren't French and German cannon as good as English, then?"

"They may be on land, sir; but hardly, I think, on Her Majesty's seas."

At these words, "Her Majesty's seas," back went the captain's head in one sudden cry of gleeful laughter. Her Majesty's seas! Perhaps there was not one living man English enough, and audacious enough, to produce that phrase, save this particular sub-lieutenant standing bashfully there.

But he, on his part, saw nothing extraordinary in the phrase—it slipped from him quite naturally, an offspring of his quietly supercilious habit of mind.

The captain's face settled soon again to gravity. This was no laughing matter.

"But we are wasting time, John Hardy," he said severely. "Will you be good enough, *now*, to leave my ship?"

"In what, sir?"

"In—in—what did you come in?"

"In the picket-boat, sir."

The captain turned his face from side to side, puzzled and irritated. John, seeing entreaty useless, was adopting tactics.

"You shan't stay here, sir—that is certain," cried the captain. "Somehow or other—you go! Get the dinghy."

"Shall I scull her ashore, sir?"

"Yes."

"And who will bring her back, sir?"

"I don't care! Take two blue-jackets, then."

"Isn't it rather late, sir?"

"How?"

"I fancy the ship is already moving rapidly through the water, sir."

The captain started.

"Boy, boy," he muttered under his breath. He loved the lad, and had loved his father.

But the captain was just now extremely busy. He tossed his hand and walked away. The strength and tenacity of John Hardy's will sometimes produced results which had the look of fate and inevitableness.

And so it happened that he was with the Channel Squadron, borne in the *Jupiter*, when it steamed at thirteen knots past Selsey Bill to meet the fleet of the Allies.

CHAPTER VII.

IN THE CHANNEL.

Dr. Yen How had his idea, and John Hardy had his. Nothing in the world is of such supreme importance as an Idea.

Dr. Yen How's Idea was this: that the cupidity and blind greed of the white races could be used by the yellow man as a means to the yellow man's triumph; the white races could be made to exterminate each other preparatory to the sweep, in hundreds of millions, of the yellow man over an exhausted and decimated Europe. Hence the grants by China of territories to Russia, Germany, and France—and the consequent war.

John Hardy's Idea was this: that the new naval warfare admitted of every bit as much constructive plan and shrewd sea-tactics as the old; that the sailor-hero was still possible—the new Drake, the new Richard Grenville, the new Nelson; that it was not (as every one supposed) a mere question of weight of metal, or superiority of gun-fire, now any more than it ever was; that a man born with the sea in his soul, and the sea-breeze in his hair, like the old sailor-souls, would still do the trick.

This was his Idea; and he had also this other, subsidiary to that first one—had it more vitally than any other modern Briton—that nothing in the world was of the least importance, except England, and the march of England, and the glory of England.

Perhaps the lad was utterly unconscious that he had these ideas, but he had them; they were there in him, radically and profoundly; and if he was unconscious of them as he was of his circulation, that was an added proof of their radicalness and profundity.

His nature was as elementary, and simple, and strong, as the nature of Dr. Yen How.

Just as the captain of the *Jupiter* flung his head irritably and turned from him, John Hardy caught the sleeve of a middy who was hurrying past, and said eagerly:

"I have got permission to see the row after all!"

"Good biz," the middy nodded, as he passed on. "I wish you joy!"

And presently he was at the sleeve of a sub. Saying:

"Here I am, you see. I have got permission to look on at the row after all!"

"It is like your ubiquitous luck, Hardy," the other said, and hurried by.

Hardy was usually more taciturn than this; the fact that he went about in this way volunteering his news showed that he was more or less excited, out of himself. He was going to see a fight—a real one this time. To this moment he had no idea what a naval battle was actually like. Summer maneuvers were a different affair.

His coldly practical nature was illustrated by the fact that the grudging quality of the captain's permission did not at all lessen his satisfaction; he had got it—that was enough. He looked only at results.

The object of the enemy was to effect a landing at Shoreham, or near it—a quiet spot, less conspicuous than Brighton or Worthing. They hoped by their prompt and sudden arrival, so soon after the declaration of war, to catch the British fleet napping—as, in fact, they partially did—and so to be able to land three *corps d'armée*, consisting of 120,000 men, 360 guns, 30,000 horses, and a fairly adequate commissariat and field-transport *matériel*, without the inconvenience of first of all undergoing a naval engagement.

Their sudden presence on the shores of Britain proved that war must have been secretly premeditated and prepared for by them some time before the declaration of hostilities—another indication of that sus-

In the Channel

picion of treachery which, all through, characterized the action of the Allies in this war. But the excellent telescopes of the coast-guards, and the brisk scouts of the British fleet, served to give a warning which, though late, was not hopelessly so. The enemy, moreover, in their over-confidence, had committed an error in tactics in approaching too near the coast while there was still a little twilight.

Off Bognor the captains and commanders of ships were assembled in the large ward-room of the *Majestic*. Rear-Admiral John Fellowes had signaled half-speed, and summoned them to a conference.

The officers sat round, hanging on his words, as the Rear-Admiral began to speak.

"Of course, gentlemen," he said, "it has been a matter of anxious consideration to me in what formation we are to approach the enemy. What makes our arrangements rather difficult is the fact that we know little of their present disposition. But it seems to me that one thing should be certain—namely, that their troop-ships and liners will be stationed well in the rear, while the whole weight of metal of their ships of war will be put forward to protect their land forces on the liners, etc. They will assume that our first care will be to destroy their land forces in our panic at the idea of invasion, and their whole effort will be bent upon protecting them, and frustrating us.

"Of course, in thus guessing our objects they are right enough. We wish, naturally, to baulk the attempt at invasion; but I must point out to you that our object, to be wise, *must* be twofold, and that our secondary object is more important than our first. I mean, that from the reports we have received of the number of transports, etc, it is impossible that they can have with them a land-force of more than 120,000 to 160,000 men, and that, even supposing these effect a landing, and the land-forces at present in Britain are possibly quite capable of dealing with them, provided the enemy be not reinforced by fresh increments of invading army-corps in the near future.

"It must, then, be our business to make such fresh

invasions impracticable for some little time by shattering, as far as we can, the enemy's powers of convoy—that is, their ships of war. For I need not point out to you that the combined countries of France, Russia, and Germany may place several millions of armed men in England, practically as fast as they choose, if only they have ships to bring them over, *and* a convoy to protect them from the battle-ships and coast-defense ironclads at British stations. And against such forces the land-force of Britain would, of course, be impotent.

"This, then, is my point of view. We must send back our invaders with such a rip in their battered metal that these particular war-ships shall have had enough of invasion for some little time.

"In the effort we shall all probably perish, but that, I take it, is not with any of us a matter of salient importance.

"What I propose is this: that we approach to within five miles of the enemy in our present formation; if they approach us in line abreast, or in a semicircle convex or concave, then we echelon right and left respectively, each battle-ship fastening on the nearest antagonist as fortune may decide; while gunboats, torpedo-boats, and fast third-class cruisers like the *Pelorus*, will deploy right and left in an attempt to get behind the enemy, where they will do all the damage they can, special attention being given to the destruction of rudders and screws, so as to obviate their ramming-power.

"If, on the other hand, they confront us in line ahead, then we retain our formation, the first ship attacking the first, the second the second, and so on.

"My instructions at present cannot, of course, but be general, and much, in any case, must be left to individual initiative—happily so, I think, in the case of British commanders. Further orders will, if necessary be sent out by trumpet-call, and passed from ship to ship in both files."

A bow of acquiescence went round the table. The policy was felt to be bad for the immediate present, but wise for the immediate future.

At that moment the flag-lieutenant of the Rear-Admiral entered the room.

"The enemy's fleet is reported in sight, sir," he said.

"Ah! what is the hour?"

"Nearly three bells, sir."

"What has been made out?"

"Only three electric search-lights in a line—probably they are thirteen miles off."

"Are preparations well advanced on board?"

"Yes, sir."

"And the same, I presume, in all your ships, gentlemen?"

They all expressed assent.

"Well, then, gentlemen, here, you see, we are in for it—'it' meaning the first really great naval battle of modern times. I dare say that we shall conduct ourselves with credit, fighting as we do in the name of justice and our country. In half an hour, say, we shall be face to face with these people. I recommend that a ration of grog be served out to all blue-jackets meantime, and that final preparations be pushed forward. My flag-lieutenant will send up as signal the words 'For England.' I think that is all I need say now, except to wish you a very hearty good-by, and a fine fight, and the aid and favor of Almighty God."

The officers, having saluted, trooped hurriedly forth with mutual *adieux*, and half-satiric, half-sad *morituri salutamuses*, and went away through the gloom each to his own ship.

The snouts of the ponderous bulks of metal were plowing leisurely through the sea.

Yonder, lit by flash-light on the flag-ship, fluttered the battle-word of the coming combat—"For England."

But the night now had darkened. A wind freshened from the sou'west, and drove somber expeditions of slow cloud over the face of the scurrying and struggling moon. She seemed affrighted at the pregnant silence of this gliding navy—a silence pregnant with a thousand thunders. But the sea was fairly calm, crisped only with short low fringes of foam driven by the wind.

The *Jupiter* was the second ship in the port file— that is to say, on the side nearest the coast as the fleet forged eastwards.

Her captain had been so preoccupied with affairs during the bustle of the afternoon that he had eaten nothing for hours. Almost immediately on reaching his own ship after the conference, he hurriedly descended to his quarters, and sat to swallow some cold mouthfuls.

Happening to lift his eyes as he ate, he saw, sitting on a couch in the apartment, and quietly watching him, his guest, John Hardy. He had forgotten John.

"Well, John," he said, across a gag of mutton, " so you have dared, after all. In spite of my orders, eh, sir? Well, I suppose I must make the best of you, as you are here. But you are a foolish lad, you know."

"It can't be of any consequence, sir," said John. "I wanted to see a fight. It is always experience."

"Yes, yes. But a young man like you. Have you no care for your life, sir?"

"It can't be of any consequence, sir."

"'A day less or more,
On sea, or on shore,
We die—does it matter when?'"

Is that the sort of sentiment, eh, John?"

"Something of that sort, sir."

"Well, you might do worse, perhaps. But what is the matter with you? The sweat is rolling down your face.

"They have been allowing me to help a little about the ship, sir."

"What, with your own hands, sir?"

"Yes, sir."

"Well, John Hardy—I shall never have another chance of telling you, so let me tell you now, boy—I

In the Channel

must say that I regard you as a most worthy specimen of the Navy. Your school and cadet careers were not very brilliant, were they? Rather—ahem—well—we will say nothing of that. But in other respects—you know what I would say, perhaps—I give you my Certificate—that sort of thing. Certainly, you are as bold as a fly, modest, thoroughly English—a little—er—original, perhaps, eh, sir? Like your father, eh, sir? But with the makings of a great sailor in you, John Hardy. Pity you should be throwing yourself away like this."

John was blushing.

"You are very kind, sir," he just muttered.

"Do not mention it. The circumstances excuse one, you know, in being quite frank."

"Quite so, sir."

John, all the time, was burning to ask a question. Suddenly he said:

"Might I ask, sir, what are the proposed tactics for the battle?"

"Well, John, there's going to be plenty of fun, apparently, for you to see. The idea is to concentrate all our efforts upon the battleships and big cruisers, so as to render it out of the question, if possible, for this particular fleet again to act as convoy to an invading force."

"And the liners and transports, sir?"

"They are to be left severely alone this time."

"To land their troops on British soil, sir?"

"Yes, boy—yes—*this* time."

Suddenly John Hardy leapt to his feet, his hands clenched, his face inflamed.

"Oh, *sir!*" he cried.

The captain looked at him in surprise, saying:

"Well, what's the matter?"

"Captain MacLeod, England will never bear such an indignity!"

"Well, my boy, but war, you understand, is not fun and heroics—it is dead earnest. England will *have* to bear it, I'm afraid."

"*She shan't, by God!*" cried John Hardy, striking

out his right fist, suddenly riven and smitten by the Call of Heaven within him.

Then, immediately, he fell back upon the couch, sobbing bitterly into his two hands.

The captain stood over him, patting his shoulder, murmuring :

"Poor John ! poor John !"

CHAPTER VIII

THE BATTLE

THE fleets drew nearer, vaguely revealed to each other by electric search-lights.

That morning, as early as five o'clock, the French, Russian, and German national anthems had been played on board the fleet of the Allies at Brest, and the colors saluted. Immediately afterwards the ships steamed out of harbor. The land-troops were already massed on board the transports.

To prevent their movements being watched and reported, they had proceeded at a high speed, never very far from the French coast, till they reached the longitude of Fécamp; then, striking directly northward for Beachy Head, had slackened speed about five o'clock, forty miles from the coast; then, as the twilight gathered, they had deflected their course to about west by north, making in a leisurely way for the neighborhood of Shoreham. When they first became aware of the approach of the British fleet, they were moving almost directly westward, as the British were moving directly eastward.

The formation of the enemy was in a quadruple line abreast. In the front were fourteen first-class battleships at twelve cables' interval; in the second, cruisers of the three classes; in the third, gunboats, torpedo-boats, and composite gun-vessels; in the fourth, the array of liners and troop-ships bearing the land-forces.

The British Rear-Admiral had rightly surmised what

would be the action of the French Contre-Amiral; his primary thought was for the troop-ships. Out from the flagship went a trumpet-call, repeated far over the ocean in a long line of sonorous and brazen-lunged iteration. Down the files of ships it went braying, a voice that died and instantly rose in vibrant outcry again, commanding all troopers and liners to go pacing backward twelve miles to eastward, and there maintain a hollow square till further notice.

Through the wide region of black smoke which poured forth now over the Channel from the entire allied fleet, flocked the captains of ships to a hurried conference with Contre-Amiral des Vismes de Monthier on the *Amiral Baudin*.

His recommendation was that the allied battleships should form in two double lines, converging inwards toward the British ships, just as the British ships (as could be already surmised) were diverging outward toward the Allies. He said: "We have fourteen battleships—they, I take it, eight." (In reality, the British battleships only numbered seven, for the *Majestic* was gone.) "I propose, then, that the four battleships of our present line now farthest to starboard will form the outer converging line of starboard attack, and the next four the inner converging line, parallel to the outer; thus, toward the coast, two starboard lines of eight allied battleships will have between their broadsides a line of four British battleships—and the contest, I think, should be short.

"In the same way with our port battleships; the three farthest to port will form the outer converging line, the next three the inner—thus two port lines of six allied battleships will have between their broadsides a line of four British battleships, eight to four, and six to four. The contest should not be long, messieurs. I even suggest, as a point of tactics, that, in view of our preponderance, we should make our victory instantaneous by placing a very short interval between the combatant ships—say, a kilomètre at the most; for, of course, the shorter the conflict the less our damage—a point of immeasurable importance to us, considering the rôle we have to fill in convoying more invading land-forces in the near future. I need not point out, too, that an enemy's ship, hemmed in between two hostile ships, will be the more hampered in ramming, the closer the quarters. But we have little time for talk; cruisers, gunboats, and composite vessels will find their work cut out according to the dispositions of the enemy's less massive flotilla. I can only hope that these recommendations meet with your approval, as I know they do with that of my colleague, Vice-Admiral von Grüdenau. Adieu, then, messieurs! This interruption to our progress will, in a quarter of an hour, be overcome. *Vive la France! Vivent—vivent—les Alliés!*"

"*Vive la France—vivent les Alliés!*" repeated the allied commanders round the table, as they raised to their lips wine poured from the carafes; then, saluting, they hurried to their gigs.

And none too soon. They had hardly reached their ships, and turned them to the performance of the prescribed evolutions, when the fleet of England was upon them.

The Contre-Amiral had made a small error in guessing the formation of the British battleships. He had assumed that, their number being small, they approached the allied fleet in two divergent single lines of ships; but the British Rear-Admiral, hoping for some unknown hypothetical advantage, had, as we have seen, decided to advance in two divergent echelons, or step-shape formations. The error was of little importance, for the Allies would quickly detect the formation, and modify their movements accordingly.

Unfortunately for them the eyes of John Hardy, with their faculty of sight and insight, were abroad over the sea that night.

He had burst into sobs in the captain's quarters of the *Jupiter*. The captain stood over him, patting his shoulder, wondering at the intensity of the lad's pride and patriotism.

But it was neither pride nor patriotism which was

then rending the frail frame of Hardy with sobs—it was something far more. To hear irresistibly the Heavenly Call to be up and save the world, and then, at once, to be overwhelmed with the bitter sense of the strong Commonplace, and with the feeling of sheer impotence in the face of it—this is the tragedy of genius.

John sobbed. There had risen in him a sublime strength, an immoderate arrogance, and with it the tingling consciousness that, were he that night the Admiral of the Fleet, he would and could somehow save England from the shame of an invading foot; then, all at once, he remembered that he was by no means the Admiral of the Fleet. So he sobbed.

But his sobs were in the nick of time, for he had the trick of luck. They softened and touched the captain, just at the right instant.

"Well, John, I must be going," he said.

John lifted up his hot face.

"Where shall I take my place, sir?" he asked.

"Your place? I should stay here if I were you."

"May I, sir, if it is not asking too much——"

"What?"

"Come with you, sir."

"Where to?"

"The conning-tower, sir."

"My good fellow!"

"If it is not asking too much, sir. One must see the fight from somewhere, as one happens to be here."

"Well—but—the conning-tower!"

"I shall make myself small, sir. You won't talk to me, nor I, of course, to you. A guest chooses his lodging in a case of doubt, you know, sir."

He was smiling now, and when he smiled his face was wonderfully winning.

The captain hesitated, and was lost. He said:

"Well, you are an original, John, that's all I can say—like your poor father before you, boy. Come along, then—come along!"

They ran briskly up.

The Battle

Suddenly the still night was a-sound. The two fleets were about to mingle.

At that moment so great was the disparity of weight, that the wildest hope of patriotism could have predicted nothing but swift destruction to the British; nor was the objective of the British captains victory, but only the disablement, as far as might be, of the enemy.

To explain the appalling ruin and havoc which one pair of seeing sailor-eyes brought upon the entire allied squadron, we must employ diagrams.

The following is the formation in which the seven British battleships approached the enemy, with an interval of about a knot, or nautical mile, between each pair of ships, A being the Rear-Admiral's ship, the *Magnificent*, A' the *Prince George* leading the starboard echelon, and B' the *Jupiter*, bearing Hardy.

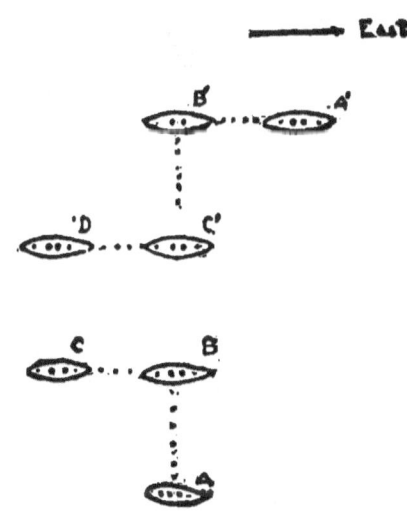

The following is the formation in which the allied battleships advanced, about the same interval being preserved among ship-pairs as among British ship-pairs.

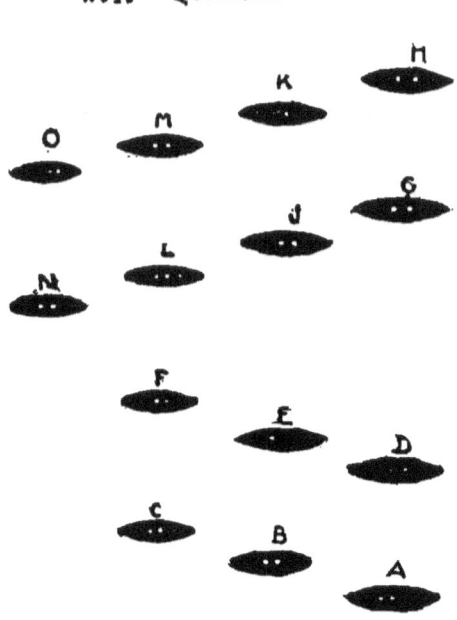

The fleets were no sooner on the point of mingling than Hardy, standing now with Captain MacLeod in the conning-tower of the *Jupiter*, was in full possession of their method of advance ; and he was no sooner in full possession of it, than he started, his eyes widened, and words burst from him.

"Sir," he cried, "the enemy are advancing in two double files. It seems clear to me that they suppose us to be advancing in two single files."

"Yes, that is so," said the captain, proceeding to give the order in which John had interrupted him.

"But, sir, sir," persisted John.

"Well, John, well," said the captain.

"It seems to me, sir—really—that if the *Jupiter* and the *Victorious* both put out external lights and lie low, the enemy will *continue* to think that we are in single file instead of in echelon, and then——"

The Battle

Up leapt the captain's arms.

"By gad, you are right, boy!" he cried, staring hard at Hardy, his head struck into a sudden sideward suspension of silent meditation.

Then, in a flash, he saw it all—the whole inwardness of the boy's suggestion—the long vista of results —the whole huge drama of the enemy's disaster.

"Sir—Captain MacLeod——" said John, all eagerness.

"But to warn the *Victorious* in time?" mused the captain.

"Send *me*, sir! Water from the engines—the picket-boat! The *Victorious* is only two miles off; I shall be there in three or four minutes."

"Well—I say yes. You understand, of course, that you will never come back."

"Thank you, captain—good-by—they are done for, captain, by the Lord——!"

He was gone, rushing.

On board Her Majesty's ships of war things were done with a certain nimbleness; everything was oiled and easy, and went off with the gliding smoothness of lightning. The *Jupiter* was carrying at her masthead the bright white steam-light, on her starboard bow the usual green, and on her port bow the usual red light; by the time these were out, and the whole ship plunged into darkness, the little picket-boat was driving her head through two combs of foam, herself in darkness, with Hardy and three blue-jackets, in a direction nearly south.

The picket-boat passed before the ram of the *Repulse* (C), and in less than two minutes Hardy was at the conning-tower of the *Victorious* (B).

Suddenly the *Victorious*, too, vanished into darkness. The night was now very gloomy.

There remained a third ship, the *Mars* (D), whose presence it was desirable to conceal for the time being; the concealment was not so necessary, as she was more remote from the advancing fleet, and by the time the significance of her presence in her then position was understood, the mischief might be done.

But Hardy would leave nothing to chance. It was quite out of the question now that, if he attempted to reach the *Mars*, the little picket could live in the shattered sea-surface, into which, surely, in a minute's time all that area of water would be torn by shot and shell. Yet he dared. The little boat, in a very passion of haste, throbbing as though she would throb her little heart out, went panting northwestward toward the *Mars*.

Was he too late? There was a sudden shock and roar from the east, and in the night a dull glare red and morose. He sat, the tiller-ropes in one hand, the other holding a double-glass to his eyes. A gust of wind had blown away his straw hat; the breeze was a-play in his hair.

A British first-class torpedo-boat rushed sounding past him, hasting wrathfully to battle, washed in spray from stem to stern. Close by his starboard bow she dashed like an angry darting fish, leaving the little picket nodding and dipping in a choppy sea which almost swamped her hurried embassy. The next moment a shrapnel-shell burst into light a hundred yards before him. The fight had commenced—Bellona was abroad.

Was he too late? He knew now that to reach the *Mars* he must perish. Certainly, he could never return to the *Jupiter*. But he held on his way. He was full of a great joy. Now he knew verily for what he was born; it was for this—the mixed and multitudinous roar of cannon sounding over the sea—England's sea—*his* sea! Something in his heart, in his life's blood, and in his very soul's soul, answered to it, was akin to it. Never had he been really glad till this night. He held on his rash and desperate way.

His eyes were alight with battle.

Suddenly he said under his breath: " Bravo ! "

The lights of the *Mars* had gone out into darkness.

Her captain—Captain Henderson—had noted, first, the extinguishing of the *Jupiter* lights, and had been puzzled; then the going out into darkness of the *Victorious*. He had stood with knit brows for two

The Battle

minutes, and had understood. A few seconds later the *Mars*, too, was invisible.

At once John Hardy put his helm to starboard, running about northeast, to regain the *Jupiter*. He was now hurrying into the very region of the starboard limb of the enemy's fleet, and by the time he neared the *Repulse*, that ship was already engaged with two of the enemy. In another half-minute the sea around these three was a white tempest of thrashed and spurting spray, as when thronging hail flogs stingingly upon a lake, and the sky about them was a vague domed cavern of coppery flame. Never did sailor, in so small a craft, run the gauntlet of a more ticklish peril, passing through a sea crowded with torpedoes and cracking shells, and balls of fire. But the picket-boat never so much as swerved; straight onward she throbbed, through the region of lurid half-light, at her sternpost the Union Jack; then once more into darkness. John Hardy sprang up the side of the dark *Jupiter* and ran to the conning-tower.

"You have done it, then, John?" cried Captain MacLeod; "I congratulate you from my soul."

"Thank you, sir. Now, perhaps, I think we may see these fellows banged a little——"

"We may, John, we may—thanks to you, boy. Wait, wait—let us see."

It did not take long to see.

In a very few minutes the condition of the battle was this: two French ships, one on each side of her, were battering the *Magnificent* (A,) into shambles; two more, one on each side of her, were making a wreck of the *Prince George* (A); two more were tackling the *Repulse* (C); the *Jupiter* was not fighting, the *Victorious* was not fighting, the *Mars* was not fighting—the Allies being unconscious at the moment of their presence in their then unsuspected position; one German ship was in collision with a French on the starboard side of the *Resolution* (C); one French ship was ramming another French ship between the *Resolution* and the *Mars* (D); another French ship was blowing a German ship out of the water at a point a long way to the west of the British

76   The Yellow Danger

fleet; and two German ships were cruising about in the same longitude, searching in vain for two enemies which should have been there, and were not.

Thus, of the fourteen allied battleships, six only were engaged in actual conflict with three British vessels, while a fourth British vessel (C) was pouring a tempest of barbette, quick-firing, and machine shot into the ships in collision on her starboard, and watching the sinking of a French ship rammed by a French on her port side. How this complexity of tragedy overwhelmed the enemy will be readily seen by the following plan, published in every London newspaper the next morning. Black squares and small letters stand for allied ships, circles and capitals for British, the three British which put out their lights being printed black.

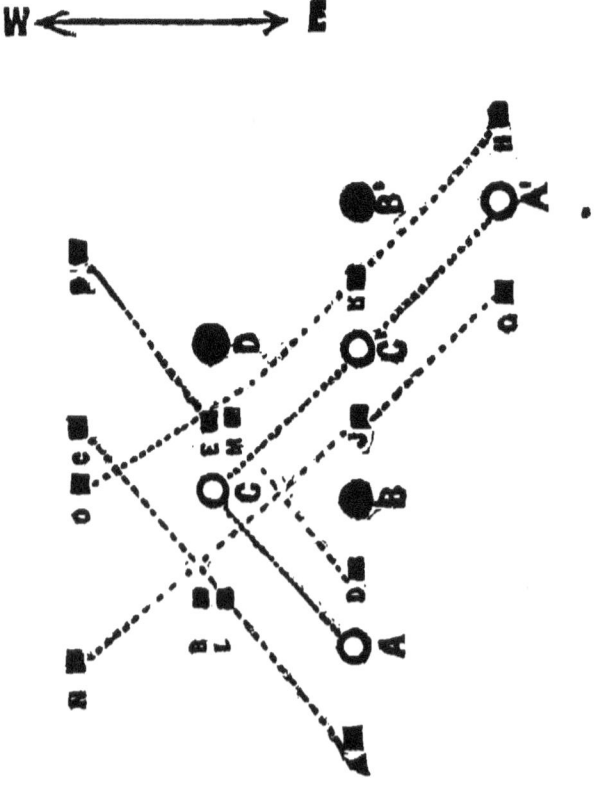

The Battle

It will be seen from the plan that, the lights of the three ships being extinguished, the starboard limb of the allied squadron saw a straight line of British ships —namely, C, C', A',—consisting of the *Resolution*, the *Repulse*, and the *Prince George*. This made them certain of their conjecture that the British were advancing in two single lines, and they accordingly proceeded to port and starboard of these three, in order to attack on both broadsides ; but expecting not three, but four, British vessels in each limb, the allied ships *n* and *o* went on south-westward to seek them.

Meanwhile, on their port side also, the allied ships saw a straight line of British ships, namely A, C, consisting of the *Magnificent* and—once again—the *Resolution*. Believing that this limb, too, consisted of four distinct ships, two of which were farther on, and not appreciating the fact that the same *Resolution* (C) was about to be attacked by two of their starboard fleet, they steamed forward. Two of their ships, *c* and *f*, reached the stations indicated on the plan, surprised to find no enemy ; while two others, *l* and *m*, came into contact with two of their own starboard limb, *b* and *e*. Before she could stop her speed, *m* had hopelessly rammed *e*, and the *Resolution* was pouring a murderous hail upon both *b* and *l*, which had similarly collided, *b*, at this time being an inert mass floating helplessly with screws shattered by *l;* while yonder to the west, *c* and *o* both searching for the missing enemy, made a sudden discovery, and began to batter each other with shrapnel, before ever guessing at the hopeless error, and the blind delusion, and the harum-scarum of disaster, in which they had been involved by the simple expedient of Hardy.

At this moment—simultaneously—the three darkened ships opened fire ; and peaceful merchantmen, heading with slow industry on their diverse ways, heard far and wide over the Channel the cry and rumor of that complex war.

It was a fearful battle. Nearly all the allied ships which were in actual combat with British ships, having taken position in the hope of pouring a double broadside on the British ship, one from each side, now suddenly found themselves in the predicament which they had planned for the British ; for, without warning, a dark unsuspected ship opened fire upon them, placing between two fires those who for others had planned two fires.

Thus, the ship *k* was between the fires of the *Jupiter* and the *Repulse*, the ship *j* between the fires of the *Repulse* and the *Victorious*, and the ship *d* between the fires of the *Victorious* and the *Magnificent*. As yet, no colors had been struck, but the *Friedrich Wilhelm* (*b*), whose stern-works had been shattered by the *Duguesclin* (*l*), was a barely-floating ruin, with only one water-tight compartment uninvaded by the waters ; the *Prince George* (*A'*) was just plunging—with screws high in the air, and a shriek from her burst and hissing engines that reached the clouds—to her last resting-place ; the *Masséna* (*e*), with a strange fatal suddenness, had sunk on being rammed by the *Hoche* (*m*) ; and almost immediately afterwards the *Hoche* herself cracked in twain amidships, struck by a torpedo intended for the *Masséna*, which had been launched by a second-class torpedo-boat lowered in the dark by the *Mars ;* while the *Mars* herself, having not yet relighted her lamps, was rammed at her central armor-belt by a second-class British cruiser, the *Charybdis*, the smaller ship sheering away with broken bows to go down by the head three miles away amid a crowd of allied cruisers.

Yonder to westward of the thickest region of battle, the *Amiral Baudin* (*c*), with a single 37-c.m. shell, had annihilated both funnels of the *Brandenburg*, while the *Brandenburg*, before she could detect the ruse by which she was made to destroy her own flagship, had rattled the ribs of the *Amiral Baudin* with a rain of thousands of rounds of machine and quick-firing 10½ and 8-c.m. shot, and had sent a barbette shell shrieking into the bowels of the French ship, where it ripped her armored deck, and in a nightmare of fury rent the whole central interior of the vessel into débris.

It was shortly after this that even the din of that

wide and various warfare received, as it were, an added shock of horror, when a broad sheet of flame was seen to rise and ride in quivering glare toward the sky, and the next moment a bang of thunder where the *Repulse* had been shook the universal sea. A fire had run through her entire length between-decks, and ignited at nearly the same moment every atom of explosive within her into one splendid detonation. She did not burst—she crumbled to fragments. At the same time, at the other end of that line of ships, the *Magnificent* was quietly going down by the poop, where a French submarine-boat had affixed a Whitehead.

In a very few minutes after the actual commencement of hostilities, four of the seven British battleships had disappeared, and nine of the allied fourteen.

Of the intricate and incalculable warfare that was darting in furious wrath in every direction in the shape of the less massive armatures little was salient where all was vast. The enemy was preponderant in number, but deficient in weight of first-class cruisers. The mutual havoc went on rapidly with complex disaster and success. Ships about to disappear rose again, blown high by torpedoes; men on the point of going down in the wheeling suction of some great vessel were arrested in their descent to be mangled by distracted shrapnel, or scalded by some flight of stinging steam; crafts were destroyed and destroyed again, and ten times destroyed again, before they sank in scattered shreds. It was an anarchy and blindness of rage, which rent the already rent, and mutilated the already murdered.

The *Jupiter*, by some favor of her position, was still seaworthy, when Captain MacLeod, a minute after the blowing up of the *Repulse*, said aloud to himself:

"Now, I think I might very well ram that ship."

"That ship" meant the French battleship k, which, now that the *Repulse* had gone, was turning, together with her sister-ship j, her whole attention upon the *Jupiter*. Part of the *Jupiter's* fore-deck had already been ripped, and a fore barbette gun unshipped.

At once she went wheeling in a sixteen-point curve

to starboard, pouring at the same time a broadside upon the enemy. But it was at once seen that the most delicate seamanship would now be required, for not only was the *Jupiter's* intention detected, but *k* began to maneuver to anticipate the attack by herself delivering the ram, while the chase was promptly joined by *j*, which had just lodged a finishing shell in the *Victorious* (B).

The three vessels, though one of them was sinking slowly, and all were more or less ruined, were intact in engines and steering-gear, and went careering in swift flight on evolutionary curves whose outcome only the nicest commanding skill could determine. To destroy a funnel of one or both,—this was Captain MacLeod's hope. He started a rattle of quick-firing shot as the three vessels wheeled nearer. But there was a racket on board the *Jupiter*—a bursting shell—a clatter of broken plate—a stream of blood poured down John Hardy's face—Captain MacLeod fell limp at his feet.

At that moment, from the conning-towers of *both* the French ships there went forth the command: "Prepare to ram." The *Jupiter* was between them; and her captain was laid low.

But a born sailor now commanded her.

Hardy gave the order to slacken speed. With his eyes on both the hurrying, impending ships he waited thirty, thirty-five seconds; and at the right fraction of a second he ordered: "Full steam ahead!"

Blood covered his face, and the breeze in his hair gave him an aspect of wildness and disarray; but his brain was cool.

As the poop of the *Jupiter* slipped elusively from between the two advancing rams there arose an outcry on both the French ships. But it was too late. No celerity of hand, no power on earth, could now avert the awful catastrophe. The two bows met, and crashed.

One of the French ships leaned to port, as if fainting in despair, then languidly sank.

Was he really in command? Captain MacLeod lay at his feet. Who knew? Would not his, John Hardy's, commands be obeyed tacitly, if he tacitly assumed the

The Battle

command? And *he*, at least, was under no orders from the Rear-Admiral. He ordered three points to starboard, and full speed ahead. The *Jupiter* went hasting at once directly northward.

Hardy was running from the fight.

The first clear necessity seemed to him now to get out of the battle, while the *Jupiter's* engines were still intact.

He suspected, indeed, that she was already sinking. But there was hope. She went plowing northward. Her position on the outskirts of the battle favored him.

Of what particular crime was it that he was guilty? He knew well that it was a crime. Was it treason, or piracy, or mutiny, or felony? The place which he occupied should have been filled by the commander of the *Jupiter*, now that her captain was senseless. Hardy knew that; but her commander was under flag-orders. *He* was not.

Three miles to the north he turned the ship's bow from north to northeast; three more miles and he turned it from northeast to east. Now he breathed freely; the *Jupiter* was well beyond effective range of the battling ships.

Her lights had long since been again put out. On she went through the darkness, east by south now, battered and broken in her upper works, but tolerably sound below—and with funnels still whole! and with a ram plowing through the water at eighteen miles an hour! and absolutely safe now from shot!

John Hardy stood in her battered conning-tower with the wind in his light hair, and the blood on his face, and a slight frown on his brow. And on through the darkness drove the silent battle-ship.

In little more than half an hour she was upon that hollow square of troopers and liners, which were here just forging through the water till the conclusion of the fight. There were thirty-eight of them, and they contained over 120,000 men.

Suddenly, out of the darkness, the *Jupiter* pounced upon them.

6

Has the reader seen a thoroughbred, long-snouted fox-terrier, the prize-winner perhaps at some show, let loose in a small room among a hundred hoarded rats? With a gleeful, sudden spring he is among them, as they scamper into a huddled heap at the corners, seeking to hide from the very sight of their little, leering eyes that countenance of wrath. He, for his part, gives one, and only one, swift crack at the bones of the neck, and disdainfully drops the limp vermin to go on to the next.

It was something in this way that the *Jupiter* dealt with these thirty-eight troopships and liners. One after another they cracked like teapots, they snapped like rotten twigs, they sank at a touch. Hardy rammed one on one side of the square, and went straight on and rammed another opposite; but in the rapid passage from opposite to opposite, he had sunk five others with barbette and broadsides of quick-firing guns. The *Jupiter* rushed among them like a fury, dashing through a multitude of complex evolutionary curves, and heaping havoc all around. It was a scene of unparalleled carnage. In a short time the ram of the ship was forging through masses of men and horses struggling in the water; what was left of the sides of the square was shooting forth flames; and the *Jupiter* herself was being swept by tempests of bullets from the land-forces. Without visible result, however. Three only of the transports, sufficiently uninjured by the time they could get speed, escaped. The rest went down.

It was now a question with Hardy whether he could save the *Jupiter* by beaching her. She was already low by the stern, and the coast was miles away. The moment his work was ended, he gave the order to turn her bow directly northward.

He only just failed.

Half a mile out from Brighton, he bent over Captain MacLeod, looked close into his eyes, and put his hand over his heart. The heart beat, but a splinter had gashed all the chest.

"Sir, sir," said John, "can you not——"

The Battle

He shook the Captain. A moan came from the prostrate man; his eyes opened.

"Try to understand," said John; "you will have to *swim* or be lost. Can you understand?"

The Captain stared stupidly, but nodded; and John stripped him hurriedly, then himself.

The next moment he gave the order:

"Hands to leap overboard and make for shore!"

There was nothing resembling a boat any longer left on board the *Jupiter*.

In two minutes three hundred blue-jackets were in the water, and the *Jupiter*, left alone, took in a smooth cascade of sea over her poop.

A blue-jacket on one side of Captain MacLeod, and John on the other, made slow progress forward. Toward ten o'clock they felt bottom; they dragged themselves forward, and fell upon Brighton beach.

CHAPTER IX

JOHN HARDY GIVES AN ORDER

Hardy in a faint on Brighton sands—Hardy waking on a down bed in Cavendish Square—the transition is rapid, but that is what in fact occurred.

Captain MacLeod, though gashed over the chest, woke to consciousness before John. John had his constant wound *inside* his chest, and gave signs of it in the form of those pathetic, clandestine coughs of his. He woke wheezing with asthma. Besides this, he had a scratch on his brow from a shell-splinter.

No. 11A Cavendish Square had been the town-residence of Hardy's race for some generations, and here, in solitary state the young man lived when in London.

London, lately, had seen a good deal of him, though he liked the country when on shore. This new attractiveness of London was concentrated for John in a certain house in Hampstead.

When he opened his eyes, torn by a cough, they met two others bending low over him—old ones, surrounded by wrinkles; anxious ones, full of solicitude. It was half-past eleven o'clock.

"Well, Bobbie," said John with a smile, and stretched a little.

"I am pleased to see you so much yourself, I am sure, Master John," said Bobbie; "how are you feeling now?"

"I, Bobs? Much the same as usual, I suppose. Where on earth am I?"

"You are in Cavendish Square, sir—in your own chamber."

John Hardy Gives an Order

"Oh ay—I see that. I remember now, Bobbie. The battle, eh? and the swim, eh? The old *Jupiter* did not do so badly, after all. Did any of the enemy escape? And Captain MacLeod—how is he, Bobbie?"

"He is said to be doing fairly well, Master John. He has a wound in his chest, which is not serious. He is better off than you, I am thinking. It was he who brought you here, sir."

"When?"

"About four in the morning, sir."

"Ah, I fancy I recollect something of it. Well, that's all right, then, Bobbie."

"Ah, Master John, not all right, perhaps! When, when, sir, will you learn to take care of that chest, sir?"

"Oh, bother the chest, Bobs, boy. A fellow has got to do his duty, I suppose, Bobbie?"

John Hardy's eyelids lifted as he said this, and he turned upward the pure cerulean azure of his eyes in clear open query upon old "Bobbie," the aged butler of his father and grandfather.

"Well, sir—well—if you put it in that way, of course. But still, there is this to be said: it was not, so to speak, your *duty* to go through this; you had not, as one might say, any right to be there——"

"No, Bobbie, but I *was* there, you see. And being there, it was natural that one should do what little one could for the old country, don't you think——"

"What *little*, sir?" cried Bobbie. "Ah, that is like your way of speaking, sir—like your father before you, Master John! This is a proud day for poor old Bobbie, Master John—forgive me for these tears, sir, the tears come quickly when we are old, Master John —a proud day, and the tiptop hour in the life of your father's old servant, Master John, making dying easy to him from this day onwards, sir. It was what I predicted of you, and to-day you have made true your old Bobbie's word before all the world, Master John. England this morning is ringing, sir, with the name of Hardy, ay, and France, too, sir, and Europe and America; and the servants down at the Hall have sent a telegram to poor old Bobbie, sir, all of them in a body, congratulating me on the man you have shown yourself, and it's a proud day, sir--a proud day—for poor old Robert Mason, Master John, is this that you have brought me."

Robert's flow of words was choked by sobs. John put out his hand, drew him nearer to the bedside, and laid one arm round the stringy old neck, the boy's affectionate nature overflowing in murmured words.

"I am so glad, Bobbie, if I have made you happy," he whispered. "You know I would do anything to do that, wouldn't I? But what is it all about, Bobbie? Have I done anything very extraordinary, then? England was bound to beat those mounseer people, anyway, wasn't she?"

Bobbie disengaged himself hurriedly. He had his proofs with him—chapter and verse. He had been poring all the morning over a score of newspapers, weeping as he only wept over his old Bible. He had brought them. He flaunted them in the face of John.

"Read *those*, if you want to know what you have done! Well, it's a proud day—a proud day—for poor old Bobbie, that's all I can say!" he cried in a weak, broken voice, treading woe-begone about, his face in his hands.

John glanced through three or four of the papers, half sitting up, while Bobbie held ever and again to his lips a glass of egg and milk.

The *Times* concluded an article by saying: "Assuming that the account to hand derived from the statement of Captain MacLeod be correct, what words of eulogy shall we find in our English tongue to extol and glorify the very young man to whom Britain this day owes her immunity from the shame of an invading foot. In ancient Rome, the people would have been acutely conscious of their inability to invent any Dignity equal to their sense of obligation to such a deliverer. This young man would have been proclaimed Saviour of his Country, and would have been entrusted with the supreme direction of affairs—naval, military, and political—with the injunction to see to it *ne res-*

John Hardy Gives an Order

publica damnum capiat. How will England adjust herself to this new-found personality in her midst ? We wait with some anxiety to see what shall be done by the Government to the man whom the nation delighteth to honor."

The *Daily Chronicle* lost itself in allusion and metaphor. It said: "What Nelson was to the ship of wood and sails, that, it is already clear, is this young man to the ship of steel and steam. That is to say, he is its genius. He is more still—he is its embodiment. Ralph Waldo Emerson, in one of his essays, points out that occasionally a man is born who is himself, as it were, the Thing in connection with which his activities are employed; thus, Nasmyth was concentrated Iron, Edison is himself Electricity, Rudyard was himself a Lighthouse. We may add, John Hardy is himself a modern Battleship."

But it was reserved for the *Daily Telegraph* to embody in its ornamented style something of that shudder of delight with which England, through all her breadth, learnt with that morning's sunrise that she had still a son with a voice hoarse enough to proclaim once more to all the earth her Empire of the Sea. No style could have been too florid to express that day the feelings of the nation; for emotion is, in its very nature, florid ; and England was in the grip of an emotion.

The *Telegraph* said : " No one has yet accused this journal of hero-worship ; and in speaking as we have spoken of Sub-Lieutenant John Hardy—whom, we confess we have for the first time heard of half an hour ago—it is partly the man whom we laud, but above all, it is the great nation that could have produced him. We have at command some special information about Mr. Hardy ; and we say with the certainty of knowledge that he is as essentially an English thing as the cliffs of Dover, or the smuts of the Black Country. No other land could have given birth to anything at all resembling him. He is doubly the child of England ; for he is the child of the sea also. The sea is part of England. The oceans are not her boundary—they are her continuation. If one were to ask Mr. Hardy, " What is the breadth of England?" he would probably reply, "Her breadth is the distance between the Poles." Such, at least, is the account we have received on good authority of the temperament of this latest scion of an old Hampshire family of thoroughgoing "sea-dogs."

"For the rest, the young gentleman is said to have an ailment of the chest; he has the typical blue eyes of the English tar, and very light wavy hair, which he wears rather long. He is small in stature, and slim. His face is said to be the gravest, saddest, prettiest girl-face in the land, and his disposition in private life is much more than usually mild, soft, and affectionate. Our informant hints at a supposed weakness for the fair sex, and confesses that, at the examination stage of his career, the man who bids fair to become the national hero proved himself far from brilliant.

"So much we have been able to gather; and this fact also, that from boyhood Hardy has seemed to be deficient in one of the ordinary instincts of humanity —the instinct of Fear. Nothing, so far, has appeared to have had any tendency toward alarming him; to use our informant's words, "He would remain cool if the earth were bursting to pieces." Such is the man who has ranged himself on the side of England against the allied nations of the Continent.

"This is no time of ordinary routines and gradual processes. The moment is ecstatic—the hour is immense with Fate. Let the nation for the nonce fling to the winds its old Shibboleths of Use and Wont, and now, without delay, proceed to garland with its fairest laurels the head which has been its salvation. It is certain that, but for Mr. Hardy, we writing here should be writing with a boom of cannon in our ears. What guerdon is high enough for the man who has averted such a doom? Fleet-Captain—Vice-Admiral—Admiral!—these are the honorary titles that occur to us, as in no way commensurate with the reward which England owes, and will insist upon paying, to her deliverer. Nay, we know little of the English people if it do not straightway find something so akin to its own secret temper, something so precisely like its own inner

John Hardy Gives an Order

self, in John Hardy, and in the cool rashness of John Hardy, and in his contemptuous way, and in his audacious gallantry, and in his homely, Cromwellian grandeur of mind—that a burst of enthusiasm from the entire nation shall at once proclaim him its chosen and darling. England, as Mr. Matthew Arnold said, is a Nation "in the grand style"; John Hardy, we do not hesitate to say, is a Man "in the grand style." It will not be surprising if these two, having once come across each other, shall, without delay, strike up a friendship perhaps unparalleled in history. The beginning of such a friendship, we to-day announce."

So the *Telegraph*. The *Standard*, on the other hand, came out with an essay on Blood. "A democracy without an aristocracy," it said, "is like an egg without salt. It was necessary for Sub-Lieutenant Hardy, before he could annihilate the navies of Europe, to have behind him a long line of ancestors whose home was the sea. He is the apex of a pyramid, the rest of which consists of centuries of the ocean-life and ocean-culture of a race. It is Blood that tells."

The *Morning Post* was the only organ to suggest that the country should insist upon the importance of order, and see to it that, if only formally, the young lieutenant should be court-martialed; while the *Evening News* covered itself with horrid fame by saying: "By the Goddess of *Victory*, Nelson has slain his thousands; but by *Jupiter*, Hardy has slain his ten thousands!"

There was no journal which did not join in this chorus which rose to greet John Hardy as he woke on the 17th of March. He was the only person who saw his praises with anything like equanimity.

He glanced through three of the articles, then pushed the heap from him.

"Well, Bobbie," he said, "it is decent to see one's name all about in the prints. But what is it all for?"

"There is the opinion of England," said old Robert, "about a son of John Nelson Hardy, sir!"

"Of England, Bobs?" said John; "don't you believe that. These writing fellows are not England.

England is silent—great and silent. She means more, Bobs, and says less. She will love me, too, for what I have done, perhaps—but different from this talk—in her own silent way——"

He stopped, coughing.

"Ah, that cough, Master John!" said Robert.

"Bother the cough! it is rather bad this morning, though, isn't it? Do you know what I think I shall do, Bobbie?"

"Well, sir?"

"Go to a hot country at once."

"A hot—what, sir?"

"A hot country, Bobs."

Bobs was alarmed. He at once suspected diplomacy. John was whimsical, and wilful. Bobs knew what it meant when those dry rose-lips closed tightly.

"Which country, Master John?" said the old man tremulously.

He divined horribly that the bird was about to fly from the old cage.

"Which country, sir?" he repeated before John answered.

"I am thinking of China, Bobbie," said John.

The old man's hands met in terror.

"China, Master John? Oh, don't, don't say China, Master John!"

"I believe that China is a hot country—in the summer, Bobbie?" said John in innocent query.

"I know nothing about China, Master John. Certainly, it is no fit place for such as you."

"Oh, I don't see that, Bobbie."

"But why China, Master John, if you really think of going anywhere? China, recollect, is at the other end of the world."

"But that's where my ship is, isn't it, Bobbie?"

"Your ship? What, ships *again?*—and you coughing there like an echo among the Chiltern Hills? Well, well, I suppose it's no use an old man talking,—who has served your father before you, and your grandfather before him."

"Yes, it is, Bobbie; believe me, it is, Bobs! But

John Hardy Gives an Order. 91

still—really—you will try and be good, won't you? I must go, Bobbie."

"Well, that sea!" said Bobbie, a hand over his mouth, shaking the head of contemplative wonderment. He was thinking of that "sea-fever" which, in the history of the house of Hardy, had more than once resulted in domestic tragedy and disaster.

"Well, that sea!" he said—"those ships!"

"No, it isn't quite that, Bobbie; it isn't the sea," said John. "Don't go blaming the sea. Of course, one is fond of the sea, and all that; but that isn't quite the reason now. I feel that I must go, and I must really."

"Well, but isn't that what I said, Master John?— that it is no use an old man talking? That no one pays any heed to him? no one whom he has watched over, and yearned his heart over, more than any son? Ah——" suddenly the old man fell half over the bed, imploring with tears. "Listen to me, Master Johnnie, do, now—give up these wild thoughts! What good can come of them? So, from a boy it always was—and did old Bobbie ever lead you wrong? Do, now, don't think of such things—it is the Enemy puts them in your head—drive them away! Here is all England going to make much of you—why not stay with old Bobbie? Don't go, my son! Don't you go! You are not in a fit state, and it is no fit place, among a pack of heathen men, fighting fiends—what good can you do? Stay here with me! Can you suppose that I would tell you wrong? Come, now, comfort old Bobbie's heart—tell me——"

John Hardy rubbed his pink face against the old man's shriveled cheek.

"It is so hard to say no to you, Bobbie," he said. "I hardly think it is right of you to urge me in that way. You see, I have made up my mind, and it is hardly—kind, is it? If one's mind is made up in a certain way, it is beyond one's power to change it, is it not? Go I must, you see."

The dry rose-leaves were pressed close now, and Bobbie should have noticed them; but he went rashly on.

"Only listen to me, Master John," he said. "Hear me out——"

"No—no more," said John. "I bid you be silent now. Pass me a sheet of note-paper and a pencil."

Old Bobbie, mouse-quiet in a moment, hobbled to a desk, and then back.

John scribbled a few words, handed them to the old man, and said :

"It is all right, Bobbie. I am not the least cross, you know. But there are times when one must be allowed to go one's own way, aren't there ? Have that telegram sent off at once, will you ? And bring me a good big tumbler of champagne, will you, Bobs ? "

The telegram with which Bobs shuffled off contained these words :—

To Selby Captain of *English Bird*, lying at Freshwater.

Please have *English Bird* ready to sail by Sunday night at latest. Going coast Spain. JOHN HARDY.

The *English Bird* was a 74-ton schooner-yacht of Hardy's own, with an easy speed of ten knots.

CHAPTER X

JOHN HARDY AMONG WOMEN

JOHN HARDY had this trouble : he was "non-intellectual," and his passion had fastened upon a person all intellect.

Had his entry into the Navy depended upon his passing the usual examination as a competitor, he would certainly never have entered it. As it was, he was a "service cadet," and had received a nomination as the son of an officer of the navy who had performed long and distinguished service. Even so, he had had to pass a test examination ; and in this very elementary ordeal he had failed in the subject "French." Once more he received a nomination, and once more he was given a chance in the examination-hall of the Commissioners of Cannon Row—his very last. All that half-year he was "swotting" like an elephant at the fatal "French," to the neglect of "Composition," another of his weak points. During the hot week in June preceding the examination he was a true slave of the lamp ; but his strong will this time was at work. With his lucky knack, he scraped through. The number of "pass" marks was 660 : he got 662.

Hardy was not a book-man ; he had even a secret contempt for book-men and book-learning.

Moreover, as we said before, he got into trouble later on. While in training on board the *Britannia* he had been reported to the Admiralty for "unsatisfactory conduct" and had been "warned." The "unsatisfactory conduct" consisted in walking arm-in-arm with a girl of the lowest class though the streets of Dartmouth, both the girl and John being pretty far gone in a state of intoxication.

These, then, were his weak points: That he was far from literary; that he was too fond of fermented things; that he was too fond of feminine persons.

Up to the time at which we met him, he still made spelling mistakes in common English words in writing ordinary letters.

In five or six of the ports of Europe there was more than one young woman unforgetful of the crinkled hair and angel-eyes of John Hardy. He was, indeed, painfully shy in the presence of women, and was a very clumsy and heavy lover—but he was also very good-looking, and *naif*: and one thing made up for the other. On the whole, he "arrived."

He loved every woman in the world; and this love was, in general, returned.

But most of all he loved Miss Isabel Jay, known to her friends as "Bosey"; and Bosey, apparently, did not love him. Her love was already taken up by something else—a thing which she called "Art."

He went to see her on the day of the telegram to Freshwater. A strip of black plaster concealed the scratch on his forehead. He was in the habit, even on visits of ceremony, of wearing a rough and heavy pea-jacket, such as pilots wear, with brass buttons, and thus attired he went out into the streets, a soft cap an his head.

Could he have been recognized, he would have been lifted on the shoulders of the people, and carried to his destination.

A servant ushered him into a very dainty inner room at Hampstead—a kind of studio-boudoir, in a Greek style, with Corinthian pillars, and flimsy saffron hangings. Miss Jay was rather an heiress, and lived with an old aunt in stately solitude. There now she sat before an easel, with brush and palette.

She was a lady of many accomplishments: of that unspeakably "new" kind; had written two novels of the "problem" sort; she was a preacher of land-nationalization; she had painted one knows not how many pictures; she was not yet nineteen; and she was pretty.

She had a substantial body, with a waist quite as large as that of Eve or Venus. She wore her red-gold hair in coil upon coil of *négligé* richness about her head; her eyes were green.

In her large countenance there were intelligence and strong self-assurance. The hard bones of her corset were not more visible through her bodice than the Will of her character in her face.

"Oh, Mr. Hardy, I am glad!" she cried. "Ah, and I have heard!"

"About the battle, and so on?"

"Yes, if "so on" means yourself. How very brave you must be!"

"Englishmen are that, you know."

"Are not a good many great cowards? Men do so live in regions of fantasy! Women are more prosaic—and clearer. Did you ever see an average English girl in the presence of a mouse, Mr. Hardy?"

"Girls are different," said John.

Bosey's lips tightened. This was the kind of ancient point of view, purely male, to which she had the most touchy antipathy.

"Oh, different of course," she said, "in pose of nervous structure, and so on, and so on. But substitute for the mouse the broker's man, and you get at once a measure of the average Englishman's courage."

"Somebody has been misleading you," said John. "Englishmen are brave. Foreign people are afraid of things."

She looked at him with real pity, for his insularity, his unintelligence.

"But why *misleading?* Can it be that you think an ordinary girl incapable of observing for herself?"

"I? Why if you only knew how much I like girls!'

"*Merci!*"

"Ah, now you are sarcastic."

"You are too shrewd."

"I never know whether you are making fun of me or not."

"Well, what does it matter, Mr. John?"

"But it is not nice to be made fun of by some one whom you like."

"Really *like?*"

"You know!"

"You are too complimentary."

"Like isn't the word. I think I like you better than any one in the whole world."

"Now you are—what is the word?—spooney."

"I should be as happy as the Queen if you would only like me back."

"Spooney!"

"You are not making fun?"

"Don't be suspicious. You are too penetrating."

"Well, what do you say?"

"To what?"

"To my liking you so much?"

"I can only say that it is distinctly spooney."

"But do you like me back?"

"Oh, *I!* Well, yes, as you ask me. I like you—back. But in my own fashion, you understand; not in that designingly spooney way."

"I do not understand you," said John. "You are not like other girls."

"Then logically you should not like me, since you like other girls so very very much."

"I do, though. I like you much better than any of the others. You must not go by logic."

"Ah, but I am nothing if not logical, Mr. Hardy."

"But facts are facts, aren't they? If logic contradicts a fact, then you must throw the logic overboard to the sharks. I tell you I like you better than any one. That is enough."

"Enough for what—for me?"

"It should be."

"But our human nature is more or less complex, I suppose? Do you mean that the mere fact of your caring for me should be enough to lead me to corresponding actions? That is wrong, you know. Listen,

John Hardy Among Women

Mr. Hardy: we first met—how long ago?—about five weeks, I think—at Lady Sinclair's, you remember. And since then, how many times? About six, perhaps. Well, I can see that you are used to easy conquests, you know; and at once I detected that you were laying yourself out to be captured by me, if I chose to take the trouble to capture you. But I did not choose! I have other things to think of; and it will be as much as I can possibly do, supposing I live for eighty years in tolerable health of body, to get through the little all I have in mind. I am not going to say that it is out of the question that some day I may not allow myself to be seduced into marriage by some man or other; but, at the moment, it is a thing so remote from the actual strain of my thoughts, that, I assure you, it has quite the look of an impossibility. All the time, mind you, I am secretly alive to the fact that it must be very nice to be petted and kissed by charming lips; but it is not, you see, precisely what I have chosen for myself. You know about "scorning delights and living laborious days," don't you? Well, that is my way. So I beg, once and for all, that you will be more sensible with respect to me for the future, Mr. John."

Bosey delivered this lecture with brush uplifted. She bent and gave a touch to the picture.

As the last words passed her lips, a sigh escaped Hardy, and this sentence, barely whispered:

"*You* are the mate for me, by the Lord!"

She heard him and cried:

"Mr. Hardy!"

His lips were pressed together. But as he was the firmest, so he was the most uncouth, of lovers. He said:

"I am going to China in a day or two. I *should* like to marry you before I go."

She broke into ripples of evil laughter.

"Not so soon! Not so soon!" she cried, angry now.

"When I come back," he said simply.

She looked into his face in unfeigned surprise.

"Have I not *told* you?" she cried, almost with alarm. "What do you mean? I am quite a free subject, you know. This is not Turkey; this is not —Peru. Do you mean that because you are to be the national hero, and so on? Oh, but that is in rather queer taste, then! Have I not answered you?"

"I love you!"
"I don't care!"
"I *do!*"
"You do not!"
"Ah, you don't know——!"
"You are to keep away!"
"I shall have you yet!"
"*Have* me!"
"Yes."
"Silly boy."
"Give me one!"
"Don't come——"
"Just one."
"What?"
"Kiss."
"Ur!—silly. Do—go—away. This is *too* absurd!"

She stamped. The dry rose-leaves had brushed her hot cheek. So far had passion led Hardy. Then he started—to this point he had never dared, on his own initiative. A shock of scarlet shyness possessed him.

"Ah, now I have presumed," he said, stammering. "Forgive me—I will go——"

"Well, it is of no consequence, Mr. Hardy," she answered, calm already, holding out her hand, "but perhaps you had better go."

"Well, then— But you understand that I am going to China?"

"Perfectly. I believe that you will find the Chinese charming artists."

"While I am away you will not be marrying some one else?"

"Not I. You may be confident that I shall remain self-sufficient. Even the new National Darling, you see, cannot tempt me."

"But you will think sometimes of a poor sailor."

"The newspapers, you know, will remind me of the poor sailor."

"Good-by. I am going."

"Then go."

"When I come back from China, I shall have you."

"You said that before—whatever *having* me may mean : and I said—No."

"But I shall."

"Well, we won't discuss the matter now. I am sorry for you, you know, because you *look—épaté*. But you will soon get over it, and it will do you good. You were over-confident, you know. Will you say good-by, now?"

"May I kiss your hand?"

"Nonsense! you are just like a child."

"May I?"

"Well, if that is any comfort to you——"

He kissed her hand with old-fashioned ceremonial, caught up his cap, and was gone.

Had he been more successful, he would have walked straight home, and to bed, and so made the course of history otherwise.

As it was, he went wandering through a number of streets in a desultory mood, not knowing whither he went.

Night had fallen.

He had a deep radical love for this girl. He said to himself, walking himself tired: "I will have her, I will have her, by the Lord——"

Suddenly his own name caught his eye. He was in front of the Palace Theater of Varieties.

London was alight. The streets thronged with people. The façades of the Palace were arrayed with galaxies of jets.

There, on a board, the ink still wet, appeared the attraction of the night:

MISS LOTTIE COLLINS

Will Appear To-night

In Her New Patriotic Song,

Entitled:

"BRAVO, JOHN HARDY!"

The song had been composed, learned, orchestrated, and rehearsed, all in the course of a single day.

He stood looking at the placard, smiling. He felt in his pocket ; he had some money. It was about time for the entertainment to begin. He went in.

His mind was, in some of its aspects, as unstable as water. It shifted like phosphorescences in the dark. All forms of pleasure, especially, had great power to deflect and draw him. He could be won from grave to gay by the simplest means. He had not only the soul of a hero but the mind of a baby.

He remembered that one could smoke and drink in music-halls. By heaven ! he would make a night of it. If there was blame, the blame was Bosey Jay's.

He never took the dry-land quite seriously. To him it was " shore "—rather a foreign place—a place for "sprees."

He put his hand into his pocket again, and looked at what money he had. There was plenty. Now then for Bacchus and Terpsichore ; wine, and song, and—Woman ?

Nearly all the afternoon, at this very hour, a stream of carriages, containing ecstatic photograph-hunters, Mr. Goschen, Lords of the Admiralty, pressmen rabid for an interview, distinguished persons, were moving toward, and away from, the door of No. 11A Cavendish Square. John Hardy was not at home.

He found himself in one of the " pit-stalls " during the performance of a ventriloquist. In a few minutes he had provided himself with cigars, and a goodly tumbler of spirit-and-soda-water.

A girl, sitting next to him, touched a companion on the other side of her—a soldier, whose name was John Brabant—and whispered :

"Just look at him ; isn't he handsome ? "

Her name was Ada Seward. She was the woman who, alone in the world, had been able to melt the ice of Dr. Yen How.

She was a small creature, with skin of a warm yellowish color, and little quaint Chinese eyes, and light hair with the whitest tinge of red in it ; not perhaps pretty, but with some unspeakable attraction of piquancy about her uncommon, saucy little face, which had caused her to receive twelve offers of marriage before she was twenty. Her friends declared that she was the living image of Miss Marie Tempest, the "Geisha" *prima donna*. In figure she was typically English.

She was perishing to speak a word to the sweet pink face by her side, to its delicate aristocratic lines. At last, during a loud song consigning the German nation to perdition, she found her chance.

"Now, young gentleman," she said, "that is *my* dress, please; it won't be fit to look at to-morrow if you throw any more brandy-and-soda over it."

John gave her the sweetest smile she had ever beheld on mortal lips, and said :

"Pardon me."

At the same time, he looked into her face, and liked it.

The waiter had already borne him three whispering glasses of beverage.

"May I ?" he said; "here, waiter—may I order for you and your companion?"

John Brabant bowed low with a hearty "Thank you, sir!"

But Ada, who was quite three or four grades higher in the social scale than he, being in his company only owing to old associations, nudged the soldier deprecatingly, objecting to the obligation.

It was too late, however. The offer had been accepted. In a few minutes John Hardy and Ada were talking—Ada laughing, John smiling. Brandy-and-soda became the order of the day. Hardy had soon a good deal more than enough.

The audience was in a queer mood, impatient, intolerant. There was neither an empty seat nor a spare inch of standing-room in the place; but the people's interest was all bent upon one future point in the entertainment—the entrance of Miss Collins—and meanwhile they took not the least pains to conceal their indifference. There was something rowdy in the tone of the assembly.

"By Jove, I *am* liking you!"

His lips were at her ear.

"Ah, now, that's the drink talking, not you."

"The drink? Nonsense!" I am, really. Are *you* liking me back?"

"Ah, that would be telling!"

"You are!"

"Go away with you! Why, I have only just seen you!"

"That is of no importance."

"Oh, isn't it, though!"

"Don't be a cruel girl. Here, waiter——"

"Do you know what I think you are—from your ways?"

"No; tell me."

"*You* tell me; let me see if I am right. What are you?"

"You mean my profession?"

"Yes."

"I am a sailor."

Had Ada's ears been more delicately nurtured, she would have detected there, half-drunk though Hardy was, a very slight intonation of imperial arrogance.

"A sailor? You? Go on! Show me your hands."

"Oh, my hands are not very rough, I admit. But still—I am a sailor. You may believe me—in the navy, you know."

"I see. Well, do you know I had an idea of something like that? A sailor! Yes, that is what you *are*. You come to the point so soon, don't you?—like sailors do."

"Well, but do you like me back, now?"

"No, thank you. No sailors for me. They are here to-day, and gone to morrow."

"That is because they must. You can't punish them for doing their duty to their country, can you?"

"The country is one thing, but girls have got to look after themselves, you see."

"You are too practical."

"I have got to be."

"But you will have me for your sweetheart?"
"Perhaps I will, and perhaps I won't. It depends."
Here was an Achievement in Indefiniteness. John Hardy fled from the mental indeterminateness in which the answer left him, by turning to his glass for a drink.

The shifters of the indicating numbers removed the card 7, and put up the card 8; "8" meant Lottie Collins. A murmur of expectancy rumored through the building. The air grew electric. Every one knew that great things were coming. Already the nerves of the audience were strung high and tense.

"That is very indefinite."
"I can't help it. Wait and see how we feel to-morrow morning."
"Only say now that you like me."
"Well, suppose I say—yes. No, no—it's too stupid!"
"Sweet of you, Nell! Is your name Nell?"
"Yes. How on earth did you know? It is my second name. They call me "Ada."'
"Ada—what?"
"Ada Seward."
"I shall call you "Nell." I like that better."
"And what is yours?"
"John."

Ada was smitten by Coincidence. On each side of her was a "John"—one a soldier, the other a sailor. She was the link which united and disparted Her Majesty's forces.

"John—what?"

Here John paused. He was now in a high state of fuddlement, but was capable of remembering that his name was on placards all about the town, and about to be proclaimed by "No. 8."

"John—what?" came the question again.

But Miss Collins rescued him. There was the rattle of a drawn-up curtain—an intense "Sh—h—h" swept through the building—and at once there followed a clap and cry of applause as the whole audience leapt to its feet. Miss Collins had bounded on to the stage, be-draperied from head to heel in the Union Jack.

The air was electric. Every heart bounded in every bosom. John Hardy's right arm had stolen and twined round Ada Seward's left, his fingers kneading and palpating the soft flesh of her forearm. With his left hand he lifted the glass to his lips. He alone, on the subject of himself, remained careless.

Amid a dead silence the artiste lifted up her arm, and so for a minute stood. Then she gave a sharp, shrewd twist to her wrist, and passionately shouted—

"Bravo, John Hardy!"

And again the audience leapt to its feet, with howls of rapture, which lasted five minutes.

The boxes were packed with some quite distinguished people.

At last there was quiet. The artiste began to sing. The tune was simple and stirring—the words were like raw rum, as crude and as strong:

When the Allied fleet came over, and passed the Straits of Dover,
 They thought they'd have it all their little way;
But a knowing little cardy (they call him Johnnie Hardy),
 He crashed them his Ta-ra-ra-Boom-de-aye.

    CHORUS

 Oh! isn't he a jolly little boy?
  And *don't* he know his little way about!
 When he handed in his card, and the French saw "Johnnie Hard,"
  Lord! transformation scene, you bet, and wild, distracted rout!

There's a little sailor lad, and his eyes are mild and sad,
 And you'd think he'd not one blooming word to say!
But holy Moses guard ye (he's known as Johnnie Hardy)
 When he crashes his Ta-ra-ra-Boom-de-aye!

    CHORUS

 Oh! isn't he a joy, that jolly sailor-boy?
  And *don't* he know his little way about!
 When he winks his little eye, you may just lie down and die,
  For his red right hand is thunder, and his eyes shoot lightnings out!

By this time the audience, wrought to a high excitement, had caught the lilt of the tune. When Miss Collins repeated the last chorus, the house vociferated it, utterly drowning her voice in the wheeling tumult which now prevailed. She pretended to retire, loaded with the masses of flowers showered upon her from the boxes; but at once returned at the call of the audience. She sang:

Ah, boldly they came over; and they crossed the Straits of Dover;
But "Hardy!" was the answer England hurled that day;
And Johnnie winked his eye, and they all lay down to die,
When he crashed them his Ta-ra-ra-Boom-de-aye!

CHORUS
So isn't he just bricks, with his little crafty tricks?
And *don't* he know his little way about!
For his head is crisp with curls, he's a devil with the girls,
But ten thousand times a devil when the Dogs of War are out!

Once more she repeated the chorus, the audience taking it clamorously up. Then she tripped from the stage. But the house roared after her with the frenzy of men parting with their last earthly hope. She had now utterly mesmerized and enthralled them. The moment was ecstatic with an electrical tension impossible to describe. They bawled, they yelled, they stood up straining forward with gesticulations, tears pouring down many faces, handkerchiefs waving. At last she reappeared. She had a verse in reserve. She sang:—

Old England is the mother, and each of you a brother,
To this stern brow that bids the world obey;
And now we shan't be tardy (God bless you, little Hardy!)
In crashing more Ta-ra-ras-Boom-de-aye!

CHORUS
So isn't he a joy, this British sailor-boy?
And *don't* he know his little way about!
He couldn't hurt a fly, but he's tricky, and he's sly,
And he makes the sky to redden, and the roaring deep to spout!

She rendered this last verse with almost distracted verve and heat; and before proceeding to give the chorus a second time stretched forth her arms, and in a fierce tone of command, cried : "Stand all !"

The audience sprang upright yelling the male part of it uncovering. The singing of the last chorus burst forth universally. And there too, was Hardy, hopelessly drunk now, with an arm round Ada Seward's arm he, too, standing, he too—with an empty glass brandished in his left hand—laughing and singing :

So isn't he a joy, this British sailor-boy?
And *don't* he know his little way about!
He couldn't hurt a fly, but he's tricky, and he's sly,
   And he makes the sky to redden, and the roaring deep to spout!

No sooner had Miss Collins disappeared, amid an unparalleled tempest of sound, than the audience scattered. They were capable of no more emotion for that night.

Hardy found himself in the street, leaning on Ada Seward's arm. They were alone. Where the soldier Brabant had vanished to, neither Brabant himself nor any one else knew.

"Shee cheers for ole Nelson !" cried John Hardy. "Ha! ha! ha!—ole Nelson. Shee cheers, by the Lord——"

"Come now, be good," said Ada. "Get into this cab, will you ?"

"Where you live ?"

She gave him the Pattison address, and impressed it upon him.

"Mind, I shall expect to hear from you," she said, as she shoved him into the cab, and kissed him.

John going home in the cab, murmured, with fainting, intoxicated breath :

"Bosey! Bosey! I shall have you yet,—by the Lord——"

And Ada waited in vain. The next morning he had forgotten her address.

But he remembered—*her name.*

CHAPTER XI.

JOHN HARDY AMONG THE NATIONS.

THE next day John Hardy shut himself up in a fit of sulky moroseness, flatly refusing to see any one. The day after that was Sunday, and on Sunday evening he was at Freshwater.

His yacht was ready to sail.

He had in his breast-pocket letters of credit from the bankers of his solicitors to business houses in Paris, Berlin, Petersburg, Pekin, and Shanghai.

He had also with him a French dictionary, a German dictionary, a bible, and a very elementary French conversation book.

He had also with him a portrait of Boscy Jay, which he had obtained that morning from Lady Sinclair.

He had also with him a Colt's revolver.

He had also with him a shilling map of Northern China, and four sorts of foreign coin.

As he stepped from the train from Newport at Freshwater, he saw a late Sunday-edition placard announcing that 100,000 English troops were about embark for Havre for a French invasion; and this made his heart rejoice.

The *English Bird* weighed anchor at 8 P.M. He was under requisition by letter to attend at the Admiralty the next day, but he took not the least notice of it, leaving it to be supposed that he had set out before receiving the requisition. He was a free subject, he said to himself.

Before sunrise on Wednesday morning he arrived at the old town of San Sebastian on the north Spanish coast.

He had taken the precaution to bring no linen marked

with his name. He intended to travel as an American citizen, under the name of Petersen. From San Sebastian he sent back the yacht to England, and at once proceeded with a small trunk by train to Bayonne, thence to Bordeaux, and thence by way of Angoulême, Poitiers, and Tours to the French capital. He reached the Gare d'Orléans on the Thursday morning at 9.30, nearly a week after the battle of Shoreham, and proceeded westward to a hotel in the neighborhood of the Madeleine, reporting himself in the hotel bulletin as having traveled from Spain.

The first thing that happened to him was that he fell in love with that charming courtezan, Paris.

He had been so exceptionally and scrupulously insular, that he had always shrunk from leaving England, except in the ships on which he served. Hence he knew some of the ports of Europe very well, but had never been to Paris. Now was revealed to him the *fille de joie* of the cities of the earth, the pure feminine, as queer, and treacherous, and lovely, and indescribable, as woman. Whoso truly loves woman will not escape her witchery. She is the divine sinner.

Hardy intended to leave Paris at three o'clock; but he put off his departure till the next day; and meantime he got into trouble.

The news of the disaster to the allied fleet had four days since reached France. But the whole thing was incredible; it was not believed, or believed with only half the mind; and for this reason: that the news had come by the roundabout way of the Mackay-Bennet cable—from New York! What lent some color of truth to the report was the incomprehensible fact that the Contre-Amiral and General de Rosney had sent no despatch-boat to announce the landing of the troops on English soil. Yet the nation refused to believe the incredible. They waited, with suspended mind, with bated breath, wildly hoping.

In the impossible contingency of their fleet having been defeated, they argued that at least *one* ship would have escaped to bring them the news. But no ship had come: the fleet could not be defeated.

The fact was that *five* ships had escaped—three liners and two battleships. But of the three liners one was towing another at the rate of about half a knot an hour, and the third was just forging through the water against a head wind under sail alone. The two battleships were German, and in sorry plight. One with a broken screw, and one with disabled engines, they were making their slow way north-eastward with a vague outlook toward Bremerhafen in the mind's eye.

Of the British ships not one craft had remained afloat.

However, on the morning of Hardy's arrival in Paris, one of the three liners drifted on to the French coast, near St Valéry en Caux, having on board an infantry brigade, and a crew, perishing with hunger, on the verge of frenzy with thirst. By noon Paris knew.

Then there was *brouhaha* and *houlabalu*, or, as we say, "ructions."

Paris, in her rages, as in all else, is like a woman. She tears her finery and ribbons to shreds; she foams at the mouth; her hair is "all over the place!"

Her last exuberance had taken the shape of the Dreyfus riots. Monsieur Zola had been the scapegoat. He had been declared a "*dégénéré*" by the University; had been regarded as a "*cas*" by the *aliénists*; had been hopelessly caricatured; was regarded as a man done for.

He waited. On this Thursday morning he had his revenge.

Under the great statue of France in the Place de la Bastille he stood, and the crowd around him spread far up the avenues, leading into the Place. He was recognized: "*C'est M. Zola!*" And he harangued them.

He had always been known as a very decent orator. And he three times used the word "*trahison*."

This word "treason" has a strange glamour for the French mind, carrying with it an extraordinary hint of the blackest infamy.

It was a word which Paris could ill bear at that moment. It simply made the crowd a kennel of rabid dogs. Already in other parts—in the Cité, the Place de la Concorde, la Vilette—excited throngs were rushing riotously about the rues and avenues and boulevards, without the incentive of M. Zola's "*trahison.*" And in the midst of M. Zola's crowd, in the deadliest peril, stood John Hardy.

On his forehead was the strip of plaster which covered the scratch received at Shoreham.

By some sure intuition, the French know an Englishman at once ; they say of you at a glance, "*Il est anglais.*" And Hardy was very much of an Englishman.

If ever human boy enjoyed himself, it was he at that moment. He loved a row for its own sake, and here was the sweetest of all rows—a French row.

What added a touch of exquisiteness to his enjoyment was his inner knowledge of the cause of the row. These children had dashed themselves like impotent waves against the rock of England, and were now astonished to find that rock was hard, and could shatter them.

John could hardly understand a word of the harangue, though he once heard his own name, but he guessed what it was all about, and he saw it in the distorted faces of the people. He stood looking up into the startling eyes of the orator, quietly smiling.

At the first sounds of uproar he had run from his hotel, and followed a crowd eastward. No thought of his danger occurred to him. His attitude of mind towards the people among whom he found himself was one of quiet and assured dominancy.

M. Zola was about to complete his oration, and the mob to rush with some indefinitely hostile purpose toward the Elysée, when Hardy felt himself touched with a deliberate tap on the shoulder.

He looked around and up.

He was confronted by an extremely foreign-looking person, a middle-aged man to judge by his face, but with a head of quite white long hair, and a splendid white beard and moustache. He wore a gray, broad-brimmed, soft-felt sombrero sort of hat, which drooped on one side like a lady's Gainsborough. But the part of him that attracted attention was his two hands ;

John Hardy Among the Nations

they were simply two constellations of bulky flashing jewels : on each of the eight fingers being several huge rings, glittering with every variety of luminous stone.

His face was very excited. But he said to Hardy, with perfect polished politeness, lifting his sombrero :

"*Ah, monsieur a marché sur mon pied !*"

"*Je ne comprends,*" said John.

"Ah ! it is as I thought. Monsieur is, then, English."

"That is so," answered John incautiously.

"Ah ! English—good. Very-well—all-right. I wished to say that monsieur has marched on my foot."

John knew that this was a lie. But he made a concession ; with a condescending nod and smile he said :

"*Merci !*"

He meant to say "*Pardon.*" But "*merci* and *pardon,*" somehow, were very much mixed up in his mind ; he often used one instead of the other.

The very-foreign person said with a bow :

"I cannot help to think that the action was intentioned on the part of monsieur."

"Go away, will you ?" said John Hardy.

"But monsieur has not answered my question."

"Yes, I have. Be good enough to go to the devil."

"To the——? Very-well—all right." And at once he lifted his voice high, interrupting the orator, crying out :

"*Voilà, messieurs—un anglais—de la Marine anglaise——*"

John had committed the indiscretion of wearing his mariner pea-jacket, with brass buttons engraved with anchors.

There arose an outcry round him. A commotion spreading wider through the crowd, like circles round a pebble-splash, had him for its center. M. Zola ceased to hold forth.

They pressed round stiflingly. Hardy began to cough feebly. He pushed back with his elbow a rough-looking, brazen-eyed fellow in an *ouvrier's* smock. But his effort to free himself was poor in force. In a moment or two his jacket was rent off him, and a cruel fist smote him heavily in the jaw. He saw clearly now that he was on the point of being torn to pieces.

He wondered what he could do ; and having calmly measured the situation, and seeing no chance of escape, he broke into a laugh at his own expense, calling out loudly :

"*Cochers! Cochers!*"

By "*cochers*" he meant to call them "pigs."

In a moment he was on the ground on his back.

But whatever force it is which underlies the world had this frail and dauntless lad in its keeping for the time being. He was necessary.

A diversion was caused by a loud pair of lungs, which cried :

"*Mais, messieurs, écoutez-moi, écoutez-moi——*"

It was the very-foreign person, who was also vehemently interposing his utmost bodily vigor to the rescue of John.

"You know me—you know me all—listen to me—I am Edrapol——"

"*C'est Edrapol! Edrapol!*"

Instantly the rumor spread far, amid *vives*. Edrapol, the duellist, the Bulgarian, the world-renowned master of the pistol and the rapier ; it was he.

He explained. The English sailor had committed upon him a personal outrage. He begged—it was his simple right—that the life of the miscreant should be spared to make the *réparation* which was only his, Edrapol's, plain due. The stranger's death was certain either way, but, in short, messieurs, the other way was more neat—more *convenable*.

And so Hardy was, as it were, torn from the rough hands which had seized him. Edrapol's popularity in Paris was paramount. The mob, led by Zola, rushed westwards. Hardy and Edrapol were alone.

The *escrimeur*, bowing, handed his card to Hardy, and requested a return of the favor.

John Hardy Among the Nations

"What for?" said John. "I have no card."
"But monsieur will meet me?"
"Where?"
"In the Bois, monsieur."
"But what for?"
"Why, to fight, monsieur."
"You don't mean a duel?"
"Why, naturally, monsieur."
"I see. But an old man like you?"
"Not *too* old, monsieur, perhaps! Does monsieur then hesitate?"
"I do. It is absurd."
"Monsieur is, of course, sensible to the interpretation which one would naturally put upon any hesitation from his part?"
"No. I am not sensible of it. What interpretation?"
"That monsieur is a coward."
"Well, but I am not one, interpret as you please."
"Still, monsieur, I say the *natural* interpretation. I am sure you will realize my point of view if you recollect that I have the reputation of being the deadliest swordsman in Europe."
"Is that so? Oh, I didn't know."
"Now I think monsieur realizes my point of view?"
"I do rather."
"And monsieur will now fight?"
"I don't mind. What with?"
"All that will be arranged for us by others, monsieur. If you will give me your name, your address, and the address of a friend to whom I may send a friend of mine——"
"I have no friend worth mentioning here. Send your friend to me personally."

He gave his real name and his address, and turned away from the bowing figure before him. He set out for his hotel.

Later in the day he found himself in front of the Chambre des Députés, and dropped in with a stream of the public.

A glance showed a full house—Zola, Papa Sardou,

the young novelist, Pierre Louys—and the Parisian pressmen overflowing into the foreign press.

Below, no dull uniformity, as in the House of Commons, but variety, colors, races. There is M. Grenier, the Mussulman deputy, his white Arabian burnous, near the "passage of the Left." The center is packed —Republicans and Opportunists—Government-supporters these. The Right is the stronghold of the Clericals and Legitimists. To the Left, the Socialists.

In the center of the circle, the tribune—a pulpit; and behind the tribune, but towering above it, the throne of the President of the chamber, M. Brisson.

M. Brisson wears no wig like our Speaker; but his patriarchal beard is full of awe.

M. Hanotaux, in the Tribune, is explaining that "nothing in the actual situation so far is of importance as regards the annihilation of the British Empire in the near future!"

Applause from Center and Right. Queer sounds from the Left. There is going to be a row.

"It is a coalition whose very name is Victory."

"It has already been defeated!" yells a voice from the Left. (Huge hubbub; M. Clovis Hugues, the long-haired poet, screaming something ecstatic through the din.)

President Brisson rises. He bids them recollect that France looks to them for an example of calm and sage deliberation. "*Délibération calme et sage!*"

Hardy understands the words, because they are like English words, and he throws a gasp of laughter behind his head, crying:

"By the Lord . . . !"

M. Hanotaux proceeds, though interrupted. His peroration is a touching appeal to the honor, the glory of France. He descends.

From the Left a cry: "Jaurès! Jaurès!" And the young leader of the Socialists, large, blonde, swings himself up to the Tribune. "Hanotaux is an *infame*. France has been made the tool of Russia and Germany!" President Brisson calls the speaker to order. But there is deaf obstinacy in the curve of the broad back turned towards the President. He makes M. de Mun, the orator of the Catholics, the object of his bitterest thrusts. M. de Mun retorts. The two men glare. Like a ball flung from hand to hand, so the stinging and witty retort darts quickly to and back between them. The Socialists egg on their man with cries, the Right their man.

A voice from the Right: "You are the paid spy of the British Rothschilds!" This from M. Carnet, a little fat man, a mere sphere of flesh. "You are a liar and a coward!" roars M. Jaurès.

There is a struggle on the front right benches. It is Carnet held back by his friends. The air is electrical. The journalists in their cribs stand and yell their own various views of the world.

Suddenly, from the left, a figure reels through a blind and drunken curve. He dodges the stray members on the floor, wheels, and fetches Carnet a blow.

Ha! sits the wind *so*, then? Hardy chortles, rearing with glee. In the passage leading from the Right to the lobbies there follows a scrimmage, from which a figure darts up the Tribune; Carnet has given Jaurès a blow under the ear.

Then all is chaos. Everybody is rushing everywhere. Wherever any one sees a head, he drives his fist at it, yelling. The whole Chamber rolls and tumbles in a tumult. They are like bits of vegetables wheeling promiscuously in a boiling and bubbling pot. President Brisson puts on his tall hat as a sign that the *séance* is at an end. The *mêleé* forces itself into the lobbies. Outside there is a clash; a sound of pistols. John Hardy has seen—France.

Meantime, all over the city the Garrison of Paris was in the streets, trying to clear them of the rioters. Night fell.

At eight o'clock a gentleman waited upon Hardy from Edrapol. But he could not speak English, and the interview was a fiasco. Hardy sat down and wrote the following letter, which he handed to Edrapol's second :—

SIR,—This is to let you know that after consideration I have changed mind about the duel for the present. If you like to think I am afraid of your fine swordsmanship, you can, but that is not really the case. On the contrary, when I tell you my motives, you ought to consider the writing of this letter, if anything, a rather brave and worthy act on my part. The fact is, I am a servant of Her Majesty the Queen, and have already, in my way, been able to do some good for my country. As you know, England wants men just now, and that is why, after consideration, I do not see my way to expose my life wantonly, while things are as they are, for a mere trifle. I am sorry to have to disappoint you, and myself too, in our little duel; but that is how I look at it. However, I make you this promise: that on the day this present war is over I will seek you out, in whatever country you may be, and present myself before you for the purpose of getting through with our little duel; and on that you may rely. I keep your card.—I remain, sir, your servant,
JOHN HARDY.

The amount of self-suppression, of noble patriotism, which the writing of this simply-worded letter implied for the arrogant spirit of Hardy may be assumed: when it was finished, he gave it, with a curl of the lip, to the ambassador of Edrapol.

The next morning he left Paris, and reached Aix in the evening, whence he proceeded to Berlin. To Berlin the bare news of the disaster had been flashed the day before; but it was not until the next morning that more detailed accounts came from the two ruined battleships, now arrived at Bremerhafen. Hardy found the Unter den Linden boulevard quite a Babel with the bawling of the news-vendors; it was rapidly being filled by groups rushing thither as to the main channel of intelligence from all directions of the city, while the Foreign Office in the Wilhelm-Strasse was being besieged by a great crowd clamoring to hear the truth, and spreading away to the Schloss, where, it was said, the Emperor was closeted with his Chancellor and his Chief of the Staff. The humor of the crowd was sullen; but it needed only the appearance of Wilhelm, accompanied by the Empress, on the front balcony of the Schloss, to turn discouragement into elation. Wilhelm suddenly drew his sword and flashed it in the sunlight. Then there was joy. No people cheer like Germans. Demonstration was their *specialité*. They excelled in looking pleased. Their *forte* was to claim the Future with verve and assurance, whether it really belonged to them or not. Hardy was in the midst of the crowd round the Schloss. He saw the flash of Wilhelm's sword. An hour later he was with a throng cheering itself hoarse in front of the Austrian Embassy, opposite the old home of M. Benedetti, so closely associated with the outbreak of Germany's last war. The Austrian Minister had unexpectedly appeared before the people, who now went wild with delight, a large area of the crowd presently starting to sing old Schneckenburger's "*Wacht am Rhein.*" Hardy observed every gesture, and every expression of every face which came within his range of vision, and he said to himself:

"So much for mein Herr, then."

He reached Königsberg the next morning, and thence went on to Vilna, Pskov, and St. Petersburg.

Everywhere there was commotion, excitement, crowds, posters, *mobil*.

In the Nevski Prospekt at St. Petersburg, in the Izak Platz, on the "English Quay," there were throngs, proclamations, printed heads of the Tsar, and every open space was gaudy with banners. The town, however, was fairly quiet, though there were some arrests of Nihilists. The Russians were the most English of the Continentals, or tended to be, when once their races became homogeneous. They had the ruralness, and something of the Stoicism, the Puritanism, and the nimbleness of the British; with this was mixed a certain Orientalism—a vermilion line in the gray of their character.

At his hotel John found an ostler of the Simbirsk Province, an adventurous and cosmopolitan man, who had been a sailor trading between Hull and Copenhagen for some years. He understood English. He struck up a friendship with John, and told him his history. John offered him 500 roubles if he would undertake to deliver a letter by hand in England, setting out at once. And this offer Ivan accepted.

The letter which John wrote was as follows :—

"MY DEAR BOBBIE,—Here I am in St. Petersburg after passing through France and Germany, and just about to set out to get by the Trans-Siberian Railway over all that great continent of Northern Asia to Vladivostok on the other side of the world, and so, please God, to Pekin, and my ship.

"Dear Bobbie, this is what I have to tell you, and you can write a letter to the *Times* yourself, so as to let the country know what little I have to say. The French are about to mass four Army Corps in the direction of Havre, and I don't think that for the present we can do much with them there, though later on, when we get our pecker up a bit, I know that ten Frenchmen won't be able to hold out against one Englishman. The German Cock-of-the-walk has telegraphed for the King of Saxony, and Prince Albrecht of Prussia, his Field-Marshals, and for Count Waldersee, Chief of the General Staff. Seven of his twenty Army Corps are mobilizing—namely, the 1st, or East Prussian ; the 17th, or West Prussian ; the 12th, Kingdom of Saxony ; and the 3d, 4th, 5th, and 6th, belonging to Brandenburg, the Province of Prussian Saxony, Posen, and Silesia respectively. But whether all these are intended to go to help the French, or to defend his own northern coast, or what, I do not know, not knowing much about fighting on *terra firma*.

"Well, dear Bobbie, I have seen my full of the people with whom I have been. I saw some splendid fisticuffs in the French House of Commons, and no end of fun ; and some very excited people in Germany and Russia. My opinion of the French is, that they are very nice people, the French women especially. But they are *old*, they are no good any more, they have not got any youth and go left in them ; you know what they are like, Bobbie ? Like *patté* (*sic*) *de foie gras*, nice but tainted. They are over-civilized, like an old dowager that's not fit for anything, but to make love-matches. France is no good any more, except for ornament and for tourists to come to. For energy she has got vivacity, and for nerve, verve—like a frivolous old *beau!* The world has nothing to expect from her. They are wonderfully ahead of us in some things—their lower class especially is far far ahead of ours in everything—but they do not move, their legs are heavy with age. The future belongs to *us*. At the rate we are going now, we shall soon have all that France has, and a thousand thousand times more, for we shall have youth and energy and vastness as well. The Germans are a young nation and they have all the enthusiasm of a young nation, and they will go ahead perhaps alright (*sic*). But they have not got anything in reserve, Bobbie. Froth is enthusiastic and young, too, but not very strong. I think the Russians would make mincemeat of the Germans, just as the Germans would of the poor pretty French. But the Russians are raw, new, and not, I don't think, a nation at all. Not one of them is the chosen race, dear Bobbie, '*the peculiar people*.' If you want to find that, I think you had better look nearer home.

"Well, no more at present. I shall expect you to take good care of yourself, mind, while I am away, so that I shall find you hale and hearty when I come back, if I ever do. Don't be getting up too early in the mornings, now; and don't forget your bottle of porter regularly every night, as something is wanted at your time of life.—With love to Bobbie, from his son,

"JOHN HARDY."

From this letter it will be seen that John Hardy could not only express his ideas with force and point, though in simple words, but that he possessed a large tract of brain, capable of taking in the world, and summing it up, and passing right judgment upon it, "as one having authority."

The letter reached England three weeks later, and could not escape the keen scent of the pressmen. It was published bodily in all the papers, bad spelling and all, the public gloating joyfully over its gentle wisdom, its humor, and its simplicity.

All this time Hardy was traveling, partly by train, and partly by camel caravan, towards his fate in the capital of China.

CHAPTER XII

THE AWAKENING

Dr. YEN HOW was seated in a garden of the Imperial City, reading.

He was arrayed in sumptuous robes of the softest, richest silk, embroidered with the tongue-darting Dragon, in token of high rank.

His pigtail reached to his calves: but at present only one inch and a half of it was of the doctor's own hair. The rest was artificial—made of fine black silk. Many dignitaries of even the highest rank in China adopted this convention.

Yen How, a minute or two before, had drawn the chop-sticks between his lips as the final ceremony to a dainty feed on rice-birds (just then in season), and the juiciest, tenderest tea. The meal had been held before him by attendants in gorgeous robes, themselves of high rank.

The ice-bound winter of Northern China was over. The sudden, hot spring was here.

By the right hand of Yen How was a stand of ebony arabesqued in walrus-tusk. On it was some of the pigment which the Chinese use for ink, and brushes such as they use for pens; there were also some folios of fine silk paper; there was a silver gong; and, half falling to the ground, the *North China Daily News*.

In Yen How's hands was an old copy of the *Shanghai Mercury*. Yen How was reading it; and as he read, his eyes went small in a smile. Something amused the doctor.

It was this: Herr von Bülow, the German Foreign

Minister, had, a good many months before, made a remark in the Reichstag which was reproduced later on in the *Mercury*. Von Bülow had said : "The Chinese Empire has already lasted 4300 years ; it will last another 3000."

"He did not mean it," murmured Yen How, "because he is a fool. But a fool may sometimes say a true thing, without meaning it."

At the same time he touched on his breast the decoration of the Red Eagle of the First Class which the German Emperor had conferred upon him immediately after the grant by China of the territories to Germany.

Then he went on with his slow, contemplative reading.

We have spoken of the meteoric career of this man in China ; we said that he " rose like a rocket." But he did not do all this by miracle. A rocket will not rise of itself ; it must be impelled by an upward, accountable force.

To what did Yen How owe his supreme authority ?— for his authority was now far more absolute than that of any Brother of the Sun and Moon who ever occupied the throne of the Hsüs. He owed it first of all to his Learning ; secondly, to his intensity of Racial Instinct ; and thirdly, to his audacious Genius.

To his Learning, first of all : for in China every door was open to the learned man. The learned man's learning, however, must be *Chinese ;* and here was the miracle of Dr. Yen How's achievements in the State Examination Halls of Canton and Pekin : that he who there proved himself more instructed than the pundits in Chinese wisdom, had spent the greater part of his life in acquiring Western scientific views and methods in Heidelberg, Paris, and Edinburgh.

He began at the bottom. He passed through the examination at Canton. The "Hall" was not a hall at all, but a double row of small sentry-boxes, capable of holding one person only, in which the examinee, provided with food, ink, brushes, and paper, spent two solitary weeks, seeing no one, answering his questions.

The Awakening

He usually came out more like a dead than a living man, and, even for the most erudite, the ordeal was one of fire.

During that fortnight of dark seclusion, Yen How smiled and smiled and smiled again. He was examined on the complex Theology, the fanciful History, the intricate old Law, the amazing Astronomy of the Chinese. In all these subjects, and many more, their Learning consists of an immense range of minute dogmatism, which the whole lifetime of their wise men was spent in acquiring. Yen How's big brain knew all about these subjects—more about them than his examiners. But he differed from them in this: that he alone knew the falseness of the answers which he painted. His eyes were all smiles as he sat there writing about the earth going round the sun in so many seconds, and about the place of Confucius in the third hierarchy of the gods. It was the sweetest fun to him.

When he came from his sentry-box at the end of the two weeks among a number of wan and tottering men, his tough visage showed no sign of fatigue. He smiled always. He knew that he would be First on the list.

And First he was. Later, when the result was announced at the portal of the "Hall," he was carried to his home through the streets on the shoulders of the people.

The Chinese populace still cherished the same awe and high reverence for the Learned Man which, in Europe, was cherished in the Middle Ages for what was called "The Scholar."

Yen How at once received a summons to appear before the Viceroy of Nanking. He appeared. A choice of two things was put before him: he might either accept a Judgeship in the Province of Kiang-si, or he might go north, and compete in another examination at Pekin, where, if he was moderately successful, he would possibly obtain a post in the Inner Court of the Imperial City.

One offer was a certainty; the other hypothetical. But Yen How had not the slightest intention of going to be a Judge in the Province of Kiang-si. He had other aims.

He went to Pekin, and very soon underwent the far sterner ordeal in the famous Examination Halls of that city. Again he was easily First on the list—a feat which at once admitted him to high honor in the Imperial Court.

He had gained his *entrée*.

Another Chinaman would now have said: "I have achieved my end." Yen How said: "I have made a beginning."

But the rest was not difficult. In Oriental countries, rises, as well as falls, are rapid. "Let Haman be hanged, and let Mordecai be put in his place." The prophet Daniel rose from nothing to the supreme power in a night. Yen How did it in two months.

So great was the necessity for Western methods, and Western science, in the Government of China, that the Chinese were actually compelled at that very time to overcome their shuddering racial abhorrence of the white man, and to pay large salaries to white experts, in various departments, to plan and to administer. Germans drilled China's army, Englishmen collected her customs, Frenchmen planned her railways.

It is not possible to estimate the omnipotence which would suddenly fall into the hand of a real Chinaman, who could do all this better than either German, Englishman, or Frenchman. To the Chinese tongue he was sweet as white mice preserved in honey. He became the Emperor of the Emperor.

But then, besides Knowledge and Race, Yen How had something more: he had Genius—the large Eye—the summoning Voice—the enchanter's Wand. The vastness of his outlook—the world-dimensions of his schemes—were simply fascinating. "Talk, my son, talk," old Li would say, sitting before Yen How, holding his chin in his hand, his eyes riveted on the doctor's face; and when Yen ceased, Li would say: "Talk on, my son, talk on; your words have flavor; and the palate of the ear is led astray by them." Yen How soon became a sort of dissipation for the aged Minister, like an advanced novel for a very young girl. When Li wanted sensation, he came and sat with his chin in his hand, and listened with delicious musings to Yen. It was at Li's own suggestion that the Yellow Jacket was given to Yen How. It was among the necessities of things, and Li saw it. And at once—*without an hour's delay*—the little Heidelberg doctor began to act.

His first care was to bring about a secret treaty between Japan and China.

He had not been idle in Japan. He had taken frequent voyages down the Peiho to Tientsin, and thence to Tokio. Of his insinuations to, and relation with, the Marquis Ito, we have spoken. But Yen How kept his most delicious plum of temptation in reserve till the last. He then showed that however great China became, Japan would always be the mistress of China; when China was the mistress of Europe and Asia, that *meant* that Japan would be the mistress of the world. The treaty was signed. It was his first step.

Yen How saw that the navy of Japan would be necessary to his schemes. Without that, nothing permanent and final could be done.

His next step was to bring about the European war.

He did it so boldly, with such a grand disregard for appearances, with such contemptuous prodigality, that it was a wonder that both his present and ultimate motives were not divined. For it must be remembered that the idea of " The Yellow Danger" was no new one to European statesmen. Again and again had the more keen-eyed of politicians pointed Eastward, and said to Europe: " The Yellow Danger! the Yellow Danger!" Only a year or so previously had Lord Charles Beresford, in a speech delivered, we think, at Hull, used words like these: " The cloud at present may seem only the size of a man's hand—but it is there; and its seemingly small size is due merely to its remoteness, not to its intrinsic smallness. What appaling fate would be that of Europe, if the yellow races, in their hundreds of millions, organized a westward march, is beyond the imagination of man to conceive." Again and again had this note of warning been sounded. But the mischief lay in this very fact: that the cloud had appeared of "the size of a man's hand." It was too remote. The idea was not yet realized and assimilated by Europe.

Still, as we say, there was nothing at all new in Yen How's idea of over-running Europe, as is proved by the fact that that phrase, "The Yellow Danger," had become quite common in every one's ears; what *was* new, was first, his discernment of the fact that the yellow races would probably fail, unless Europe were, to begin with, made ready for them by a great inter-European war; and secondly, the novel means which he took to bring about that war.

No single soul outside China and Japan suspected his *ulterior* motive of over-running Europe when he made the grants of territory—for the cloud, though often pointed out, was "like a man's hand"; but three people, at least, suspected his *present* motive of bringing about a European war. One was a young student in the Quartier Latin in Paris; another was Sir Charles Dilke, who mentioned it as just a possibility at a dinner at the National Liberal Club; the third was a Hampshire gentleman, who, as we said in a former chapter, wrote a letter to the *Times* during the excitement preceding the war, making this suggestion of China's motive. The letter attracted little attention. This Hampshire gentleman was John Hardy.

His eye had seen!

Yen How's first step was the league with Japan; his second was the European war; his third was the organization of China.

This last was a great task—it was stupendous. Only a new Confucius could have done it. But Yen How was quite that.

To wake a nation which has been asleep for four thousand years! To lift the arm!—and cry aloud!—and wake them in their myriads with a "Rouse ye! rouse ye! the Hour is come! the Day breaketh!" in a voice like the Trump of Doom!

The Awakening

The little doctor could do it—and did it.

But again, he did not do it by miracle. He knew his way.

The results attained by great Talent do indeed *look* like miracle; but they are not, of course, really so. The man of talent himself knows that he must use definitely precise ways and means, which, if used by any one else in the same manner, produce the same results. Talent is Industry—the capacity of being infinitely interested—of taking infinite pains.

Yen How had been taking infinite pains from the day when he could first pronounce his name.

All his acts in the rousing and organization of China were based upon a profound knowledge of the Chinese character. The principal points of this character are an immeasurable Greed, an absolute Contempt for the world outside China, and a fiendish Love of Cruelty.

It is impossible for the vilest European to conceive the dark and hideous instincts of the Chinese race.

The first thing that happened after the outbreak of the war in Europe was a wholesale massacre of Europeans in the East. Wholesale—but not haphazard: for Dr. Yen How was directing it. For the time being, every European became precious in his eyes—he collected them with care—he preserved them scrupulously—and he distributed them with deliberate wisdom. They were conveyed over China from Yun-nan to the villages round the Ming Tombs and from the Yellow Sea to the Tien-Shans. No district was without its white visitor. Then sounded Yen How's first trumpet blast to the nation he meant to rouse. It is morning! the Day breaks! And at once there occurred a memorable Passover-Day through the length and breadth of China—a holiday of gore, an orgy of death, to symbolize the annihilation of the white race all the world over. When it was ended, there was not a white man or woman alive on Chinese soil, except on an island or two; all had perished in the act of undergoing the most loathsome public tortures. This Solemn Feast-day, this Sacrament of Blood, made a lasting impression upon the spirit of the Chinese race, which is sensitive to the suggestiveness of symbols. Yen How had begun well. Certainly, he knew his man.

The killing of the German drill-sergeants of the Chinese Army was left to be performed by the hands of the soldiers whom they had drilled.

The territories granted to the Continental nations were as yet unoccupied by them. The small European garrisons actually in China had been easily overpowered. And Europe was busy at home, fighting against herself. At last China was free to do as she chose.

The attitude of the nation as a whole at this moment resembled that of a sleeping cat, which hears a sound, and pricks her ears.

To say even so much of the Chinese is to say a great deal. For centuries they had lain in deep, stolid slumber, without one prick of the ears. There were still many millions of them who, as Li Hung Chang had said in Europe, had never so much as heard of the Chino-Japanese war.

How to stir up such a people? How to get at them, and fire them, and make them act? Yen How knew.

He must, first of all, now that he had given them a morning Dream of Blood, kick them hard to wake them, bruising their flesh, if necessary : then, as they rubbed their wide and startled eyes, he would preach to them the Gospels of Greed—and Race—and Cruelty.

Already, by the time John Hardy had reached Vladivostok—just about four weeks after the battle of Shoreham—the kicking process was in full progress. There was a strange stirring, a movement, a new something, in old China. Men said : "What is toward? What is to be? Can these dry bones live?" The Spirit of a Man was abroad in the land—an intense Mind, a vitalizing Leaven—kneading, fermenting, energizing, creating.

The massacred drill-sergeants were replaced by Japanese officers. But where there had been one German there appeared now a thousand Japanese.

The Awakening

Yen How's scheme was nothing less than this: that every Chinaman should be a soldier.

Conscription in China. . . . !

Here was a lesson learned from Europe.

But when we say "soldier," we mean something different from what is understood by the word among us. We do not mean a man equipped with smokeless powder, and magazine rifles, with Lee-Metfords, and Martinis, and Sniders. We mean only a man having some sort of arms—a club, or a dart, or a match-lock or a poker—anything which would give him the idea that he had to fight, and which would perhaps delay his death a moment while myriads of others swept over those who had killed him. The Chinese host was to resemble a flight of locusts, covering the entire sky from horizon to horizon each member of which was armed with some implement, not so much for the purpose of killing, as for the purpose of protracting his own death, while the rest of the host pressed forward, blighting as they went. His duty was hardly to fight, but to occupy time in dying. For this service none were too old, few too young—and women were as good as men. Yen How's army would consist of the 400,000,000 which formed the population of China.

The organization of this war-host he planned principally on the French model.

He divided the whole of China into 240 army-corps regions, each containing about two million inhabitants. This arrangement included Thibet, Mongolia, Manchuria, and Korea, the heads of which countries he had long since brought into line with his plans.

In each region he quartered the principal elements of the field army-corps with the necessary staff, setting up in each region a large number of recruiting depôts, and depôts of artillery, transport, supplies of food and forage, with clothing and camp-equipment.

The whole of the troops and organization for this purpose was put under the command of the General of that particular army-corps and its region. And this General was, in every case, a Japanese.

Each region was divided into two hundred subdivisions, each of the subdivisions furnishing one regiment of infantry of the line, twenty subdivisions forming an infantry brigade command, and forty subdivisions an infantry divisional command. Divisional commands were also entrusted exclusively to Japanese; brigade and regimental commands to the most trustworthy of the Chinese officers of the regular army.

Each corps was furnished with a vast corps-cavalry-brigade, the horses—to use an Irishism—being mules, and the weapon the long spear.

Each regiment was subdivided into three battalions each battalion into four companies, and each company into twelve squads.

Each squad contained from sixty to sixty-three persons, who were known by numbers, from No. 1 to No. 63.

They contained children over the age of nine, women (except the wives and daughters of mandarins and other upper classes), and old men tottering on the verge of the grave. The priest and pundit·classes were exempted also.

The nation was organized into an army.

This was one method which Yen How employed to kick and prick it into wakefulness.

Each army-corps contained, beside its squadrons of cavalry and its eighteen batteries of artillery, six sections of artificers, six artillery parks, thirty companies of pontooners, six telegraph sections, and forty field-bakeries.

But there were no field-hospitals or hospital orderlies, no ambulances, no medical provisions. Yen How could afford men.

One important feature of the army-corps was the provision of armored carts. They were to serve not only for transport, but for defense in battle, and their shape was contrived with this view, being long and low with small wheels, and rather ponderous. One had been made, cr was to be made, for each " peloton."

All this was now in rapid and intense progress. And the world knew nothing of it!

China, north of Tonquin, had telegraphically isolated herself.

The Awakening

In Japan the manufacture of guns, swords, spears, and small-arms was going forward with agonized activity; and these were coming over to China. China's chief manufacturing energies were directed to the making of armored carts and tents.

But the drilling of China was only one-half of Yen How's method of rousing it. He knew that it was necessary to drive the nation further still. He did this by taxing it.

Let it not be supposed that any part of his motive was a need of money for all this war preparation. The loan raised in the previous year, which should have been spent by China in paying Japan's war-indemnity, was still, except for one instalment, in the pockets of China.

The loan had not been necessary to China at all! She could have raised sufficient to pay Japan by an issue of Treasury bonds, the purchase of which may be made compulsory in China, if not subscribed to voluntarily.

Or she could have called upon the Viceroys to wring enough out of the mercantile and agricultural classes.

But neither loan, nor bonds, nor Viceroy extortion had been necessary! Japan's mere credit was good for the building of the vessels she needed; and the money, paid over to Japan, would simply have lain in the Bank of England to Japan's credit. As a matter of fact, in the secret treaty between the Marquis Ito and Yen How, the payment of the indemnity was remitted.

From this source alone China was, for the present, rich; but under the guidance of an exact administrative brain like Yen How's she was vastly richer still from quite other sources.

China, in reality, was never a poor country; on the contrary, she was potentially about the richest in the world. Manchuria was an El Dorado of gold. The mineral mines of Kwang-tung, Heilung-Chiang and the Kirin provinces had been the envy of the nations. But the curse of China had been her official class. The heavy *likin* charges, which went, nearly all of it, into the pockets of its collectors, stifled many an industry. The Government income was estimated at two hundred and ten million taels, but only seventy million of this —one-third—was accounted for. On the remainder the mandarins wallowed in fatness.

Yen How's eyes screwed into a smile, and he said : "No more of that, my sons !"

The substance of what he said and what he did was this : "You are to extort, you are to squeeze, and plunder, and grind the people ten times—a hundred times—more than ever before—till they perish like sheep of it. But this time you are going to do it not for your own benefit, but for *my* benefit, and for the benefit of China. I, Yen How, have said it, and will see to it."

Within two months from his attainment of the supreme power, he had created a Board, formed on the lines of the Imperial Maritime Customs Board, for a clean-handed collection of the internal revenues. It contained some Chinese officials, but more Japanese.

The immediate effect of this change was an increase —by tens and hundreds—of the revenues which began to pour into the Treasury of Pekin.

From the working of the mines, specially organized and superintended by Yen How himself, a great increment of wealth began to flow into the swollen coffers of China.

Yen How was not popular. He was kicking and pricking China into unpleasant wakefulness. But he knew that he had the sweetest oil in store to salve her bruises at the right moment.

All these measures of his would have meant insurrection, revolution, at another time—the introduction of the Japanese element, especially, into the new life of China was distasteful to the people. But now the stern universal military organization nipped every thought of rebellion in the bud.

To turn a two-legged beast into a man—drill him, straighten his spine, make a soldier of him. He will never be a hopelessly unintelligent animal after that.

Yen How was drilling the Chinese beast, straightening his spine. By the time the beast could look round

The Awakening

twice to tear whoever it was that was disturbing his slumbers, lo, he was already turned into a man with sufficient intelligence to see that there was no resisting this new Power which had him in its grip.

The Chinese, when they saw no help for it, began to fraternize with the now ubiquitous Japanese element. Yen How had foreseen this. They had already, more or less, learned to submit to the domination of white men. And the Jap was much less a foreign devil than the white man. On reflection he was judged to be an improvement. On reflection, Yen How, too, would, in time, be judged to be an improvement.

But, meanwhile, he wore a secret steel plate over his breast.

For the people of China were being terribly oppressed and badgered.

The order of the day was drill, drill, drill—tax, tax, tax—work, work, work—all over the land.

As yet no one knew why all this was—what was in the mind of the gods above. Yen How had not yet begun to preach his three Gospels to the people.

So matters stood when, on the 18th of April, Yen How sat in his garden, reading an old *Shanghai Mercury*.

An attendant opened a door in the courtyard, walked softly towards the great little man, and prostrated himself before him.

"Speak on," said Yen How.

"A white man has been captured at Moukden, your Excellency, by soldiers of the Liao-Tong division, and sent on to Pekin. They have just arrived at the Palace—and await your instructions."

"Let him be taken to the Imperial Prison-house for the night," said Yen How, "and beheaded at sunrise to-morrow."

He went on reading. The servant made an obeisance, and turned away.

Do not call the man back, Yen How! Let him go and do your bidding, and read you your paper, and be at peace! For this is John Hardy that you have ordered to be slain—and he is as strong as the rocks, and the strong earth, and the sky, and the stars in their courses fight for him!

But Yen How called the man back.

"Stop!" he cried.

The attendant returned.

"What nation is he of?" asked Yen How.

"His interpreter says that he is an Englishman, your Excellency."

"Let him be brought before me here."

And Yen How went on reading his paper.

CHAPTER XIII

JOHN AND YEN

JOHN HARDY, having arrived at Vladivostok, had engaged an interpreter, and spent two days in trying to charter a craft for Nagasaki, where he hoped to meet his ship, or hear about her *locale*.

His impatience was fevered; for he heard that no *rencontre* had as yet taken place; but that, within a week, it was expected that the allied French, German and Russian vessels would meet the allied English and Japanese. Such was the report brought by junks from Nagasaki and Fusan, and by caravan from Newchwang and Kin-chow.

An engagement had not occurred, for this simple reason: that the Allies had practically been in hiding from the English; and the reason was this simple one: that they were finding extraordinary difficulties in the matter of coaling, the English and Japanese having, as a matter of fact, created a "corner" by buying up all the coal in the East; so that from Singapore to Vladivostok the cry had been coal! coal!

Now, however—so said the reports—the French, German and Russian vessels had coal in plenty! Whence this supply had come, no one could conceive. It was a mystery—but a certainty.

The battle, therefore, so long delayed, must come soon.

Hardy's pulses beat faster; and his chagrin was intense when, after anxious search, he found no *compradore* willing or able to secure him a passage to Nagasaki. The East was in suspense, waiting for the future, without interest in the present. It turned a listless ear to Hardy's pleadings.

Nothing remained for it but Port Arthur, where, as he was told, he would be sure to find a willing junk. But the journey was immense. Hardy almost gave up hope of the battle.

But with strong heart he set out. He anticipated no danger. China was not formally at war with England. He did not know that, even in times of settled quietude, no traveler's life was worth a rush in Northern China—as in the case of Sir Harry Parkes.

He had with him quite a little retinue; and he traveled in a palanquin borne between mules.

The northern Chinese were a hard, ferocious, and treacherous race—considerably more so than the southern. They were also larger and stronger men,—rascals tall, and lean, and brawny, their bony toughness being derived from the Tartar blood with which their tribes were infused. Their language, too, was different; above all, their walk. The southerners walked on the flat foot, like Europeans; the northerners swung along on their heels, with a backward slant of the body, like a statue put to lean with its back against a wall.

At Hunshun Hardy stopped for a night at a two-roomed inn; and here it was that, as soon as he was asleep, a consultation occurred between the villagers and his retinue of five.

The next morning he went forward, this time in a springless *jinricksha* or mule-cart. He could no longer bear the swinging between the palanquin mules. It had reduced him to a state of weakness; he was now spitting up phlegm streaked with blood.

At every village now they were surrounded by increasing crowds and clamors. But always John's servants spoke some words to the people, which had the effect of restraining them. As he set out afresh, a throng of those skeleton visages would be there to gape greedily after him; but still, he did set out.

A sickness of the heart—a sickness of the stomach —grew upon him.

Could Man—could Woman—be like this?

Every nerve in his gentle and loving nature rose in shuddering revolt against this race.

He saw the whisperings and confabulations between his men and the mobs, and, with his instinct for truth, suspected treachery. But he was quite helpless.

Everywhere, as he advanced, his eye noted the drilling, drilling, to which the nation was being subjected. But he was now very sick, and languid, and day by day sat propped against the cart, staring wearily before him, under the growing heat. He was compelled to keep up his strength with sips of the deleterious Chinese spirit *samshu*; and the only food which he could procure for days was the sickening mass of rice and greens which forms the staple Chinese diet.

He descended the river Yalu in a gorgeously painted junk, drawn on each bank by a mule. Here he had some rest, lying on the deck in long dreams of quietude through the starlit nights of a Chinese spring. Never had the heavens and the earth seemed to him so lovely, enthralled in a mystery of peace, as in those vast sheeny nights of his descent of the Yalu. Near Wiju he commenced the land-journey again, on muleback this time, somewhat recovered in health.

He was given now to understand that he was being guided to Port Arthur. Instead of this, he was being led northward, toward Moukden.

At Moukden was a garrison of the old regular army; and the railway from thence to Tientsin had lately been completed.

At an inn at Moukden he was eating, when a Japanese officer, accompanied by an interpreter, entered the room, and bade Hardy follow him. It was Yen How's decree that any white man found by chance in Northern China should be sent on to Pekin.

Hardy was ineffably surprised, first, at finding himself in Moukden, and next at being hustled into a queer, low, dark railway train, in the keeping of half-a-dozen gigantic pigtails.

"But," he protested through his interpreter, "England is not at war with China!"

"No," said the Japanese with a grin, "but China is at war with England."

In the train John's wrists were bound. His interpreter and servants had disappeared.

They reached Tientsin by train, and thence went on to the village of Tung-chow, five miles from Pekin, by junk up the Peiho. Just as the sun set they arrived at the mighty walls of Pekin, and had only time to rush between the gates, when the ponderous jaws of the city-portals clanged and roared behind them.

Pekin! multitudinous, unfathomable city, place of beauty and of horror, of romance, and of infamy! city of vast triple-boulevards, grand as the imagination of an architect, loathsome as the stench of a sewer, city of gauds and colors, vermilion, and emerald, and blue, and of temples, and avenues, of palaces and lakes and forests, immense, a world in itself, resembling in its tone and aspect no other of the cities of man!

Here may the hoariness of our race on the earth, the vast age of the old world, be read even by the blind.

Whoever is a Dreamer, let him bury himself in Pekin. The city is itself a dream—an opium-dream.

It was necessary for Hardy to pass through both the Tartar and the Chinese cities before reaching the Imperial City. Each of these three is enclosed within its own massive walls, independently of the great wall of the whole town. The Imperial City was sacred ground. Here resided the Supreme Power, and here also the Legations. The profane foot entered it on pain of death.

They passed through a number of thoroughfares, broad as three or four Holborns laid side by side, and long as vistas; streets thronging with camels, and jingling mules, and the booths of small merchants, and swaying pigtails; and in an hour reached the Imperial Portal on mule-back.

The leader of the little band produced his brevet, and found admittance. They proceeded slowly through a park, leading their animals now, and after traversing a number of secluded granite street, and a long marble colonnade, entered the courtyard of a vast, low, white palace.

John and Yen

Hardy, as they halted, leant wearily upon his mule. There was a hollow pain at his chest, and at the back of his shoulders. His lips were dry and cracked.

A door opened in the courtyard, and a soft-footed official came to learn the reason of this intrusion.

A few words were spoken, and he turned away. In a quarter of a hour he was back again; and five minutes afterwards Yen How and John Hardy were face to face.

For quite a minute Yen continued to read his paper. Then he lifted his head suddenly, and said to the official:

"You may go; wait in the vestibule: when I want you I will sound."

The man went away. Yen How looked at John Hardy, and John Hardy looked at Yen How.

Both were smiling.

Yen How had still under his eye a scar where the fist of the English soldier, John Brabant, had struck him. So he smiled.

Hardy's hands were unbound. This had been done when he reached Tung-chow, where it had been necessary to mount a mule. He had on the usual blue pea-jacket; and under this, in the breast-pocket, his loaded revolver.

In the colloquy which followed, one of these two men spoke an English as perfectly grammatical as that of Tennyson or Macaulay, though with an intensely foreign something in his way of speaking it; the other spoke broken English. It was Yen who used the good, and John the bad, English.

"Who are you, sir?" said Yen How.

"Me Englishman," said John, "name John Hardy."

Yen had heard of the battle of Shoreham, and he never forgot a name. He said:

"Don't talk pigeon English. I can understand you. I have lived some years in England."

"Oh, veer goot. Me no knowee that. Me talk good English to Chinaman."

"As you please. What is it you have come to China for?"

"Me sailor. Me come from Russia to Vladivostok to joinee me ship. What for you no letee me join it? Englishman and Chinaman good friends."

"Since when?"

"For always!"

"You got a sister?"

John was surprised.

"No," he said.

"A female cousin?"

"Yes. Well——"

"Will you give me your cousin for my wife?"

John grinned.

"Why, you queer Chinaman . . . !" he cried out.

"Ah, you say no, you see. Englishman and Chinaman are not such very good friends, then."

The chief fact about John Hardy was that he had eyes which saw a fact. As these last words fell upon his ears, he looked keenly into the placid face before him; and at once he realized that he was in the presence, not so much of a Chinaman, as of a mind.

And at once the instinct to speak pigeon English left him. Unconsciously he began to speak naturally. This was a great compliment to Dr. Yen How.

"But look here, Mr. Chinaman," he said, "what is all this for? Who are you?"

"Well, since you ask, I am called Yen How."

John started.

"Ah, you know my name, I see," said Yen How; "I know yours, too."

"Yes. Very good—I am glad that I find myself with you, since you are who you are. You are acquainted with European ideas, and certainly a man of sense. I wish to throw myself on your benevolence. I find myself in such a silly sort of scrape. I am a poor sailor trying to join my ship. Knowing China as a friendly country, I thought I should have no difficulty in passing through. Yet here I am! What for? Isn't it very absurd? Please help me to get out of this! If you cannot set me free of your own power, you can at least put me in communication with the British Ambassador."

John and Yen

Yen How's eyes went small in a smile.
"There isn't any British Ambassador any more," he said.
"How do you mean, sir?" asked John.
"It is the Chinese custom to hang thieves by the heels, head downwards," replied Yen. "The British Ambassador has been hanged by the heels in the square before the Pekin Temple of Confucius, and died while the people were torturing him with hot irons."

John Hardy's left eyelid lowered in intense menace.
"That is not really so, Mr. Chinaman?"
"It is, my son."
"And whose doing was that? Not the Government of China's?"
"It was *my* doing, my son."
"Yours, Yen How?"
"Mine."

Now the two men were really in contact. They looked into each other's eyes, searchingly, eye to eye.
"You shocking little devil!" said John Hardy.
"Call me what you like. I will repay your insult by a compliment: you are a brave fellow."
"You will be strangled like a frog for this, Mr. Chinaman!"
"Whom by? All the Englishmen in China are dead."
"All?"
"Every one."
"A massacre?"
"A regular sacrament of death."
"But the Chinese believe in a God above, I think?"
"Poh! not much."
"*You* do not?"
"Not I."
"And the white men of other nations, they were massacred, too?"
"All—all."
"But with what motive?"
"It would take too long to tell you."
"Ah! I know."

"You do?"

"Yes! I know! I know! I had a queer, dim idea long ago. Now I know! I know!"

"You are shrewd then, as well as brave."

"Yes! I know!"

John Hardy was in an ecstasy of discovery. He saw the skies growing black, black over the earth.

"Well, will you give me your cousin for my wife now?" asked Yen How, all wrinkles.

John did not answer. His brows were knit. It was only after a minute's thought that he made two steps forward, and laid his right hand on Yen How's shoulder, the doctor looking up into his face as he began to speak.

"Now, look you, Yen How," John said, "I know now, as I tell you, what your idea is like. Let me put it in plain words: you mean to sweep with this Chinese nation over Europe when our war is over, and Europe is prepared for your coming. I was a fool not to see it quite before—but that is it. And this idea is *yours*, yours only, Yen How: I see that. You have the face of a devil, you toad, you have! Well, I have got an offer to make you—a challenge—if you are man enough to accept it. Get me out of this—put me on board my ship. And I will undertake to fight you, and beat you. I alone, Yen, against you alone. If you beat me, I give you, not my cousin, but the Queen's daughters for your wives. If I beat you, I squeeze the life out of your throat, you frog. I promise you that I shall breathe not a word of this plan of yours to a living soul—no one shall know from me: and no one shall know from me about the massacre and the drilling of the people. I make you that offer, Yen."

John Hardy had recognized the great mind in Yen How; now it was Yen How's turn to recognize the same in John Hardy. Here was the full stature of Man, the world-big Thought, the sun-kindled Imagination.

Yen How answered.

"Take your hand from my shoulder my son,"

"Well, what do you say, Yen?"

"I say that your thought tickles me, boy."

"Well——?"

"And I say, that if I were to accept your offer, you could go to your ship saying to yourself: 'The great Yen How has recognized me as one of the two kings of the world.'"

"Still, I wait for your answer."

"How am I to count upon the silence you promise?"

"Well, you know something of English life. I come of a family of English gentlemen. We never break our word."

"Well, come, we shall see. Your thought—what shall I say?—tickles me, my son. We shall see—come now. But first—do you know that I gave an order for your beheading? And then I said I would see you. Do you know why? I had a question to ask you."

"Well?"

"Have you lived in London?"

"Yes—sometimes."

"Ah, well—there is just a chance, then. Did you ever know a lillee girl called—what's her name?—Ah! Ada Seward."

Yen How could destroy a world without the quivering of a nerve; but as he uttered this name in a whisper, he slunk, his voice trembled.

Hardy did not answer. The name sounded familiar. He hung his head with knit brow, thinking. Suddenly he blushed. He had remembered—the music-hall—the drunken night—Lottie Collins—Ada.

Yen saw the blush.

To this man, drunk with his passion, it was inconceivable that any other man could see this girl, and not straightway go mad for love. Men will sometimes get so intoxicated with wine, that the sober state becomes inconceivable to them; and they will say to a sober companion: "Oh, you *are* drunk, boy!"

Yen saw the blush, and he noticed now that Hardy's face was more than usually lovely, even for one of a lovely race. It was a face made to be loved by women.

"You have seen her?" He half rose from his seat, and brought his mouth in an intense, secret, cunning whisper close to Hardy's ear.

"I have," said John.

He had an instinct, even then, that he was running some frightful danger in making this avowal. But he was truthful in a very rigid, rather old-fashioned sense. He had never told a falsehood.

"You have?—in real truth?" whispered Yen.

"I have."

"And—kissed her—eh, boy?"

The Chinaman's face worked. He hissed rather than spoke these words.

John grinned.

"Why,—you most queer person——!"

He was ready to laugh a puzzled, anxious laugh.

"You have!"

"What?"

"Kissed her—eh, John Hardy?"

"Of course, I have kissed her."

"Then you die!"

"What, not for kissing Miss Seward?"

"You die, I say!"

"It was she who kissed *me*."

"You die! you die, you little white devil! you die! you die!"

Up went the fingers of Yen's right arm, twinkling in ecstatic wrath.

There was no mistaking Yen How. He meant this. He pounded the gong twice with the hammer.

"In one half-hour——" he said, with a furious nod of the head at John.

Hardy, perfectly cool, saw clearly that all hope for himself was lost. But he had no intention of leaving Yen How behind, to work his mischief in the world.

The second sound of the gong had hardly shivered and clanged, when Hardy, with the revolver whipped from his breast-pocket, blew Yen How—passions, schemes, ambitions and all—out of existence.

In intention, that is—in absolute, cool unerringness of aim. The bullet struck Yen precisely over the

John and Yen

center of his heart. But it struck a plate of steel mail, and did not penetrate.

John was about to fire a second shot at Yen's head, when suddenly the two men were locked in desperate conflict. Yen had flung himself upon John.

Yen's eye had long before noted the bulge of John's pea-jacket over the breast. He was half prepared for what had happened.

The struggle was carried on with the entire physical force of the two combatants, the revolver being the aim of both efforts.

John, though below the middle height, was quite an inch or so taller than Yen ; and he was able, with his left hand, to seize Yen's pigtail, and draw it in a single coil tight round Yen's throat ; while Yen enclosed the other's right arm and ribs in a grip of iron, squeezing with all his energy, and heaving and slanting his adversary in the effort to effect a throw.

The force of the tough little Chinaman was quite two or three times that of the frail English lad.

This contest of strengths was a foreboding—and a resemblance—of the larger national contest which was impending.

Hardy was comparatively weak. But in his right hand was a revolver, representing the Science of Western Civilization, which, however, Yen's grip rendered ineffectual ; and in his left hand was Yen's pigtail, representing the barbarism, the superstition, the repulsive soul of the East.

Yen's face darkened. A gurgling came from his swollen lips. The rat was being suffocated by its own tail. The West was strangling the East.

Suddenly the revolver went off, and the bullet entered Yen How's left foot. The Science of the West had uttered a cry.

But the West was breathing its last gasps under the stringent ferocious grasp of the East.

The contest was short, and it ended suddenly. A little spout of blood welled and rolled from Hardy's lips ; and at once he lost power, and fainted.

Before he could fall to the ground, an attendant had

come up, and struck him a blow on the brow with a heavy bamboo. He fell at once flat on his back, his face covered with blood.

Almost immediately Yen How was cool.

"Take him away," he said. "He has attempted my life—he must not be killed."

"The torture, Your Excellency?"

"Yes. But I will direct it myself. Go away."

He sat again, as the attendant lifted John in his brawny arms. He commenced once more to read the *Mercury*.

There was a bullet in his foot. But he would not move ; the racking pain was sweet to him.

The intensity of the Chinese instinct of Vengeance is a mystery—it is not human—it is not bestial—it may be demonic. To us, at all events, it is incomprehensible.

To them pain is joy, if, at the same time, they can gloat over the knowledge that it is in their power to take a thousand-fold vengeance on the causer of the pain. They hug their pangs—they wantonly put off the hour of their revenge—they roll in a secret luxury of malice.

In the matter of Torture, the Chinese have excelled all nations in a devilish cunning. They have investigated the nerves of man, and adapted their plagues to them with a nice and minute ingenuity. And Yen was more ingenious than the most ingenious.

He intended to give his mind to this matter. Meantime, he went on reading.

CHAPTER XIV

THE VANISHED FLEET

IT was twenty hours before John Hardy, in some absolutely dark place, opened his eyes. At about the same time, the battle at which he had hoped and striven to be present was going forward.

For over a year the question which had been agitating many an English mind was this : Is our weight of metal in Chinese waters enough ? Is it commensurate with possible contingencies ? Is it not too hopelessly small ?

This anxiety had been somewhat allayed by the spectacle of ship after ship of the British navy—the *Barfleur*, the *Bonaventure*, the *Hannibal*, the *Gibraltar*—steaming away in mysterious haste to the East.

On the other hand, they had not steamed away alone : they had followed—they had been followed by —a host of the choicest, mightiest ships of Russia, France, and Germany, all hasting eastward, eastward, as if in the sweep of some law of gravitation, all with the same secret urgency, the same suggestion of mystery, and flurry, and design.

Heavy Russian armaments like the *Vladimir Monomach* had hurried after French craft like the *Pascal*, and German craft like the *Gefion*. An addition of some 30,000 tons to her Chinese navy was made by Russia alone in her ships, the *Rossiya*, the *Cissoi Veliki*, the *Navarin*.

This Eastern fever had infected even nations not precisely in the running. Away in the sweep of the

Chinese Current went battle-ships from Italy, from Austria, from America.

In a few months the seas of the Far East were gravid with the navies of the world.

China herself, by way of pantomime, had been building cruisers at the Vulcan Dockyards at Stettin; and at that very time was promenading the boulevards of the seas, quite like one of the *chic*, with the new *Hi-Chi*, *Hi-Tien*, and *Hai-Shen*.

The *Hi-Chi* had a speed of twenty-four knots, and was a cruiser carrying an armament as heavy as many vessels twice her displacement.

The fleet of Japan was in prime fighting order, modern, as smart as it was swift and strong. It was worth any two of the fleets in Chinese waters put together.

Was England's weight of metal sufficient? This was the question.

The fact was, that England had ceased to be acutely anxious when it was once known that her weight was greater than that of any two of the European nations combined.

She had added 37,000 tons, in round numbers, to her former Chinese squadron; Russia 36,000; France 11,000. But, all told, she had concentrated 126,700 tons in those waters, whereas Russia's total was only 83,000, and France's 26,000. It followed, therefore, that Britain had a preponderance of some 17,700 tons over these two.

This had seemed enough, considering that some of Russia's terra-cotta colored ships were old fashioned.

It was hardly remembered that there was Germany, too, with a weight of 27,000 tons in Chinese waters. Russia, France, and Germany together had a preponderance over Britain of 10,000 tons.

The fact was sufficiently impressive in itself; but it had not been terrifying, even to those who remembered the possibility of the German element being hostile to the British, when they also remembered the splendid fleet of—Japan.

Here was an additional element of 200,000 tons—all on the side of Britain.

The Vanished Fleet   149

For was not Japan the friend of England? Were not their interests identical? The Britain of the East, and the Britain of the West—how natural that they should stand shoulder to shoulder!

But there was one question, in connection with this queer, outlandish, yellow ally of England, the correct answer to which would have sent as great a shock through England, could she have known it, as she had ever received in her history. The question was this: "Where on earth, during the early part of April 1899, did the Allied fleet in Eastern waters get their supplies of coal?"

We have stated that England and Japan, by a clever deal, had, weeks before, effected a corner in all the Welsh and other coal in the East.

Yet on the morning of the 19th of April the whole Allied navy, which some little time before had been almost immobilized for lack of steam-fuel, and had been hiding and dodging, each ship for herself, all about the northern Chinese coasts, now steamed gallantly past Quelpart in search of the British fleet, supposed to be somewhere in the neighborhood of Chemulpo.

They were steering northwest; Nagasaki lay south-east; they were therefore coming from Japan. Could it be that from Japan they had obtained this coal?

And where was the fleet of Japan? For two days Vice-Admiral Sir Edward Seymour had been expecting it, by previous arrangement, to appear off Chemulpo. But as yet it gave no sign.

The Vice-Admiral was not at first precisely anxious; for his only ground of suspicion that anything was wrong in China was the fact, reported to him at Hong-Kong six days before, that all communication between that island and the mainland had mysteriously ceased. Yen How had left the Englishmen on Hong-Kong alive, having no desire to have every Chinese port shelled by British guns. Hence, when the Vice-Admiral coaled and started northward hurriedly on receipt of a telegram from Tokio stating that the Allied fleet had managed to procure some coal, and were steaming eastward upon Japan, he had no suspicion of the massacre. His reply to Tokio was that he was starting northward at once, and would avoid an engagement, until the junction of the two fleets; and he instructed the Japanese fleet to join him at Chemulpo.

But at Chemulpo he received a shock. There was no white man in the place.

All he could suppose was that there had been a rising in the town, and the white men killed.

But he hardly attached any political importance to the fact. Such things were common in China.

He waited with perfect confidence for the Japanese fleet.

The next morning he received a cable despatched from Nagasaki to Fusan, and brought two hundred miles on mule-back to Chemulpo. It was as follows:

"The Allied fleets, plentifully supplied with coal, are about to steam eastward in search of you. Japanese fleet will follow."

"Steam *eastward!*" "Supplied with coal!" "*Will* follow!" Certainly, now, if ever man was puzzled, it was the British Commander-in-Chief.

For if the enemy were steaming eastward supplied with coal, that meant Japanese treachery. But if Japan were treacherous, and had joined the Allies, why on earth did she take the pains to warn the British of their advance?

And why "*will*" follow? They should have set out, according to the Vice-Admiral's instructions, long before. If they had not already set out, they were treacherous; but if they were treacherous, why did they give this warning of it, instead of taking the advantage of a surprise?

That they were not neutral seemed proved by the fact that they were "following" at all.

The Vice-Admiral's brow was a heavy cloud of care. He decided that the missive was a hoax, then that that was impossible, then again that it was a hoax.

He sent an expedition of blue-jackets by road to Seoul to see who was there. They returned with the announcement that there were no white men in Seoul.

The secret of Japan's action, though inscrutable, was

The Vanished Fleet 151

this: she coaled the Allies in order that they might destroy the British; and she warned the British in order that they might destroy the Allies.

She helped both sides, being the enemy of both.

But this policy was too subtle for the British Commander to divine without an absolute clue.

The absence of white men at Seoul, as well as at Chemulpo, was merely an added shock. It brought no real light to the mind. He waited on, with anxious heart, for the appearance of the Japanese.

Two days he spent in coaling the fleet out of four colliers which had accompanied him from Hong-Kong, and in taking in stores from the store-ships. At the end of the second day there was still no sign of the yellow ally of England.

The thing was so inexplicable, that even wonderment could find no guess. Japan was a nation among nations, responsible, presumably careful to keep her pledged word. What, then, could have happened?

"What, in God's name *has* happened?" said the Vice-Admiral to himself twenty times during the course of that terrible and sleepless night.

But he did not neglect the warning of Japan's cable. The next morning, immediately after the saluting of the colors, the fleet steamed from Chemulpo harbor, the flag-ship being the *Barfleur*, one of the only two line-of-battleships present.

The Vice-Admiral, in his ignorance of the real facts of the situation, had no intention of being caught at anchor without sea-room.

So far, no action had taken place in the East. The approaches to Vladivostok harbor, Port Arthur, and Kiao-Chau were crowded with mines, and defended by forts. The Vice-Admiral had preserved his fighting power from injury, till the first naval battle. After that, in the event of victory, he meant to proceed to the hostile ports.

He went cruising southeastward under half steam. A bright, breezy morning of Spring.

But what now is that, away yonder on the southern horizon? A long streak of gray mist, which has the

property of growing swiftly broader and darker. The Japanese fleet at last, surely!
No. It is the fleet of the allied enemy. That is quickly determined by the look-outs.

They numbered twenty-nine, and occupied the whole region of the southern hemi-horizon.

The British ships were thirty-three. Among them, however, was a very large number of smaller-tonnage craft, torpedo-boat destroyers, first-class gun-boats, second and third-class cruisers, despatch vessels, and sloops of war, of varying weight, from about 4000 to as low as 260 tons. But there, too, on the other hand, were the great *Terrible*, and her sister-cruiser (in whose books was the name of John Hardy, absent), the *Powerful*. These had each a tonnage of 14,200. There, too, were the *Revenge* with 14,150 tons, and the *Gibraltar* with 7,700.

The weight of the enemy was greater; but it was not much greater; and even so, it was not the custom of Englishmen to count as a deterrent from battle a preponderance of the enemy in physical power. The Vice-Admiral banished from his mind for the time the mystery of the Japanese fleet, and sent forth his command with a high heart.

Nimble Jack, below decks, belted his trousers with a determined snap, and stripped himself of blouse and shirt, prepared to sink, to fight, to swim, to die, to live.

Already from the conning-towers could be discerned the pea-soup color of some Russian ships, though both fleets were pouring round the horizon two regions of dark smoke.

The British approached in a very wide wedge, the *Barfleur* leading at the apex of the formation, while the enemy maintained a double line, the whole of the first line being composed of Russian vessels, the heavy *Vladimir Monomach* occupying the central post.

The barb, so to speak, of the British wedge was as strong as possible. On each side of the *Barfleur*, somewhat astern of her, came the *Powerful* and the *Terrible*. It was the intention of the Vice-Admiral to

The Vanished Fleet

begin well, and to derive all the moral prestige which this fact might afford. At the moment when the *Vladimir* was two miles from the *Barfleur*, and three from the *Terrible* and the *Powerful*, the battle commenced on the British side. All the three British vessels had kept their forward barbettes trained upon the *Vladimir*, and they fired simultaneously. The result was just like magic. Before the smoke had cleared, the Russian ship was no longer on the surface of the waters.

An instant afterwards, and the battle was general.

In the fury of warfare which now ensued, let the reader fix his eye upon a middle-sized and comparatively unimportant ship which stands far back in the starboard limb of the British wedge. She is called the *Iphigenia ;* a second-class cruiser ; tonnage 3600, horse-power 7000 ; not very wonderfully armored. but agile in the water, and capable of showing a clean pair of heels. On board of *her* is—Fate.

Yonder is the *Gefion* engaged with the *Terrible*, and yonder both the *Pascal* and the *Indomptable* with the *Revenge*, and yonder again the *Barfleur* with the *Admiral Nachimoff*, and the *Powerful* with the *Jean Bart*. Wide is the war and various. The British wedge has penetrated the fleet of the Allies. The navies of the world are mixed together in a hotchpotch of combat. Either with design or without, the battle, within five minutes from its start, has become a mere *mêlée* of thunder.

There are instances, on one side and the other, of splendid maneuvering, of the right thing done at the right moment. But these all are individual, between ship and ship, captain and captain. Neither on the one side nor on the other is there any wide plan, or grand plot, or omnipresent eye. On the whole, it is a question of weight of metal against weight of metal. The great man is not there.

. . . .

Slowly, in his dark prison, the Chinese iron is entering into the soul of John Hardy. He is being taught the meaning of Fear, and familiarity with the face of Pain. This, too, was necessary for him.

. . . . . .

But see what a mess the *Terrible* is making of the *Gefion* yonder in the very thick of things. Some of the ships are fighting at a little more than pistol-shot distance; and the *Terrible* is well within half a knot of the dismantled *Gefion*, when Commander Maddern, careering to starboard, trumpets forth through the uproar in a kind of German: "Haul down your flag, or I'll ram!" And half a minute later down sails the flag of the *Gefion*; and half a minute later still, down dives the *Gefion* herself to her final harbor at the bottom of the Hwang Hai, which swallows with her all that part of her crew which a pinnace of the *Terrible* is unable to rescue.

But the *Revenge* has lodged a 12-inch shell in the fore port magazine of the *Indomptable* in vain. The French ship shudders—then, a little forward of amidships, there is a red belch that spouts high above her mast, and curves outward in a lurid rain far over the sea—then there is a long reverberation of clattering thunder—and the *Indomptable* bursts and sinks. But this row is mingled with another, caused by the ram of the foundering *Pascal* which is working and ravening in the central armor-belt of the *Revenge*. The three vessels disappear from sight within a minute of each other.

There, on the far starboard edge of the British line of battle, the *Iphigenia*—on board of which is Fate—is leveling her whole port battery in one incessant roll of Gardners and Nordenfeldts upon a small approaching second-class torpedo-boat; growling harshly is she, like a hound which bristles and gnashes and snarls, retreating backward, at the sudden apparition of an advancing cobra.

The torpedo-boat lances one of her needles of steel, but it is caught by a wave, tossed upwards in a whiff of spray, and sent flying to starboard, where it explodes under the stern of the French first-class battery-cruiser *Aréthuse*. As the tube of the torpedo-boat sends forth another explosive, the ram of the *Iphigenia* passes into and over her small assailant; the torpedo explodes ten yards away, but tears a hole in the for'ard protective bulkhead of the *Iphigenia*. She commences to settle down by the starboard bow.

But what is this phenomenon which now suddenly appals every eye—the eyes of friend and of foe ; something appalling by its mere novelty, not hitherto seen in sea or land warfare—something in the air—with all the properties and the powers of a spirit of evil ?

It is a balloon—narrow, low, and long—French in origin. It can be steered backward and forward even in the teeth of a light wind; and its operators have the power of dropping dynamite shells with a steel casing, containing liquid oxygen and blasting gelatine, upon the hostile ships. It has come sailing with the light breath of the S. W. monsoon from a French ship which has studiously kept far on the outskirts of the battle.

It is not a toy ; nor is it sent up as a curiosity for the amusement of the British ships. It becomes stationary high over the *Barfleur*, a black dot is seen to disengage itself from it, and a moment or two afterwards ninety-five British sailors are dead, and the engines of the *Barfleur* are no longer there. Then, sparing of its shells, it moves on in another direction, and then swiftly in another, and another, letting fall each time, like some evil bird, its deadly droppings. Except two, which fall into the sea, every shell destroys a ship. One bullet of a rifle would be sufficient to prove fatal to it, but it is high, its movements are swift and sudden, and when at last it tumbles, pierced, into the sea, the battle is all but over. It has done its work.

This had been the wisdom of France, in the time of peace : that she had not despised the ingenious man, and his ingenuities ; she had invited the thinker ; she had welcomed the dreamer of dreams.

This was the second time since the beginning of the war that the British had come into contact with the

Forges et Chantiers de la Méditerranée, and had shuddered intensely at the contact.

But we are an ocean race! Every cock on his own dunghill—and England on the sea. But for the French balloon, the British would very likely have won the battle by five seaworthy ships, and one unseaworthy. As it was, they won by two seaworthy ships, and one unseaworthy.

The last shot fired was fired by the *Iphigenia* at a German third-class cruiser, which she sank. This was the last but two of the Allied vessels left afloat ; the other two, having some time since struck their flag, were now sinking fast.

Besides the *Iphigenia*, which had engines, funnels, screws, and rudder intact, but had a considerable crank bow-wards, three were afloat of the British craft the *Daphne*, a twin-screw sloop, practically uninjured, and the *Barfleur*, floating a mere log, unable to move. There were fifty-seven men alive in her.

The *Iphigenia* had one boat, and the *Daphne* two, still capable of passing over the water ; and these were soon out, two of them making towards the *Barfleur* to take off her crew, and the third in the direction of one of the still floating two ships of the Allies, for the purpose of rescue.

The sea was oilily smooth ; the breeze had died to a mere breath ; the sun had climbed to noon.

All was still. Over four buried navies the water swung lazily—as a cradle which one has ceased to rock, of its own motion.

Weirdly sad is that vast and wandering grave of the sailor ; and careless is the great heart of the sea.

So intent were all who floated during this quiet noontide in the central ocean upon the humane work of rescue, that no one noticed the swift approach upon them of a growing cloud from the east ; and it was only when a shrapnel shell came screaming upon the already shattered *Barfleur*, that the British sailors, to their consternation, discovered that yet another enemy was upon them.

Presently, as though the new arrivals had found

an entire fleet to oppose them, the air was full of fire.

Five large cruisers were seen to be steaming at full speed upon the small remnants of the four fleets.

But cruisers of what nation ? They carried no flag !

The two vessels of the Allies—small torpedo-boat destroyers—had long since struck their colors. And at once, as a precautionary measure, the three British vessels did the same.

But it made no difference ! The rain of fire continued.

Happily, before the boat of the *Iphigenia* reached the *Barfleur*, the *Barfleur* dipped, and sank. So also did one of the Allied ships, and also one of the *Daphne's* boats with her crew. The other of the *Daphne's* boats, and the *Iphigenia's* boat, at once turned to hurry to their ships.

For the moment, the *Iphigenia* was still beyond effective range of the shells of this strange enemy ; but one of the screws of the *Daphne* was shattered by a semi-submarine explosion.

At once, as their boats reached them, the two British ships turned tail under forced draught, flying straight westward from this sudden, dread, mysterious foe.

Both were very swift ; but the *Daphne* could now only move with half her speed. On board the *Iphigenia* the pumps were at work.

The strange enemy, seeing that there was no longer target for their shot, ceased fire, and slackened speed. Only the swiftest of the cruisers was told off to continue the chase of the fugitives.

She gained upon them both, especially upon the *Daphne ;* but a stern chase is a long chase, and it was an hour before the first shell, shattering every gun in the *Daphne's* port central battery, warned her that further flight was useless.

The *Daphne*, as she fled, had again hoisted her ensign, and now again she struck it ; and *again* was surrender met by a hail of shot from this extraordinary adversary.

The *Daphne* at once re-hoisted her colors, spun sharply round to port, and bore straight down upon her pursuer.

Her commander was at least determined to sell the life of his ship dearly.

But he was met by such a cataract of shell and shot that he perceived that he must certainly founder before accomplishing the ram which he meditated.

He determined, far off as he was, to risk the launching of his last torpedo.

It proved a happy inspiration.

The little needle of disaster went hasting, in steadfast headlong flight, in spite of swinging wave and baffling spray, straight upon its victim. It fastened upon her beam at the level of her armored deck, a few inches below the water-line, and burst.

The strange vessel started, and, with a cough that rent her, threw her fragments over the sea. She was the Japanese cruiser *Tschiyoda*.

A minute later, while the *Iphigenia* was still hasting back to the scene of the duel, the *Daphne* sank with all hands.

The *Iphigenia* was now miles out of sight of the four Japanese cruisers. She continued her course eastward, very slowly sinking all the time.

About midnight of the next day she was beached on a sandy bottom not far from Kiao-Chau.

She had on board a hundred and eighty men.

CHAPTER XV

THE SUICIDE OF EUROPE

AT the time of the battle in the Hwang-Hai nearly all Europe was at war.

If any one had imagined that Russia, France, and Germany could declare war against England, and that there the matter would end, he must have been blind to the actual meaning of the then conditions.

Shortly after the defeat of the Allies at Shoreham, a burst of Homeric laughter was caused over England and the Continent by the announcement that the Prince of Monaco (an independent sovereign, possessed of the magnificent army of sixty body-guard carabineers) had declared war against England.

The episode, amusing in itself, was not without significance.

The Prince was not a mere pantomimist. He had been compelled by some intricacy of the actual situation to act as he had acted, and his action only meant that so complex and finely-poised was the machinery of modern European polity, that it was no longer possible for any considerable portion of Europe to be at war without plunging into war the rest of it also.

With the sound of the first cannon a thousand slumbering passions of the people started into life. The hour had struck for the placing upon the stage of a thousand schemes of long-meditated revenge, avarice, and aggression.

Servia rejoiced. Her secret vow to settle the long-standing account with her Bulgarian victors might now be fulfilled. Bulgaria rejoiced. Now at last would she be free of Tsar and of Sultan alike.

Sweden looked round with something of the aggressive enterprise of her old hero, Gustavus Adolphus, wondering if now, at last, she could not accomplish the deliverance of her Finns from the oppressive hand of Russia.

The Cretans, certain now that the Sultan would have his hands full of matters other than their small selves, girt on the dirk and carbine of massacre. Austria turned her eyes toward Salonica with languishing, and her right hand crept out to steal.

Roumania dreamed that Russia's only motive for war was to furnish an excuse for *her* destruction, and rushed in arms to her frontiers. Italy had territories still "unredeemed": and was not this the time to "redeem" them?

Denmark had been nipped and curtailed, and her day was come for vengeance; Portugal was alert to stab in the back her British rival in Africa in the hour of his preoccupation.

At Athens, at Belgrade, at Sophia—from London to Batoum—from St. Petersburg to Meglo-Kastro—the sword leapt from its scabbard.

Mobil!

The Sultan pressed his fez tight upon his head, sitting among cushions; and the panic of the sinner in the day of his calamity gripped coldly at this man's heart. He had heard that the main body of the Servian army was moving eastward from its headquarters at Knnzevatz, and were being massed upon Nisch and Vranja, while fresh levies were being made in order to form a strong reserve; and he had hardly heard it, when the further news arrived that a bloody battle between Servian and Bulgarian divisions of infantry had occurred near Vlassina, in which the Bulgarians had been routed.

The messengers of evil followed fast one upon the other, like the messengers of Job.

The same night a considerable Austrian body crossed the Save, and quietly occupied Belgrade.

The next morning Austrian troops bivouacking in the open spaces of the city, and Austrian officers taking *déjeûner* on the boulevards, met the astonished eyes of the waking citizens.

It seemed as if the Golden Horn was in danger of being broken.

For this action was tantamount to an act of hostility against Russia on the part of Austria. Within a few hours after the occupation of Belgrade, another Austrian brigade, without firing a shot, was installed in Scemendria. The same day telegraphic communication between Constantinople and Odessa was interrupted.

Macedonia was in flames, and a land of *émeutes*,— both Anti-Turkish and Anti-Bulgarian,—from end to end. The Vali of Saloniki was assassinated and mutilated in the streets of his city.

The Porte had called out the last class of rediffs; and rediffs from Smyrna and the Tripolitaine, to the number of 70,000, were being massed with a view to the protection of the frontier line. Fifty thousand men, still left around Stamboul, were distributed along the chain of forts from Roumalie Kavak to the Golden Horn. A fleet of Turkish torpedo-boats without torpedoes, and ironclads without ammunition, steamed northward through the Bosphorus. But before they reached the latitude of Midia, a fleet of Russian Black-Sea battle-ships, torpedo-boats, and transports crowded with 90,000 troops from Odessa, had shelled and occupied Bourgas. (Bourgas is in direct railway communication with Constantinople.)

The uncalled-for action of Austria in occupying the two Servian towns was Russia's defense for her occupation of the Bulgarian town.

Events followed one upon another with an ever-increasing frightfulness of rapidity. Developments which at other times would have required weeks for their outcome, now required hours. Europe wheeled in a delirium of haste. The next day half-a-dozen sotnias of irresponsible Cossacks pushed forward across the Galician frontier to Lubica; and without delay Austria declared formal war against Russia.

Here was a topsy-turvydom of things—brought about by the festering greed and the old malice of the nations. Germany was the pledged ally of Austria; Germany was the pledged ally of Russia against England; and Russia and Austria were at war!

Look, too, at those Italian Bersaglieri and Alpini climbing like chamois over the Alps, with batteries borne on nimble-hoofed mules, by the Mont Cenis route. Italy means to get back, now, old Savoy—which is *her* Alsace-Lorraine—and is engaged on the one hand with French dragoons and mountain-chasseurs among the Alps, and, on the other, is shelling with her fleet the batteries that defend the Riviera, preparatory to landing three corps, her 2d, 4th, and 6th, in the neighborhood of Nice and Mentone.—Yet Germany was the ally of Italy; and Germany was the ally of France; and France and Italy were at war!

Mobil, then, ye sons of men! Set briskly to it—for it is now or never. *Mobil* for your lives!

In England there was no longer a nation: there was only a Militia. The nation had become an army.

After three days of a terrific artillery battle between British ironclads and the forts de la Floride, de l'Heure, and de Tourneville, an English army under Lord Roberts had occupied, first Havre, and then Harfleur. A series of disastrous battles, between Harfleur and Yvetot, had followed, in which the British, though outnumbered, were generally successful in claiming nominal victories. But they made no decided advance. The hitherto unknown results of modern contrivances were found to make victory almost as fatal as defeat. The very small bullets of the Lee-Metford and Lebel rifles—the enormous range of the magazine rifle—the use of smokeless powder—were discovered to be elements whose effects were, on the whole, ten times greater than had been anticipated. Division after division hurried over from Britain to the support of the Havre army; and corps after corps of the French massed upon Rouen, upon Harfleur, upon Confréville, and the neighboring towns to oppose them. It became a question of men.

The Suicide of Europe

Five British ships, which were all that was left of the Mediterranean Squadron after a great engagement in the Bay of Algeciras, were reducing Marseilles at the very time when the Italian ships were engaged in an incessant artillery duel with the forts along the Riviera coast. Yet Italy and England were not formally allies.

North and south a dark cloud of tragedy widened over France. In less than six weeks from the commencement of the war her 7th, 14th, 15th, and 16th Corps d'Armée had ceased to exist, in consequence of signal Italian victories in the south; while in the north a steady deluge of British regiments had accounted for seven more of her corps. Toulon, the impregnable, was in the hands of General Ricotti. Havre was a British base.

Already the reserve of the territorial army was being mobilized for probable service.

France was shrinking under the intolerably harsh frown of England. The Joy of the whole earth was about to perish.

England herself, in her tough, silent way, was in the grip of bitter suffering. The Government had established public granaries over the kingdom. But the price of bread was prohibitive. Whole villages perished.

Singular as it now seems, she had had no separate cable connecting her telegraphically with South Africa, which was to a large extent her life. When she was disconnected with the Continent, she found herself disconnected also with her most important colonies. It was necessary to adopt the method of sending a despatch vessel round the Cape in order to recall the Australian and Pacific Squadrons. The Suez Canal had long since been blown up by the French officials at Port Said.

At the Cape a naval battle had resulted, by some few ships, in a victory for the Allies, in consequence of overwhelming odds. Cape Town and the British seaboard of South Africa had been shelled. Sierra Leone had become French.

But Australia and the seaboard of India were already

safe. The enemy needed all their still floating navies nearer home.

On the strongly-fortified German coast England's success had been hardly less than marvelous. A small fleet of British war-ships and troopers had appeared at the entrance of the Kiel Canal, and captured Tronning.

There the two great branches of the Teutonic race measured strengths. England had sent 100,000 men to fight a nation boasting the most exquisite military organization the world has ever conceived, and capable of placing in the field an army approaching three millions.

The first result was mere disaster for the invaders,— but not moral defeat. They retained Tronning, and, by a *coup*, the remnants of the scattered army under Sir Evelyn Wood possessed itself of Stralsund. They did it under cover of a bombardment by a British fleet, among the British ships being the three Swedish cruisers *Göta*, *Svea*, and *Vanadis*, which suddenly appeared, and joined in the action.

Nor was this England's last word to Germany.

It can never be that guns and swords alone can rule the world. The nation with the stoutest heart and the hardest brow, she is the mistress.

What happened at Havre, happened at Kiel and Stralsund. England with astonishing, steady pertinacity sent men to fight—only, *here*, the rigor of the thing was greater, the flame hotter.

In all that low-lying tract of land between Wismar, Neu Brandenburg, Anclam, and Stralsund a series of murderous conflicts took place, Wilhelm himself directing the course of the campaign, and the English being entrenched for the most part behind a semicircular line of earthworks stretching east and west, with Stralsund for base.

The three lines of railway, west to Lubeck and Hamburg, east to Stettin, and south to Berlin, were in the hands of the British; and after a day of fearful carnage in the neighborhood of Neu Brandenburg, in which the German army was routed with a loss of 150,000 men, a successful rush was made for Stettin, which, in the course of a night attack, fell into British hands.

The same night nearly the whole of Berlin was destroyed by fire, a catastrophe attributed to the action of Socialists.

And ever England came to Germany—raw levies, meager Cockney-born lads, boors from the Downs, Lancashire bodies, persons in kilts : not terrible to look at : terrible to meet in battle.

Their chief characteristic is not that they are brave, and agile, and cool ; but that by some unknown national quality of mind they really contrive to do what they try to do. Their results always produce a certain effect of surprise.

Before these nimble invaders the *tapfere Krieger* of the Fatherland slowly receded.

From Thon, that Metz of the East, from Königsberg, and Dantzig, and the great military depôts of the Northeast, troops were drafted to repel this obstinate, rock-browed, small, unseasoned foe.

But the more the English poured their levies upon the German seaboard, and the greater the draughts by Wilhelm upon the as yet inactive corps, and nearer the possibility of a call upon the Teuton shopkeepers and burghers of the reserve, so the more Socialistic seemed to become the opinions of the German nation.

Socialism—with its absurdities—with its heavenly gospel of salvation for the world—had, for ultimate good, or ulimate ill, got into the blood of the nations during the latter half of the nineteenth century, far more than any one then supposed. Men who most hated the word, thought Socialism, and did not know it. It was bound to come out when the great moment for its birth arrived.

Wilhelm walked on an abyss, and the ground beneath his feet was parchment.

He had no sooner withdrawn a large portion of the Army of the Vistula, than Danzig was sacked and taken by the Swedish fleet.

The most extraordinary phenomenon of this vast and complex war was the success of Sweden everywhere.

Within three weeks a division of her gallant little army, consisting of only three corps, had gained a permanent *pied à terre* as far south as Bromberg; she had wrought havoc with the northeastern coast-defenses of Germany; and she had turned West Prussia into a depopulated wilderness. Another division of her army, consisting of five corps, had in two great battles on the Banks of Lake Ulea routed two Russian war-hosts, and had pushed on to Helsingfors, which they captured from the land side, and made their headquarters. Intoxicated, they turned their faces across the Gulf of Finland toward Cronstat.

The hands of Russia were full enough.

Immediately upon the outbreak of war with Austria, she had concentrated, as fast as her defective railway-system would allow, great masses of troops, consisting of the 4th, 8th, 9th, 10th, 11th and 12th Army Corps, in the direction of Lemberg. Behind these followed the more remote 13th, 16th, and 17th Corps.

Including the Corps d'Armée doing unsuccessful battle with the Swedes in Finland, by far the greater part of Russia's vast territorial power was now in the field, three additional army-corps having advanced from Kars to the investment of Erzeroum, where a crushing defeat at the hands of a mixed army of Turks and English awaited them.

The eastern limb of the British Mediterranean fleet had steamed through the Bosphorus, conveying transports to Trebizonde, and then proceeded northwards, with the double object of a search for the Russian Black Sea Squadron, and the bombardment of Odessa and Sebastopol.

Austria had massed her forces into three armies: one in East Galicia, on the Dniester, another on the San with its back on Przemysl, the great bulwark of Middle Galicia, and the third on Cracow, the key of western Galicia, on the Upper Vistula.

The Great White Tsar was preoccupied. All around his sky were clouds and darkness. That mighty breadth of empire was already rocking to its fall.

The gray and green-coated soldiers of Russia were

swarming round her borders, more on the defensive than the offensive. In the first fixed battle with the Austrians, General Gourko, the old Invincible, had been routed with such a horror of widespread massacre that the brain of the aged General was unhinged.

And ever anew—after each orgy of blood—went forth the cry over Europe : *Mobil, Mobil.*

In a skirmish near Karatova between two demi-regiments of Macedonians and Bulgarians, not a single man was left alive.

In fact, Europe was destroying herself. Everywhere from Land's End to the Caucasus, the grin of a specter was perceived in the air—the Specter of Hunger, and grim Scarcity, and raw-boned Want.

England had America to supply her wants; but wants cannot be supplied save by the purchasing power of the party who wants. England's purchasing power had consisted in her commerce, and her commerce was near to death.

America, moreover, in this crisis, had no idea of small profits and quick returns. She had been thrown by the war into a state of financial collapse. And she raised her prices to prohibitive figures.

On paper England remained rich enough. Her consols were taken up eagerly. The chief financiers and bankers of the world filled her war-chest. The security of by far the larger half of investments depended upon her success. As a matter of self-interest the Rothschilds, and Wall Street, and the kings of finance, threw in their lot with her.

But the industry of the world was at a standstill, and there is no wealth not the direct offspring of industry.

Germany, France, Italy and Russia opened their ports to all comers, adopting the free-trade policy of England—but too late. That, of course, which they were unable to buy was not brought to them to be sold.

Russian wheat, by Imperial command, ceased to be exported. But it would quite certainly have ceased to be exported without the command.

The fields grew rich and oozy with a human sap, the blood of millions. But the hand of industry was palsied to sow the seed.

Mobil, then, ye children of Europe! *Mobil* all ye can! But know that in the end it shall bite like a serpent, and sting like an adder.

CHAPTER XVI

THE LOVE WHICH FOO-CHEE BORE TO AH-LIN

Foo-CHEE was No. 13 of the 3d squad of the 1st company of the 2d battalion of the 11th regiment of the 2d brigade of the 1st division of the 17th Army Corps of the great army of China.

Every morning and every night he lifted up both his hands, and he blessed the name of Yen How, illustrious, who by his might had changed the old flow and show of things. For why? Because Ah-lin was No. 15 of the same squad of the same company of the same battalion of the same regiment of the same brigade of the same division of the same Army Corps of the great army of China.

Every day, between four and a quarter to six o'clock, the company was drilled on the plain southeast of Pekin, half a mile from the walls. The roll was called before drill, and if any one was absent, he or she was hanged publicly, by the heels, the next morning. So Ah-lin *had* to be there, and Foo-chee saw Ah-lin, and blessed Yen How, illustrious.

Ah-lin was a girl of eighteen, very pretty, with the elongated face which the Chinese adore, and eyes so long, and narrow, and slanting. She was the daughter of a tiny silversmith whose shop was on a fifth floor in a gaudy Pekin main-street.

Her father lived his life in a corner of the single room which was his shop and dwelling. His life was a dream, and his food rice-greens and opium. When he awoke from his paradises, he languidly took up a piece of silver, and looked at it, and put it down again.

Ah-lin's father and mother and herself lived happily upon fifteen *tiaos* per week. The father was exempt from service, because one of his legs was incapable of walking. The mother served in a different company from that of Ah-lin.

But in spite of her poverty, Ah-lin had an elongated face, and peepy little bewitching eyes, and a pigtail of incredible length. Her feet, of course, had not been cramped, and she walked with a fine free swing, slanting a wee bit backward, like the true Northerner that she was.

"Foo-chee," said Ni-ching-tang, who was the father of Foo-chee, "take your eyes from Ah-lin, my son. Leave Ah-lin be. She is loved by Sin-wan, and Sin-wan is among the honorable ones in the days which are."

Ni-ching-tang knew what he was saying; for he was a very subordinate cook in the multitudinous kitchen of Yen How, and Sin-wan was a warder in the Imperial Prisons. Ni-ching-tang and Sin-wan were good nodding acquaintances, as we should say.

That Sin-wan loved Ah-lin there could be no doubt. He had more than once risked his neck in leaving the Imperial precincts at unlawful hours to make signaling gestures before the fifth-floor room of Ah-lin's parents.

But Sin-wan was of middle age, and unduly stout. His neck was thick and hard, and seemed made for hanging. And his countenance was as hideous as Fe's, the joss, as it stands carved out in the ebon idols.

Moreover, Sin-wan was addicted to orgies of the spirit *samshu*, and the impress of these excesses was left on his brutal face.

Ah-lin's eyes, though narrow, could see much; and in her secret meditations in the darkness of the room at night she would think that Foo-chee was pleasant to look at, and Sin-wan was not.

Foo-chee was a young man of twenty, and a seller of Thibet incense-sticks in the next street to Ah-lin's. And these two units, among the tens of thousands of human beings that swarmed and sweltered around them, felt within them the stirrings of that force which made the world.

Foo-Chee's Love for Ah-Lin

Ah-lin had noted the following eye of Foo-chee often, long before the strange drilling commenced ; and when she found herself almost next to him in the 3d squad, she had a presentiment and a tremor. It was the doing of the upper gods.

"Ah-lin," said Ah-lin's mother, Nan-lin, "turn away your eyes from the eyes that turn to you. Foo-chee is pleasant to look at, but Sin-wan is among the honorable ones in the days that are. A child should love her father and her mother above herself, and do all for them."

But it was the doing of the upper gods, what happened. Ah-lin was near to Foo-chee every day in the new drill ; and the drilling straightened Foo-chee's back, so that his backward slant as he walked was increased, till a woman would have died for him.

But Sin-wan, one night, beckoned to Nan-lin from the street, and Nan-lin sent down Ah-lin, and Sin-wan took Ah-lin by the hand and said :

"Ah-lin is well formed, both in face and figure. Therefore I, Sin-wan, will marry with Ah-lin."

At this directness Ah-lin hung her head. It was not difficult to perceive the sequence of cause and effect in this matter—and she was afraid of Sin-wan.

"Do you say yes, Ah-lin ?" said Sin-wan. "If you say yes, I will take you now to a meal in Hing-Chang-Li's eating-house, with fresh tea to drink."

"I say yes," replied Ah-lin, "But my father and mother—to whom all honor—do not wish me to marry now."

"That is a lie, Ah-lin. Your father and mother wish you to marry. And you wish to marry, too. But you do not wish to marry with me. You wish to marry with Foo-chee."

"Foo-chee ?"—she started—"Where did you hear the name of Foo-chee ?"

"Your mother told me his name, Ah-lin."

"It is strange. I know no one with such a name."

"It is a lie, Ah-lin. His name is written in green and red picture-letters over the booth where he sells incense-sticks. I have seen it, and I have seen *him*."

"And what do you say is his name?"

"Foo-chee."

"Well, it may be, Sin-wan. I know nothing of the matter."

"Foo-chee shall die, Ah-lin, if you do not marry with me."

"Oh! what for? Whom has Foo-chee hurt? He sells his incense-sticks, and hurts no one!"

"Now I have made you say that you wish to marry with him. For you do not wish me to kill him, Ahlin."

"Kill him, if you wish."

"I will kill him."

"But why so?"

"Because you will not marry with me."

"I did not say I will not marry with you, Sin-wan."

"Then you will?"

"I must."

"When, Ah-lin?"

"When the new drilling is no more."

"Oh, that may be never. No. It shall be while this moon is big."

"I cannot, Sin-wan—I cannot."

"Why not, Ah-lin?"

"It is my father and mother,—to whom all——"

"It is that dog's gall, Foo-chee! Foo-chee shall die, Ah-lin."

"Oh, me! I am not feeling happy, Sin-wan!"

"No, nor am I feeling happy, till you say that it shall be this moon! Nor shall Foo-chee feel happy, when my knife is rankling in his liver! Say it, Ah-lin?"

"I say it, Sin-wan."

"While the moon is big?"

"Yes, Sin-wan."

"Then I will go. And I will come again to-morrow night at this hour."

"Did you not say that you would take me to the eating-house of Hing-Chang-Li for a meal, with fresh tea?"

"I cannot to-night, for I have no time, since I must return now to the Imperial Prison. But to-morrow

Foo-Chee's Love for Ah-Lin 173

night—or the night after—you shall feed at the eating-house of Hing-Chang-Li."

So Sin-wan turned on his heels, and walked away on them. And when he arrived at the portals of the Imperial City, he was already late, and his bulging neck was in danger.

The Imperial Prisons stood in a great quadrangle of marble, fringed with stupendous avenues of long-haired trees of the banyan genus, being surrounded by a moat bridged by a number of marble bridges. The building itself is of marble, and of very great size. A stone's throw to the south stood the palace of the Austrian Ambassador, embedded in a bower of foliage; to the north, a hundred yards away, and separated from the prison by a lake overgrown with huge lilies and moon-leaved water-growths, stood the shaded palace of Yen How. The Imperial Palace itself was half a mile away by the broad avenue, but there was also a short-cut to it from the palace of Yen How.

It was the quiet hour of the evening-time, and the sumptuous landscape of the Imperial City seemed to faint and doze in a dream of lotus peace.

Leaning over one of the marble bridges that spanned the prison-moat was an old man. It was Ni-ching-tang, the father of Foo-chee. His day's work was over, and he was looking sleepily upon the dark and slumbrous water of the moat.

As he leaned so, Sin-wan approached him, passing to his duties in the prison. Ni-ching-tang would not have heard the tread of the thick-felted slippers; but Sin-wan spoke.

"Give good to you, Ni-ching-tang," he said. "Has his Might, the Governor, passed this way yet?"

"No, Sin-wan," the old man answered, and his eyes smiled; "fear nothing. He will not know."

"Know what, Ni-ching-tang?"

"That you are late—again."

Sin-wan leered.

"It comes of going to seek a little wife," he said.

"Poh! it is nothing—if you are not seen. But a wife?"

"Ah-lin is her name, and she is the daughter of Lan-sing and Nan-lin, his wife. We will marry this moon. She is well formed, both in face and body."

"What, with small feet too?"

"No small feet; but well formed in face and body."

"And she lives where?"

"In the third quarter, and the main street."

"Why, I have a son who lives near the main street of the third quarter."

"And what is your son's name, Ni-ching-tang?"

Sin-wan did not notice that Ni-ching-tang paused a second before he answered.

"My son is called Cheng-lu," he said.

Then Sin-wan passed on, and entered the prison.

As he went in, he took from his bosom a small cylinder of ebony, round which clung a roll of silk-paper.

On the paper were six lines of writing, each starting from the top and going down to the bottom. Each line started with a date, and underneath the date came the instructions for that day.

This document had been painted by Yen How, with his own hands.

Yen How had stood over John Hardy, with watch and stethoscope in his hands. John had lain bound on his back on the marble floor.

Yen How had examined him from head to foot. He had felt the texture of his muscles, had palpated the calves of his legs, had held his pulse, watch in hand. He had applied the stethoscope to John's chest, and heard the wheeze; he had laid it over his heart, and made an estimate of the exact timbre of the beats, systole and diastole, venous and arterial.

When it was over, he knew the precise truth about Hardy's vitality, its quantity, its intensity, its whole diathesis; he knew just how much mental and physical torture the lad could bear, and for how long, without an actual cessation of life.

He was not in a hurry. He waited—Hardy was well fed and nourished. It was over a week before the torture began.

Now, when Sin-wan opened the door behind which John lay in sleep, Ada Seward would no longer have recognized the pretty boy who had sat beside her in the music-hall, nor Miss Jay the gallant fellow who had made her start in an alarm of self-retention.

Broad streaks of absolute white mingled with his long fair hair. His bony hands clutched and trembled in his sleep like the hands of some aged miser.

At the first faint sound of the key, he sprang with a bound straight to his feet, wide awake. He had learned to be afraid now.

Sin-wan, as he turned the key, muttered something to two men who were now with him. They went away up a narrow stairway into a room above.

He gave a final glance at the directions under Day IV. on the silken scroll, and with studious brow ran over the points on his fingers. This was the fifth scroll of the kind, all covering a space of six days, which Sin-wan had studied.

Having satisfied himself that all was ready, and his instructions well in his head, Sin-wan entered the chamber and closed the door behind him.

The sight of that face had become a pang and a sickness to the soul of Hardy. To all his tortures it was an added torture. It grinned in his nightmares. It was the devil of his hell.

He sank back in a corner pale as death.

Sin-wan never brought him his food; so that Sin-wan's face was associated in his mind only with agony. Yen How, who knew the mind and its secrets, had willed it so.

The room was not very small, but it was of stone, and damp. However, in one corner was a bed which was nothing less than luxurious, the coverings being of fine, padded silk. Hardy had not suffered from cold; still less from hunger or thirst.

These were tortures far and away too elementary and obvious to occur to such a mind as that of Yen How. The body, by itself, is capable of intense pangs; but never is torture exquisite when it is wholly divorced from the mind.

Yen How's profound knowledge of this fact was proved when he said to himself:

"One of his tortures shall consist in the daily sight of—a Face."

Beside the quilted bed, there were in the chamber a table, on which was water and wine: near it, a cushioned chair; and a stool made of a hard greenish-colored wood, provided with a straight upright back, and cross-pieces in the legs. It could not be moved. It was cramped by iron rivets to the flooring.

The room was lighted by three Chinese lanterns which hung above Hardy's reach, let down through holes in the ceiling a short way.

Sometimes one, or two, or even the three, went out, through some carelessness of the attendants; and even when they all burned, there was not much light. But Hardy's eyes, long accustomed, saw everything.

One of the ingenuities of pain to which he had been subjected consisted in the mere appearance of Sin-wan. Once Sin-wan had entered, leered round, and retired. The next day he entered, leered round, and retired. Was the ordeal over, then? A heavenly hope leapt in Hardy. The next day Sin-wan appeared with a brazier crowded with white-hot wires.

Several times lately Sin-wan had entered, leered round, and retired. With every new entrance now, John hoped that on *this* day no new sword would pierce him. For to-morrow he cared not—only for *this* day his spirit cried to Heaven. But on many a day Heaven turned her ear from him.

He breathed in an agony of Hope, in an Arctic Hell of Fear.

In the course of weeks his great mind had quite collapsed. He was now utterly demoralized and craven.

He knew neither morning nor night. He had lost count of the days and the weeks.

He did not commit suicide, because, at first, the means were not ready at his hand. It is not an easy matter for a man to dash his brains against the wall. Later, when he looked round for the means to kill himself, an intense cowardice seized him. He clung to life—only

Foo-Chee's Love for Ah-Lin

to life. Just one little spark, too, of his innate stubbornness lingered. After a torture, he would pray aloud that Heaven would send its swift Messenger upon him; but his obstinate will to live returned, if a day of peace was granted to him.

Now, as Sin-wan showed his face, he cringed against the wall with staring eyes of expectancy.

Was this a day of torture? or a day of grace?

What added a touch of intensest horror to the relation between this boy and this man was the fact that they had never exchanged a word. They were as remote and divided as two creatures of different planets. Sin-wan did not know a word of English, nor John of Chinese.

A day of torture, or of grace? He had ceased to care for the morrow; but *to-day* . . .

A wild hope stabbed his heart. Sin-wan had no sort of implement about him. He could not torture without an implement. It was a day of—grace, then?

No. The Chinaman walked to the cabinet in a corner where lay some cords. And he lifted them on his forearm, and he came to where John, half-standing, half-falling, cowered.

John had long ceased to make any resistance to the binding process.

During the operation this time he fainted. But terror woke him. He was placed on the high-backed stool, his arms bound behind the back, and his chest, high up to the neck, upon it. Underneath, his shoeless feet were bound to the cross-pieces.

He could not move his head backward, for the chair-back prevented him; forward, he could move it about fifteen degrees, and from side to side about thirty.

What was in store for him? He was wide awake now. With starting eyeballs he waited.

Five minutes passed.

Then Sin-wan produced something.

It was a leather strap, four and a half inches broad, sixteen long. At the ends were clasps.

He put it round Hardy's neck and clasped it. And

now Hardy could move his head neither backward, forward, nor sideward.

He sat with elevated chin, staring—a gaze of horror into vacancy. Yet he felt no pain.

He waited five more minutes, and the dim thought that reeled within his brain in a vertigo of woe was this: how long? how long, O Lord?

Five minutes, and then five more: and then he felt —something.

Yet it gave him no pain.

It was a drop of fluid—water, in fact—which had fallen upon his head from above.

He waited half a minute, and it came again; and half a minute, and it came again. And so, regularly, every half-minute it came for some ten minutes.

This, of itself, to an ordinary person, would be a misery. But by this time John Hardy was so familiarized with agony that to him it was simply nothing. The slowly-dropping water collected on his head, and was trickling down his face, when he began to wonder, with a species of glad incredulity, whether this could be meant as a new torture.

He could have borne it all the night, and all the day, and thanked God for His clemency.

Suddenly he lanced a horrid shriek.

A drop of *something else* had fallen upon his head, and eaten into his scalp. It was a drop of strong oil of vitriol.

. . . . . .

Would the falling of the vitriol continue? or the falling of the water?

The next drop was a drop of water.

But if it had been vitriol, and vitriol thenceforth regularly, Hardy's agonies would have been far less monstrous than, in fact, they were.

In this was manifested the profundity of Yen How, that he knew how exquisitely to intensify the pangs of the body by means of the travail of the soul.

The next drop was water, and the next was water, and the next was water, and the next was—vitriol!

And now John Hardy cried out against Heaven, straining at his cords, and bawling like a bull.

But drop by drop from the ceiling fell the implacable fluid; not so many drops of water, and then a drop of vitriol, but with crafty variations, sometimes two drops of vitriol at a time, and then for minutes not another.

Yen How, however, knew his craft too well to make such an ordeal last very long. Sin-wan had instructions that, as soon as the victim showed signs of madness or collapse, the torture should cease.

Accordingly, when Hardy ceased to cry aloud, and a reddish stream trickled down his chin, his bands were undone, and Sin-wan cast his unconscious body on the bed.

. . . . . .

Just about the time that he did so, Ah-lin was standing before the incense-stick booth of Foo-chee.

"It is not that I am bold, Foo-chee," she said, "that I come here to speak. But I must say what I have in my mind."

Here was blessedness, and a wringing of the hands, and an embarrassment of the pleased eyelids, and the favor of the upper gods, for Foo-chee.

"It is an incense-stick that you desire," he said, "and your name is Ah-lin, for I know it. And all the incense-sticks which I have are yours. For why? Because we stand and step together each day before sundown in the same company of the drilled—no other reason."

"It is a lie, Foo-chee," said Ah-lin, "there is another reason—though I cannot guess what it can be. But whatever the reason be, you must now throw it quite away. It was not for an incense-stick that I came—though incense-sticks are pleasant, and I have long desired one—but to tell you just that. You must throw it quite away."

"And for why?"

"Because another, who is greater than you, wants just the thing that you want. If you get that thing, he will kill you. In order that he may not kill you, he shall have the thing."

"Cruel Ah-lin!"

"No, not I. You say what is not, not knowing, Foo-chee. But he will kill you; therefore he shall have what you desire."

"Then I shall kill myself, not having what I desire."

"Cruel Foo-chee!"

"You will, then, feel happy if I live, Ah-lin!"

"Yes; and therefore I shall make myself feel unhappy by giving to another what you desire, in order that I may feel happy at the same time in knowing that you live."

"To feel happy and unhappy at the same time is mixed, Ah-lin."

"But it is better, Foo-chee, to feel happy and unhappy through a long lifetime than to feel happy for a little hour, and then die."

Here was the practicality of the Woman. Foo-chee pondered it. Then he lifted his head and said:

"There is a riddle somewhere which I cannot solve, Ah-lin. Let us go, instead, to the eating-house of Hing-Chang-Li for a meal, with fresh tea. And with you take three of these incense-sticks."

Ah-lin hesitated, and was lost. Foo-chee drew down the flap over his booth, and carefully adjusted the ring to the staple; then together they walked off on their heels; and their swinging pigtails met and touched, as it were knowingly, behind them.

And at the eating-house of Hing-Chang-Li they ate a hearty meal, with a whole *mitin* of fresh tea-leaves.

They were in the sweep of the force which underlies the world. It was the doing of the upper gods.

CHAPTER XVII

THE CHINESE IRON

THE next day John Hardy, at the hour of evening, sat in his corner, watching his door with a kind of wild-beast sullenness.

His nerves had an instinct of the hour when Sin-wan was due to appear.

So sick was his soul with misery after the ordeal of the day before, that he had eaten nothing since. His food lay untasted on the table.

He sat sprawling with disjected limbs on the floor, watching the point of Sin-wan's expected entrance through the fierce and sullen corners of his eyes.

He had often had the thought of braining Sin-wan with one of the porcelain platters, or of strangling him with his pig-tail, or with one of the ropes used to bind himself. As he sat there the thought now recurred to him. His brain was in that condition in which thoughts are no longer semi-voluntary, but seem to come and go at random of their own motion, like winds through the vacant heaven. He had, however, sufficient reason left to give no entertainment to this thought. His chance, if he ever had it, was long past. He was too hopelessly frail now.

He sat long, expecting. One of his lanterns went out; then another; in half an hour the third. He was in darkness.

Suddenly the lad started as though a sword had pierced him.

He looked eagerly towards the door; and he said to himself, "No, no." It was too incredible; he must be mad.

"Mad, mad," he moaned, his head buried in his two arms, as he rocked himself slowly to and fro, with a regular motion like a pendulum. So he went on for about half an hour, his face hidden, with sometimes a moan, and sometimes a word. "What have I done?" he said wearily, in the thinnest whine: "What have I done—O God, Father, God?... But now I am mad, mad...."

It had seemed to him, as the third lantern went out and left him in darkness, that, at the edge of the door, there was a long streak of semi-light—*that the door was open!*

He had sense enough to know that the condition of his mind was one far and away removed from a state of ordinary sanity; that his senses were now quite capable of playing him tricks. But when, after a long time, he lifted his head, there, still before his eyes, was the streak of light.

He sprang to his feet, and his pallor of death assumed a hue of even more absolute wanness. Groping limpingly along the walls, he made toward the door. But, on the whole, it was rather to assure himself of the optical delusion which he supposed, than with the expectation of finding the door really open.

But the door was, really, open.

What made his heart go bumping and bounding within his ribs was the look of Providence—the hint of God's finger—in the fact of the lanterns *all* going out at the very time when the door, by some extraordinary means, had become unfastened.

But though one step meant salvation, and one instant's delay meant death, yet could he not take the step. The sudden shock of hope—the sudden suspicion of Heaven—all but killed him. He dropped back against the wall, panting, panting, trying with his right hand to force back the violent galloping of his heart.

But the instant that he could move, he moved. With wide mouth and gasping chest, he cautiously pushed back the door, and passed through it.

Toward what? Toward certain capture? It must

not be supposed that he was now in a mental condition to give this question even a single thought. He went through the open door precisely in the way in which a wild animal passes through the open door of its cage—instinctively toward liberty. He lived by moments. At *this* moment he was free ; to the next he gave not a thought. He simply walked forward as a stream flows downwards—because it is a law of nature.

He found himself in a long corridor ; and yonder, half-way down the corridor, was—a man.

The man's back was toward John ; and he was bending down, cleaning a blue-glass lantern.

It was at this sight that the first notion of the impossibility of his ultimate escape occurred to Hardy ; and with this appreciation of the impossibility, came also the ravenous Desire, the frenzied Hope. As he slid swiftly back behind the door, and drew it upon himself, he was no longer a mere wild creature of instinct. He looked forward—he reasoned.

He waited, fearing worse than death to stir the door. Then he had a sudden horror which pricked him like a goad to action—if Sin-wan came ? It was his hour !

He very slightly pushed back the door, and peeped out. The corridor was empty.

He ran now, with the stealthy feet of a man treading on hot embers. His feet were bare and made no sound. He had on a shirt and trousers. But the shirt was filthy, and the trousers flapped in long rags all down his legs. His hair reached to his shoulders.

At the end of the corridor was a door. He pushed it lightly. It did not move. He forced his shoulder against it. It was locked.

He was as much a prisoner as before, then ? Immediately after the first intolerable sinking of the heart he could not believe it. A vague, but real, faith was in him now. The mere fact that he was where he was proved Providence. He believed dimly that God now was willing him to be free, wild as the idea was, far off as the probability might be.

He looked round for some means of escape ; and

there, in fact, was a tall window in the side of the corridor, slightly open.

He ran to it, and looked down. It opened upon another corridor twenty feet below.

Twenty feet! The distance was infinite.

Underneath his flapping rags one could see the red and livid patchwork of his flesh, where it had been nipped and pinched and burned and pricked and bruised in half a hundred agonies. How could he leap twenty feet? It was as dreadful to him as to an infant. Like the very aged, he was afraid "of that which is high."

But as he looked again he saw a short rope hanging over the window-sill by which he could help himself down.

And now, at this sight, it is a wonder that some suspicion of the fact that all these happy chances were only part of another elaborate torture did not enter his head. But his brain was so preoccupied with the idea of *Providence*, that nothing of the sort occurred to him.

With endless pains he managed, with the help of the rope, to reach the lower corridor; and at once, with the same stealthy trepidation, he set out, running in the same direction in which he had so far come.

At the end of this corridor also was a door; and at his push it opened.

Now he was in yet another corridor, at right angles to the first and second. In which direction should he turn? He did not care. He would be guided right by the Hand that led him. Away to the right he went with tottering gait, treading on embers, hugging the wall.

If only his heart would cease its awful thumping! Surely, surely, through all that vast building, through all Pekin, they would hear the echoes of that laboring bosom! So it seemed to him.

His white, wide lips were twisted awry in his effort to take in and expel his noisy breath.

As he ran in this excess of agitation, he suddenly remembered the battle of Shoreham, how he had been cool in the midst of sounding cannon and angry war. Could he not still be so? Was he so much changed?

He made a weak effort—a faint self-assertion of the old John Hardy. But in another instant he forgot the effort. It was far from him.

He reached the end of the corridor, and was about to turn to the left, when, there before him, he saw two Chinamen, near to him, talking. They were standing in the middle of the passage which he had to pass.

Had they seen him? Had they not heard the labor of his heart? Apparently not: they remained deep in talk.

Must he lurk till they moved away? Would they not come his way?

Suddenly, behind him, down the length of the corridor in which he stood, he heard a sound. He looked and saw a man approaching him. He was between two dangers.

The man's eyes were bent meditatively upon the ground. He came swinging toward Hardy.

The night had not yet come, though it was near. The corridor in which the two conversed was not dark, but it was much dimmer than that in which John stood. It was necessary for him to move—the third man was coming near.

He stole forward, inch by inch, sideways, with his chest against the wall, and his face twisted round watching the two talkers. He came near them—he was opposite to them—by a stretched-out arm they could touch him.

Stealthily he crept, slowly as the movement of a glacier; he was past them. And he was no sooner past them than, with incautious haste, eager only to be on—to be on—he sped away. During those instants of slow motion he had passed through all the terrors of the grave.

The two men calmly continued their talk; the third came up and joined them. Hardy went onwards undisturbed.

For quite half an hour he stole forward, all leers and tremors, like a thief in the night, through three halls, over a courtyard, along two more corridors, without anywhere meeting any one.

The slumbrous gloaming deepened. He began to think himself lost in this endless structure, without hope of finding exit.

But at last he saw an oblong of distinctly lesser obscurity; he knew that this must be a door of exit from the prison.

Could it be true? Was he really about to escape into the open day—under the sky, the clouds? He leapt forward. And as he did so, a man stood in the doorway, and leant his back against the door-post.

It was far from light now, but Hardy would have felt the presence of that form and face in the darkest midnight. It was Sin-wan.

John was still in full career to make for the door, when his eyes fell upon this man; and like a shying horse he bolted aside. A door, as he touched the wall, gave way before his pressure. He rushed through, mad to put a world of distance between him and that face. As he hasted forward, in the dark now, he stepped upon nothing, and tumbled headlong down a flight of stone stairs.

He had hardly time to pick himself up when he heard that some one was behind him, descending the stairs, humming a tune. And he knew that it was Sin-wan.

Off he rushed again; and again, in five minutes, there was light. He stood between two walls, about five feet apart, about ten feet long; and at the end of them was a portal, painted green, half open; and beyond the portal, he saw—trees!

He was free! and yet he shuddered. Behind him was Sin-wan, coming, coming; and before him the open gate; but the whole of the space between him and the gate, and between the two walls, was paved with broken glass.

There was not an inch of harmless ground upon which to place his naked feet.

But Sin-wan was behind. Hardy stepped forward, and reached the gate, and passed through it, running.

Every footprint which he left behind now was a footprint of blood.

Still onward, panting heart! The hand with which He leads is surely rough—but still, is *He* not leading? And now for the bridge of marble ahead, which spans the moat. He reaches it, and starts and stops.

There, in the middle of the bridge, leaning over the parapet, looking at the water, is a man.

This gauntlet also Hardy must run. Crouching against the opposite parapet he crawls forward.

His lust to be free is now a thousand thousand times more intense than ever before. Every danger that he has escaped has added to his terror, a deeper terror, to his hope a wilder frenzy. Like a beast he crawls forward on hands and knees, step by step, without a sound.

But as he is exactly opposite the man, the man turns quite round. Hardy leaps to his feet. They are face to face, and eye to eye.

All is over, then. He has been seen.

But no! What mean those groping hands, that hesitating step, as the man turns slowly away? Is he *blind?* Can those eyes see *nothing?* So John Hardy believes. Here, at least, is Providence, and the leading Hand.

Away, once more, towards the palace of Yen How, and then down the long avenues to the portal of the "Imperial City." This part of the way he remembers, having passed through it before. Onward, in the shade of the great trees, he limps, leaving behind him his trail of blood. He meets no one. He is under the open sky. Among the leaves sighs the evening wind.

He reaches the great portal, and, strange to say, there is no one there. He passes out. He is in an open space—beyond the Imperial walls—which properly belongs to the "Chinese City."

So far has he escaped. A feeling of absolute security rushes upon him, and with it an overwhelming, speechless gratitude. He drops to his knees; his face turns upward in an ecstatic agony of love to the skies, washed in tears; out stretch his arms in adoration,

But between his eyes and the sky comes a face, and between his stretched-out arms comes a form. He leaps with a shriek to his feet, recognizes the face of Yen How, and faints in Yen How's arms.

The slightest possible smile wrinkled the corners of Yen How's eyes.

"Poh!" he said in English, "it is nothing. Why such a cry as that? It is your own fault, boy. You ought to have known that Providence—if there is such a thing—never works in these outright ways. Yen How's Providence does—but Yen How is a smaller fellow altogether than the Big One above—if He is there at all. Is He there? *Is He there?* Ah!—may be, and may be, not. But just now it is Yen How for you, and not He. The man cleaning the lanterns, and the men talking together, and Sin-wan, and the blind man—they all saw you, you know, boy, because Yen How put them there to see you. And it is hard to escape from Yen How, whose Ada Seward you have been kissing, and whom you have tried to shoot, lillee English boy. And Yen How is not done with you yet —not yet—not yet. But those English!"—here he ceased to speak to the unconscious form in his arms, and continued his meditative soliloquy in Chinese—"those English! They are just like devils for fighting! Only 150 or 200 of them, they say, at Kiao-Chau, and six weeks gone, and they not killed off yet. Stupid Japanese ship-captains to let them get away in that fashion. However—ah, lillee English kisser,"—he addressed John Hardy again—"wouldn't you like to be with the 200 white men at Kian-Chau now? I think you might be able to play some tricks with their help, too. But Yen How has you tight—Yen How, the toad, the frog, eh? Stop, though! isn't there something in your Bible about a plague of frogs in the land of Egypt in the Pharaohs' time? Yes, surely—yes. Well, now, how would you like a little plague of frogs in your land of England, eh? Ah, well, it is near. It is not far off now. . . . "

At this point a man appeared; Yen How handed him the limp body of Hardy, and walked up and down a long time that night under the shade of the trees of the Imperial avenues.

About this time there were two men outside the Imperial precincts who ought to have been within them. One was Sin-wan, and the other was the father of Foo-chee, Ni-ching-tang.

Ni-ching-tang went to the dwelling of his son Foo-chee, whom he loved, in order that he might see Foo-chee, and receive from him the reverences due to a father. And, lo, Foo-chee was not there; and Foo-chee's booth was deserted.

Said Ni-ching-tang:
"Now where can Foo-chee be?"

Sin-wan went to the dwelling of his promised wife, Ah-lin, to see her, and receive from her the reverences due to a husband that is to be. And lo, Ah-lin was not there.

So Sin-wan said:
"Now where can Ah-lin be?"

Now Ni-ching-tang was shrewd, and Sin-wan was shrewd. So Sin-wan said:
"Ah-lin is not far from the booth of Foo-chee."

And Ni-ching-tang said:
"He who knows how to find Ah-lin is far on the road to the discovery of Foo-chee."

And Sin-wan set out to go to the booth of Foo-chee, and Ni-ching-tang to go to the dwelling of Ah-lin. And midway between the dwelling of Ah-lin and the booth of Foo-chee these two men met in the street.

It was Ni-ching-tang who spoke.
"Ho! ho!—late hours—late hours," he said (and he half hid his nose behind a sportive hand)—"late hours, and a merry courting-time——"

Sin-wan was struck dumb. Ni-ching-tang knew that Sin-wan had no right to be out of bounds, but Sin-wan did not know that Ni-ching-tang had no right.

"A merry courting-time?" said Sin-wan at last; "but it is not so with me, Ni-ching-tang."

"Well, after all, pleasure is pleasant to feel," answered Ni-ching-tang, still harping on the same string;

"and they will not know in the prison, Sin-wan,—for who will tell them?"

"Pleasure is pleasant to feel, yes," said Sin-wan; "but it is not pleasure which I am feeling now, Ni-ching-tang."

"And why not, Sin-wan?"

"Because Ah-lin, of whom I told you, is away from her home; and my mind is telling me that she is making some one else feel pleasant instead of me."

"Ho! that is bad. And who is that some one, Sin-wan?"

"He is called Foo-chee."

"Soh! And you are now looking for Ah-lin?—I see."

"I am looking for Foo-chee."

"And for why?"

"To kill him."

"Soh! to kill Foo-chee. Well, that is the only way. But has Foo-chee no brother, no father, who will kill you back again?"

"I do not know."

"With keen tortures?"

"Poh! I do not think of that."

"With dreadful agonies of the brain and the liver, Sin-wan?"

"No! I do not think of that. He is a brotherless dog, a seller of incense-sticks."

"Well—well, do your will, Sin-wan. It is the only way. As for me, I am not feeling happy, too. I have a son, who has an enemy. 1 am going to look for my son now, that I may hear from him whether it will be necessary for me to kill his enemy or no."

"Well, then, may you do well, Ni-ching-tang."

"And you, may you do well, Sin-wan!"

And so they parted. But they neither of them found Ah-lin or Foo-chee that night; for they did not think of looking into the eating-house of Hing-Chang-Li, where they two again were that night.

So Sin-wan and Ni-ching-tang hurried back, both of them, to the Imperial precincts, making an inward vow that, on the next night, they would procure more time, and do better.

CHAPTER XVIII

SIN-WAN

THE next evening, at about six, John Hardy lay on his back on the bed of his prison.

He was conscious that it was near the hour when Sin-wan appeared.

His feet were so gashed and raw from his run over the glass, that he had not stood since he had been thrown upon the bed. For two days he had eaten nothing, being sick, sick. He was not far from death now.

How long, O Lord? How long? This was the burden of his feeble thought.

But he retained an intense interest in the nature of the added pangs which *this* day had in store for him.

When the key turned, he sprang upright, though, at the effort, the wounds in his feet broke into fresh bleeding.

Sin-wan entered, and at his entrance this time John Hardy's flesh writhed like the flesh of a twisting serpent from his feet to the roots of his hair.

Fire was the instrument of torture at which he felt the deepest horror. And Sin-wan had now with him a brazier, which swung from his fingers by a handle.

In the brazier glowed and flushed the living coals of flame.

He had in his hand no other instrument that John could see. But John, by this time, had begun to learn that when the instruments were at first invisible, then, in general, the agony was the most relentless.

And now, at the sight of the flame, feeling himself

too hopelessly feeble to pass through any further hell that day, Hardy, by an impulse, did what he had never done before. He fell upon his knees, and stretched out his clasped hands in an attitude of meek supplication to the Chinaman.

Sin-wan was a man; he had the limbs and bodily structure of the human being. Who could say if within him, too, some trace of the divine origin of man might not linger, some throe of love, some sob of pity? In John's eyes, as he knelt, cried a world of mute pleading.

But the Chinaman showed no sign of having seen him. He deposited the brazier in a farther corner, took some small metal objects from a fold of his robe, dropped them on the floor, and approached the kneeling form. He proceeded to bind him as before, arms and feet, to the chair. But this time, first of all, he took off John's shirt from the upper part of his body, leaving it to hang downward from the navel.

This done, he went towards the fire, took up two of the six small metal objects which he had dropped, and put them on the fire to heat.

The six objects consisted of four tiny Latin capital-letters in iron; they were the letters A, S, Y, H—the initials of Ada Seward and Yen How; there were also a roll of iron wire and a pair of pincers.

It was the intention of Yen How to print the four letters all over the body of John Hardy—on his breast, on his two arms, on his thighs, on his back; two at a time; two each day.

And the letters of the first day, as Yen How had ordained in compliment to his queen, were to be A and S.

But, as usual, Yen How had no idea of inflicting the mere brutal pang of a burn upon his victim; some mental refinement of pain must mix with the scream of the physical nerves.

Sin-wan took one of the two iron letters from the fire with the pincers, and holding it from him, approached Hardy. The iron emitted a red glow, and seemed to burn into the staring eyesight of the victim.

Sin-Wan

When his bare chest could feel the radiated heat, his torturer stood, holding the metal steadily still. And so, for a few minutes, remained ; then returned and replaced the iron in the fire, without having touched John with it.

And now he climbed and stood upon the table, the roll of wire in his hand. The three lanterns hung from the ceiling by hooks near to open spaces in the boarding of the ceiling, through which the candles were placed in the lanterns. Over one of these hooks Sin-wan threw a length of wire ; and over another another length of wire. The hooks were near to each other.

With one end of each of the two pieces of wire he made a half-loop ; and at once he hurried to the fire, snatched up the red-hot letter A with the pincers, and hung it upon one of the loops ; then the S, and hung it upon the other. Their weight was sufficient to make the wires run through their supporting hooks ; and they fell upon the marble floor.

Sin-wan now gathered the other two ends of wire and secured them to a point in the wall, having drawn the two letters some inches from the ground. In his hand he held a piece of bamboo, and with this, standing in a line with the wires, he struck first one of the letters, then the other, gently forward.

The two letters began to swing to and fro through the chamber, with uneven motions, one this way, one that. And right in the line of their movement sat John Hardy.

It depended entirely upon the force of the propulsions which Sin-wan imparted to the letters with the bamboo, whether or no they touched the naked chest of the bound victim.

Sometimes they touched, and left behind them, as they swung back, a whiff of smoke. Sometimes they touched twice in succession, one, or both. Sometimes they were only expected—with a shrinking horror, and whistling breath,—and did not touch at all.

It was a monstrous torture—the worst he had yet

suffered—this coquetry of pain—these fleeting, incalculable kisses of the hot and dancing letters. For every kiss—a whiff of smoke.

Let us draw a veil over his agonies. His mouth was wide, bawling—his eyes straining from their sockets; and at the tension of every fiber of his soul and body, his hair whitened—his skin grew sere—he lived through many a year—he became an old man.

It was some twenty minutes before the see-saw of the swinging wires ceased. Sin-wan hurriedly left his post, ran toward John, and bound his eyes with a cloth. What happened within the next five minutes John did not know. He strained his ear to detect a sound, though he kept on mechanically bawling in a lower key. But he heard nothing. In reality, Sin-wan was reheating the metals to redness; and his noiselessness had for its motive the fact that he wished to take the victim by surprise.

When the two bits of metal were of a bright glowing red, he passed one limb of the pincers inside the top of the A, and the other limb inside the upper curve of the S, and, holding them so together, at once trotted eagerly and silently upon John.

A beastly scream broke forth, wondrously like the cry of a cat in the extreme of physical anguish. Sin-wan had suddenly clapped the hot pieces upon Hardy's right breast, and held them there. The metal sank, as into a bed of soft luxury, into the wasting flesh, fizzling forth a steaming smoke and reeking stench. . . .

· · · · · ·

At the exact moment when his spirit fainted, and he lost the sense of pain, Foo-chee and Ah-lin met in one long embrace.

Toward this they had been drawn and swept for days, and now, as the poets say, the two trembling dewdrops had trembled into one.

It was outside the walls of Pekin, and all the members of Foo-chee's and Ah-lin's company had swarmed back into the town; for the drilling of the drilled was over. And only these two were left.

And Foo-chee said:
"Ah-lin."
And Ah-lin said:
"Foo-chee."
And Foo-chee said:
"I am feeling happy, Ah-lin; for we are here where none can see us, and the moon which is rising there is pleasant to see, though her face is round."
And Ah-lin said:
"Her face is broad in a laugh of joy, Foo-chee! And do you like a woman with a broad face, Foo-chee, or with a long?"
"I like a woman with a long face, Ah-lin," said Foo-chee, "like yours, Ah-lin."
And Ah-lin replied:
"I am not feeling at all unhappy, Foo-chee."
And it was then that the two dewdrops trembled into one in a long embrace.
A really long one: for it began a minute before the closing of the gates of Pekin, and it lasted a minute after it. And had they had any idea of the real state of affairs, they would have felt like two very shattered and dislocated dewdrops indeed.

It was Ah-lin who woke first from her trance, and she woke from it with a start that made her pigtail wriggle, and she whispered an awful pallid word into the ear of Foo-chee, and together they started towards the gates.

They were shut out, they were hopelessly late. Pekin refused them. They must spend the long night without.

Ah-lin had an instinct that this meant death for her beloved, perhaps for herself also.

They stood hand-in-hand and the upper corners of their slanting eyes went very high indeed.

Still, a whole night hand-in-hand with the beloved is not nothing. They walked away with a happiness troubled, but not destroyed.

An hour later Sin-wan and Ni-ching-tang were ransacking a certain area of Pekin, one for his son, the other for Ah-lin and her lover, but separately, unsuspected by each other. As for Sin-wan, his knife was bright and white.

"Oh, where is Foo-chee?" said Ni-ching-tang to himself. "Is my son dead?"

The suspicion grew upon him, it became a certainty. He hurried back to the Imperial City, and made inquiries for Sin-wan at the prison. Sin-wan, he was told, had obtained a scroll to pass in and out of the sacred precincts at any hour of that night.

Soh! Sin-wan was abroad then; and if Sin-wan was abroad, then it must be that Foo-chee was dead.

Ni-ching-tang went from the prison straight to the palace of Yen How, and he descended into the vaults wherein was his sleeping-room, and he held the reeking flame of a saucer-lamp of earthenware over a box, and into the depths of the box he dived. He brought up two blue phials and a broken joss-stick; one of the phials contained a poison, and the other a non-poisonous drug; and this last he put into his bosom.

Then he re-clasped the box; and at once he fell upon his knees, bowing his body and folded hands up and down, touching the cold plaster with his forehead. And from his lips came groans of prayer. And he burnt incense to the gods.

Then he went up again, and out from the Imperial precincts. He, too, was provided that night with a scroll of permit.

Onwards he went, walking very fast. And as he treaded the intricacies of Pekin, he was engaged in a strange continuous effort of mind: the effort to recall all the English words he had ever known.

Once, long ago, he had served in the kitchen of an English family in Canton, and had then been quite a master of pigeon English. But now he found his vocabulary wondrously small. On he went, cudgeling his brains, through the dark and swarming vastness of the city.

Ni-ching-tang was a great man, if patience alone can make a man great, for he searched all that night for Sin-wan, and did not find him. So was Sin-wan a great man, if patience can make a man great, for he

Sin-Wan

searched all that night for Foo-chee, and did not find him.

But towards the break of day, as he sat drinking *samshu* in a den, Sin-wan had an idea. He was a drunkard, and could be inspired by drink; nor was he now sober. His idea was that Ah-lin and Foo-chee were not in the city at all, but without it.

He went back once more to the dwelling of Ah-lin to inquire if she had not yet come home. And then, hearing that she had not, he said:

"Fearing me, they have fled from the city together, and are now at Tung-chow. To Tung-chow, therefore, I will go. For the edge of my knife has the itch this night, till Foo-chee scratch it for me."

But it happened that while Sin-wan was crying aloud from the street to inquire for Ah-lin, Ni-ching-tang had come to inquire also whether one Ah-lin was there. And as the day was prone to break, Ni-ching-tang, far behind Sin-wan, was cautiously shadowing him towards the city-gate which leads out upon the Tung-chow road.

Sin-wan waited there twenty minutes, and when the gates opened, he passed swiftly through under the bellies of the crowding camels, the gall of malice and yellow jealousy rankling bitterly in his jaundiced soul.

To kill—to hew, and slice, and stab—a ravening hunger for this red breakfast was upon Sin-wan. He had had a comfortless night, a night of dark thought and impulse, and the hot *samshu* was talking hot things to his head.

And surely the gods were on his side—anxious for nothing that morning were they but how to provide a red breakfast for Sin-wan! See how they draw up the curtains of night for him; and now the day has that very-early-morning grayness for which one can find no adjective to express its utter yawniness; and now, *just as it is light enough*, something makes Sin-wan turn his head to the left—and he sees.

But poor Ni-ching-tang is struggling frantically among the mules and camels, which press inwards and outwards through the just-opened gateway; and he has got jammed there, and the man is nearly mad in his agonized struggle to be free ; for Sin-wan has passed through, and he has lost him.

Foo-chee, interlaced with Ah-lin, was fast asleep, as was also Ah-lin, they half-propped against the outer surface of the wall, between two buttresses, not very far from the gates.

Sin-wan walked up to them, smiling, lest one or the other should be awake, and see him ; and the knife-handle was in his palm, and the blade up his wide sleeves. And when he was right over them, and saw how they breathed heavily, and how the confidence of old love was in their careless embrace, he drove the knife first into Ah-lin with a loud breath, and she sighed, and died. And then, with loud breaths, he drove it several times into Foo-chee, and he sighed, and died. And then into Ah-lin again, and then into Foo-chee again, he drove his knife.

"Dog's gall," he said, as he turned away, and found himself face to face with Ni-ching-tang.

"What, Sin-wan, is that you ?" said Ni-ching-tang; "oh, *I* can see what you have been after. Ho ! ho !"

"Those are they I told you of," said Sin-wan. "I have done what I said I would do, Ni-ching-tang."

"So I see, Sin-wan ! Well, it is the only way—the only way."

"As for you, you will tell no one, Ni-ching-tang ?"

"Poh ! not I. For why should I ? I who have known you these months, and the two dead not at all. Phew ! see how they lie—still embraced. Are you sure they are well dead, Sin-wan ?"

"Oh, well dead."

"They should be. The man—he has one, two, three, four, five stabs—yes, five—ugly wounds, too. The knife went deep each time. What was his name ? —Foo-chee ? Ah, well, no more Foo-chee now—no more Foo-Chee."

"Let us be going, Ni-ching-tang. For watching dead dogs is not pleasant to the corners of the eyeballs."

"But *I* feel pleasure while looking upon them, Sin-wan ; and the middle of the eye is not offended by the sight of them embracing together—young things, too. But *you* leer obliquely upon them, Sin-wan, having slain them, through the corners of your eye-balls, and so receive disagreeable feelings from their sight."

"Still, let us be going—let us be moving away, Ni-ching-tang."

"Well, as you wish it, Sin-wan, let us be moving. But they lie very well together, Foo-chee and Ah-lin —Foo-chee, with his five gashed wounds, and her arm behind his neck. A young man, too, he seems to me —a seller of incense-sticks, I think you said. No more incense-sticks now for Foo-chee—and no more Foo-chee now at all, Sin-wan. Well, well—well, well. It was Foo-chee and Ah-lin ; and now it is no Ah-lin any more, and no Foo-chee at all. Five stabs, too, and ugly wounds all. One would have done the work, but he got *five*, well home. Oh, they are well dead, Sin-wan!—have no fear. But Foo-chee has no father, I hope, no brother, to avenge his death, Sin-wan?"

"I care not."

"With horrid tortures, Sin-wan?"

"Poh! he was a brotherless dog."

"Well if that is so . . . But your walk is staggery, and your eye wanders. We will have a morning drink together in a drink-place which I know, and then to the day's work. . . ."

They re-entered the gates. A reaction had come now upon Sin-wan; his nerves were unstrung from their high tension, and the *samshu* swam stalely in his turgid brain. He followed Ni-ching-tang as a lamb to the slaughter.

Ni-ching-tang led him down to a foul, dark cellar, where drink was placed before them. And into one of the two calabash-cups Ni-chin-tang poured a liquid from a blue phial.

Sin-wan had thrown himself sullenly upon a plank-projection near the black-earthen floor, and Ni-ching-tang handed him the draught.

CHAPTER XIX

"THE HUNDRED AND EIGHTY"

THE draught was non-poisonous; but Sin-wan had hardly drunk half the contents of the cup when he fell back, fast asleep.

And now, when no eye but God's could see him, the malice of a fiend worked and twisted in the face of Ni-ching-tang. He took Sin-wan's knife, and he ran the edge of the blade gently, almost playfully, along Sin-wan's throat, and over his face, and round the roots of his pigtail, reveling in his sense of power, wallowing in that sweet lust of cruelty which brings to the Chinaman the same keen delight which bodily forms of enjoyment bring to the Western.

He ran the knife-edge along Sin-wan's skin; but he had not the least intention of hurting him. The pleasure of self-restraint with which he kept his itching fingers from violence was exquisite.

The Chinese theory of vengeance is not, like the Hebrew, "an eye for an eye, and a tooth for a tooth;" it is, "two eyes for an eye, and thirty-two teeth for a tooth."

Ni-ching-tang could easily have killed Sin-wan, as he slept there; but, had he done so, he would have despised himself as a weak and bungling boor.

For vengeance to be complete and satisfying, the victim must know *who* it is that is taking vengeance upon him, and *why* he is doing it; and the avenger must know that the victim knows. Under these conditions, the longer the period which the vengeance occupies in its accomplishment, the sweeter the cud of satisfaction which the avenger chews.

Ni-ching-tang intended that, for the murder of his son, Sin-wan should suffer weeks of torture before death. And although it was beyond his power to inflict those tortures with his own hand (as he would have wished), yet he knew that it was easy for him to cause them to be inflicted by hands stronger than his own.

He did not lose much time in the self-indulgence of running the knife-edge over Sin-wan's throat. Presently he put down the knife, and he dived his hand into Sin-wan's bosom. From thence he took out Sin-wan's permit to pass in and out of the Imperial gates, and also an Imperial Mandate ordering the Keeper of the Prison Keys to deliver a certain key to the presenter of the Mandate.

With these two rolls in his own bosom, Ni-ching-tang ascended the narrow earthen steps, and at the entrance above met the keeper of the drink-place yawning his eyes into invisibility against the door. Ni-ching-tang told him that a man, holding position in the Imperial precincts, was asleep below, and did not wish to be roused.

"Let him sleep: he will wake himself," said Ni-ching-tang.

Then he sallied forth. He twisted at a steady trot among a number of alleys, and stopped at a gaudy bamboo-umbrella booth where an early-morning merchant was lounging desolately. Ni-ching-tang spoke some hurried words in the merchant's ear, and the merchant nodded, listening, then disappeared down a court, and in three minutes returned, leading a mule by a rope.

Ni-ching-tang scrambled on to the back of the mule, tossed his hand in token of thanks, drove his heels into the outstanding ribs, and went galloping away.

He traversed in this way two lengths of intervening street, and, still galloping, passed through the city gate which he had lately entered with Sin-wan. He turned the mule's head eastward toward Tung-chow.

Tung-chow, as we have said, is a village about four, or possibly five, miles from Pekin. It is, as it were, the "port" of Pekin, for it stands on the Peiho, Pekin itself not being a river-city.

At Tung-chow, Ni-chin-tang had a nephew. And this nephew was the owner of three river-boats, two of them fitted with junk-sails, the third a mule boat, all three traders down the Peiho with Tientsin in millet, rice, and barley. In twenty minutes Ni-ching-tang, at the river-side, was talking to his nephew from the mule's back. And Ni-ching-tang said :

"Which of the three boats are here, Li-kien ?"

And Li-kien replied :

"The mule-boat is here, and also the *Taku*, which lies there where you see."

"The *Taku* has a junk-sail, Li-kien ?"

"Yes."

"Then I will buy the *Taku* from you."

"I cannot sell the *Taku*, Ni-ching-tang."

"It is a lie, Li-kien ; for you can, and you will. At the waning of the next moon I will pay you for her three hundred taels, which is a good reward, in silver pieces. For your cousin, Foo-chee, is dead—and there will be no more Foo-chee any more now at all, Li-kien ; for he has been murdered by five stabs, and ugly wounds all. And it is necessary, in order that his slayer should die with horrid tortures, that you sell me your boat, the *Taku*, without much talking. And now you see that you told a lie in saying that you could not, Li-kien."

"It was a lie," admitted Li-kien.

"And the part which *you* shall take in avenging your kinsman," went on Ni-ching-tang, "shall be this, Li-kien. You will put on board the *Taku* rice, and spirit, and water, and fuel, and a rudder-oar, and everything which a man may want for a voyage down the Peiho, and a voyage over the sea, during a week, or more. This you will do. And this also : you will wait here near the *Taku*, all the forenoon if it is to be so, till you see a young man come riding on a mule ; he will be wrapped up from head to foot in a great mantle, so that not much of his face, and nothing of his head, shall be seen. His face shall be yellow like a Chinaman's, but give a keen look into his eyes, and you will see that he is no Chinaman, but an English dog. You will put him on board the *Taku*, Li-kien, and you will hoist the sail for him, for he is without strength, and you will send him on his way alone. And, as you send him on his way, burn an incense, that he may go to his journey's end in safety; for, if he be recaptured, Sin-wan, who slew your cousin, will be tortured, but not killed; but, if he escape wholly, then Sin-wan will be killed after he has been horribly tortured."

Li-kien pondered, and then objected:

"But one man in the *Taku*, he must needs be cast away, unless he be——"

"He *is* a sailor, Li-kien, and do not fear. And be sure you place in the *Taku* a drawing of China, and instruments such as are used by seafaring men as the sign-posts of the ocean. For he can doubtless read such things; and it is necessary for him to arrive at Kiao-Chau, where he will meet with his countrymen, and be slain with them when they are slain: but none will know that it is *he*; and Sin-wan will die. The mule you will keep till I send for it."

Immediately the old Chinaman turned the mule's head, and galloped back to Pekin.

All his movements now were characterized by an intense haste, and yet by a certain calm which did not forsake him. He had much to do, and yet he did not stop to think of anything; he did not forget anything; everything seemed prearranged.

Within the prison he was unknown, and he had the Imperial stamp, which opens every door, in the form of Sin-wan's papers.

When he presented himself before John Hardy he had in his hands pigments, costume, and everything ready for the necessary disguise.

At a new face Hardy started—for we see the finger of God where it is not, and where it is we see it not. John anticipated now some new torture, to be carried out by a still more subtle agent than Sin-wan.

As for Ni-ching-tang, he spoke not a word, simply doing his will swiftly on the impotent captive. He painted his face, he dressed him. And all the time he was cudgeling his brains to remember all the English words he needed to tell Hardy what he was to do.

He found, however, that there was one fact of the situation which all but balked his plans. Hardy was weaker than Ni-ching-tang had counted upon. If Hardy's mind was in as feeble a state as his body, it seemed certain that Sin-wan would not die.

He took the dazed captive under the arms, supporting him, and half-dragged him forth. And while John Hardy was still wondering to what new experience of pain he was being hurried, he was in the open air. And still Ni-ching-tang spoke no word.

With Ni-ching-tang's own permit, and with Sin-wan's, the two passed beyond the Imperial precincts, Ni-ching-tang lifting after him the lagging steps of Hardy. What was happening to him John could not dream; but yonder, beyond doubt, was the sky, and there the sailing clouds, and under them a breeze of heaven which went wandering gladly towards the sea.

It was not possible that he was free? He did not believe it. In his profound distrust of heaven and of earth, he denied it. He was mad again—it was a new torture—the most devilish of all.

But when he found himself beyond the gates—and there around him spread the wide plain—and there, tethered to a tree drowsed the waiting mule—and there above him was the vast vault, and the free and wandering airs—what could he think? A strange, low, whimpering sound—as feeble as can be imagined —as thin as the plaintive whine of a very old and senile man—came from his lips, and two forbidden tears rolled down his cheeks.

He was wrapped in a long robe of soiled silk, which covered the hat of straw on his head and descended to his feet, hiding his rags beneath; and on his feet Ni-ching-tang had put felt slippers. Thus attired he was pushed and maneuvered by the Chinaman to the back of the mule. The rope was put into his hand; and it was then that, for the first time, Ni-ching-tang spoke a word.

Ni-ching-tang had need of his whole English vocabulary to express now all he had to say. For quite half an hour he went on talking, and it was evident that the scheme which he was putting into execution must have been long meditated; for his instructions to Hardy how to secure his safe arrival at Kiao-Chau were as minute as possible. In his uncouth and tentative English he gave some idea of the formation of the harbor; and he also spoke of the position in which the stranded *Iphigenia* lay, pointing out to Hardy that the cruiser would serve as the chief landmark to warn him of his destination. He gave John his own name and that of his nephew. Finally, he handed John a sharp knife with which to commit suicide in case of recapture; and he ended by saying:

"Am got you anything to question me?"

Yes: John had something to ask. He said:

"Yes—one question."

And he waited a minute before he asked it.

"I owe nothing to Yen How, do I, for my present freedom?"

He repeated the question thrice, and no sooner had Ni-ching-tang gathered its meaning, than instantly his head went shaking in a series of vigorous "No's."

"No, no, no," he went; "you no gote believe that, mind! You getee catch—getee catch! Yen How catchee you—sharp—killee you!"

Good; all this, then, was not due to any clemency of Yen How's. Even *then*—at that moment of feebleness, when he was still hardly beyond his prison-walls—John Hardy shrank from hearing that there existed anything good, or human, or redeeming in the Chinese character. He was desperately and clandestinely unwilling to hear it. Some dim and far-off instinct *even then* told him that it would be necessary for him to go on believing this bad race to be *wholly* bad, *wholly* of hell; and that it was in order that he might so believe it, that the Chinese Iron had been ordained to enter into his soul.

But, with a certain reluctance, he ventured upon yet another question. He said :

"And you, sir—what is your motive for setting me free?—Mercy? You want poor Englishman goee free?—Or you havee some other reason?"

Ni-ching-tang smiled at this simplicity of the little foreign devil, when the meaning of the question entered his head. He said :

"Poh! you no troublee head for that. Me havee other reasons. But that nothing for you."

Good again! he owed nothing to them.

Ni-ching-tang pointed along a road, and the mule moved. The Chinaman, whose presence in the Imperial precincts was nearly due, stood a while and looked after the drooping figure on the mule's back. Then he re-entered the city to arrange for the burial of his son.

John occupied two hours in accomplishing the four miles to Tung-chow, and, during this time, thrice fainted from sheer powerlessness.

But on the banks of the Peiho, Li-kien was duly waiting, and the *Taku* was in perfect readiness to receive her strange white master. By the time the alarm had spread through the Imperial precincts that, by the carelessness of his jailer, the white prisoner had escaped, Hardy was in the middle of the Peiho, already some miles below Tung-chow.

In a wondrously short time, as the boat glided down the river, he began to lift his head, to observe, to reason, to purpose. How large was the world to him! His wan eye turned whitely upward, and dwelt upon the sky; one great sob thronged in his bosom for exit from his choking throat; his face worked.

The boat was a bluff craft with an erection aft, making her there a kind of house-boat, and with stones laid round a slab of iron, for cooking, for'ard. The junk sail could quite easily be hoisted and adjusted by a single man, and gave to the boat, with a fair wind and stream, a speed of some seven knots. In a land where carts are driven over land by means of wind and sail, as in China, the navigation of the seas and rivers

is in a condition far from elementary. John found
his craft pliant and ready, and the bulge of the up-
ward-tapering lug-sail was fine to his eyes. An exhilaration of mood, ecstatic, high, grew upon him.
The day was broad and clear, and busy with breezes.
On either hand spread endless flat-lands, already sprout-
ing with the tender green of barley, rice and millet.
The river was all but deserted.

There was an aspect, not of earth, but of Paradise,
in the bright and balmy world. Henceforth—and he
knew it—he would have little to do with joy, and soft
emotion, and the throe of genial feeling; for the gentle
heart within him was turned to stone, or something
resembling stone. But for the present he was too
weak in body and mind to resist the charm of the wide
and placid landscape, and the feeling of freedom which
it brought. His heart was still not quite a dead
thing.

Yet, let us record two facts. First, that John Hardy,
from boyhood, had been of an intensely religious
nature; that he had had a somewhat crabbed habit of
reading methodically one chapter each morning from
the Bible; and that his affectionate soul had overflowed
in affection for his Maker also. And secondly, let us
state, that on this morning of his deliverance he
several times resisted and repelled the impulse which
rose in him to give thanks to God. He refused. So
much had Yen How changed him. The boy had
hardened into something more (or something less) than
a man.

Midway between Tung-chow and Tientsin, he left
the rudder-oar and searched the boat. Li-kien, apparently, had forgotten nothing; there was food and
drink in plenty, a pot, a compass of Western make,
and a curious instrument, which he assumed to be a
contrivance for taking the sun's altitude, but which
he could not at once understand.

He made a fire, for which the materials were at hand,
put on some rice to boil, and resumed his place at the
oar.

Now and again a painted junk passed him, toiling up

the river; but he was not even at the pains to hide himself, as Ni-ching-tang had warned him, so sure was he of safety.

At sundown he glided between the central space, then open, of the bridge of boats across the Peiho at Tientsin. At eleven o'clock, under a calm and radiant night, he had Taku on his starboard beam; and soon he was in the open sea of the Gulf of Pechili.

Feeling drowsy, about fifteen miles from land, he shipped his oar, lowered his sail, and went to sleep.

The point of his destination was Kiao-Chau, once German, then very much English.

Here, seven weeks before, one dark midnight, a hundred and eighty English sailors had beached the battered second-class cruiser *Iphigenia*, and landed.

The subsequent adventures of these men, when properly written, would fill volumes. At present we can merely glance at them.

At the moment of landing, the Englishmen were no longer wholly in the dark as to the real state of things in China. The absence of white men both at Chemulpo and Seoul, of which they knew, if not very suggestive in itself, was *very* suggestive when no explanation could be found of the flagless ships, which had chased them, except the one that these ships were Japanese.

The possibility, therefore, that they would be massacred on Chinese territory occurred to them; and their object in coming to Kiao-Chau, which was not very remote from the sinking ship, was to throw themselves upon the protection of the Germans, who, as they supposed, occupied the forts of Kiao-Chau.

Previous to this, the Germans had very strongly fortified the harbor and its approaches. Its waters were thick with submarine mines, and two strong forts at each of the claws of land which formed the entrance, together with one on the low-lying island in the basin of the harbor, made the position one of considerable strength.

The harbor is about six miles long, and lies N. by W., and S. by E. Around it, in general, is high

"The Hundred and Eighty"

ground, save at the northeastern entrance, where an area of sloping meadowland rises gradually to the higher levels of the inner *entourage* of the basin. And it was here that the *Iphigenia*, then on the point of sinking, was beached.

Fifty yards away, on the brow of a slope, stood the N. E. fort. Though the night was dark, and rain fell heavily, its outlines could be made out.

The blue-jackets held a sort of informal synod on the sands. There was among them only one staff-officer, a lieutenant called Edwards, who, however, was wounded in the breast, and in a kind of daze. Happily, all the special hands were in evidence except the surgeon, these including the chief engineer, engineer, and assistant engineer, the gunner, the boatswain, the carpenter, with the stokers, and all engine-room hands. Beside these there were a hundred and fifty blue-jackets.

It was decided to make straight for the N. E. fort, and though no one present could talk German, a volunteer committee of ten men, headed by the chief engineer, a Mr. Murray, set off toward the rising ground.

But these were careless watchmen, these Germans! Where was the sentry, and the challenge, and the soldier's stalk, and the rattle of the butt-end? No-where was there a light to be seen through all the dripping and desolate night.

The ten men reached the fort to find it as solitary as a desert. They called, and the hills echoed their voice, and through the open portal the night-bird fled and screamed. They passed within the gateway between the two outer bastions, and into the courtyard, and thence onward through every open door. They saw one dead Chinaman sitting in the embrasure of a window, grinning in old decay. But otherwise there was no sign of any struggle. At all events, there were no Germans there. Only the guns remained, and some ammunition, and some stores, but not a single small-arm.

What to do now? It only remained to visit the

S. W. fort, and the fort on the island. And these they found in the same condition.

The Chinese had gained possession of them by killing the unsuspecting sentries in the middle of the night and seizing, almost bloodlessly, the rest of the garrison, so to speak, as they slept in their beds. The captive soldiers were distributed over China for the celebration of Yen How's Sabbath of blood; and the forts had then, for the time being, been deserted.

There remained no further doubt in the minds of the British blue-jackets as to their own fate. But they were resoved to sell their lives dearly.

The *Iphigenia* had still a steam-pinnace uninjured, and in this they took turns in plying backward and forward between the ship and the island all the night, landing everything in the way of stores, small arms, and ammunition which might prove useful.

The gunner, Shillitoe, counseled the occupation of all the three forts; but Murray and the rest, fearing the result of a division of the little army, gave their voice for a concentration of forces upon the island-fort, on account not only of its disconnection with the mainland, but also of the fact that it appeared to be the most powerful.

This plan was somewhat unfortunate, because the island was uncultivated and furnished no other food than a scanty supply of wild orris and cassava roots, though there were three springs of rather brackish water. Moreover, at about sunrise, the movements of the pinnace were observed by some peasants on the mainland, and shortly afterward there was a considerable commotion to the east and north of the bay. Though the work of the pinnace was not half completed, it was seen that no further voyage must be attempted, nor had any effort as yet been made to spike the guns of the other two forts. At about seven, these two opened fire simultaneously upon the island fort.

At this period China was awake, or at least had opened her early-morning eyelids; she had tasted blood, and every Chinaman was feeling the thrill of

"The Hundred and Eighty"

that electrical cobweb spreading over the land, of which the brain of Yen How was the center. The artillery combat which now commenced between the island-fort and the others was fought not more obstinately on one side than on the other.

But the fixed batteries of the outer posts had not been constructed for inward attack, while the inner had been constructed for outward attack. By noon, the two outer fortresses were in ruins. But the poor *Iphigenia* also, by which the castaways set much store, had been broken by the wanton Chinese almost into nothingness.

And now commenced a series of strenuous and adventurous days and nights for these one hundred and eighty men—or rather one hundred and seventy-nine, for on the next day Edwards died. They had hardly any food; it was necessary to get it, and to get it in the teeth of the armed Chinese, directed by Japanese. And they got it.

Each night had its own tale of brilliant sortie, or crafty ruse, or ticklish enterprise, or cautiously-premeditated plan. One by one their numbers lessened—they became a hundred and seventy—a hundred and sixty. But those who remained went on furnishing materials for a new *Odyssey;* in two weeks they were the most exquisitely-trained body of men in the world; every day added to them a new supremacy of discipline and culture; eye, and hand, and brain were in it; they could twist through the grass like snakes; could climb like Alpini; could see in the dark; could shoot like machines; could plan in deliberative council like statesmen. In seven weeks they were a living monument of the adaptability to every possible condition of life of the nimble English race.

But their *Odyssey* lacked Odysseus. It was *Hamlet* without the hero.

To do anything of much greater importance than the procuring of their food, they needed a Leader; and a very decent Leader indeed was on the way to join them.

CHAPTER XX

"WHAT A FACE!"

DURING the afternoon of the seventh day from Tungchow, John Hardy, hugging the coast, arrived in the locality of Kiao-Chau harbor. The solitary helmsman had made a good voyage, being familiar with the ocean-winds and their moods, and having an old comradeship with the brine and spray. However, he had several times got wet, and every few minutes now was shaken by a moist cough, alternated by vomitings due to a constant sickness of the stomach.

He was being wafted along by a gentle breeze, when he spied a portion of a ship's bow above the thin, inaudible fringe of foam which lined the coast afar. And at once, noting his course, he put out farther to sea, and lay to, ten miles from land.

He guessed from the fragmentary look of the wreck that the Chinese had been busy with the English sailors of whom he had been told. At eleven o'clock, he ran in for the harbor. Unfortunately, all he knew about it was its locality. Ni-ching-tang, indeed, had told him that the Englishmen were upon an *island*; but when he entered the basin he saw no island, for in the darkness and distance the contours of the island, which, on the east, is near to the mainland, seemed part of it.

The moon was young, just rising; it was a night of stars; things near were visible, things remote lay in a mystery of shadow.

Hardy ran his bow upon a gravelly bottom near the east entrance, intending to mount the rising ground and search for the island. For what he knew, he might be already on it.

In this way he came to the east fort, now mostly in ruins. He passed through a broken arch, and saw guns lying at random in the court. He examined the battlemented square, and entered what remained of the heavily-armed works. But there was nowhere a human being.

His search was conducted with extreme caution. With the same care he descended to his boat, and made for the opposite side, where he saw a stonework outline against the sky. Here the ascent was steeper; he scrambled up a pebbly footpath, scraped through some scrub, and entered the fortification. There was less marked destruction on this side. He examined bollwerkswehre and glacis, aussenwerk and donjon, and saw no one. Then he entered an inner court, where was a low building with small barred windows: barracks and mess-room. And in three of the windows near the ground he saw a light.

On his hands and knees he crept toward one of the openings. As he drew near he could hear a sound of laughter, and some one protesting in harsh gibberish. He knew now that he was among Chinese. But he continued to advance, eager to acquire some sort of knowledge of the facts of his situation. He reached the window, lifted his head and peeped in.

The room which he saw was long and surrounded by beds at regular intervals. On most of these lay Chinamen asleep; three only were intently playing some sort of dice-game at a table on which was a lantern.

As Hardy looked—before he could run—before he could cover his mouth—he was seized by a sudden cough which sounded through the still night and the quiet room.

The three Chinamen sprang up at once, looked in amazement in the direction of the sound, then snatching three rifles, and making a great noise, they rushed toward the door.

Hardy, too, was off, running; but before he could cross the breadth of the yard the three were out of the door.

At the moment, he was in the shadow of the buttress of a barbacan, and he knew that if he left it to cross the strip of moonlight which lay along the exit from the yard, he must be seen. He stood still, therefore, crouching in the deepest shade.

The three, in a state of great excitement, ran toward the spot which he had left, and finding nothing, scattered about the yard in flurried search within the deep embrasures of arches, and the black shade of turret and buttress. Their eager examination was disorganized, the second again scrutinizing a spot which the first had just searched, and the third, perhaps, following suit.

It was all over in the space of certainly not more than a minute. One of the Chinamen rushed to the corner in which Hardy crouched, his hands groping; in a few seconds he was followed by the second; in a few seconds more by the third. And they dropped like a line of little wooden soldiers, upon which one blows obliquely, one after the other, stiffly, at full length. The knife of Ni-ching-tang was no sooner out of the first than it was in the second, and instantly in the third. Before the startled sleepers within had rubbed their eyes, sprung to their feet, and snatched their weapons, he had diminished the population of China by three. It was the first-fruits of his vengeance.

Now, meantime, was his chance to run, and he ran. Thirty Chinese soldiers, however, were after him, and one saw him as he slipped through the exit from the inner to the outer courtyard. This man raised the hue and cry, and it became a question of running, first towards the outer exit, and secondly through the scrub, and down the steep hillside, guns popping all the while, and the Chinamen screaming in an ecstasy of excitement.

Behind the rising ground, on the general level of the mainland, there was camped a half-regiment of the old regular army of China under a Japanese lieutenant; and these, hearing the firing, quickly set off at the double up the gentle incline at the back of the fort.

Hardy was saved from the shots of the thirty on the top of the plateau by doubling and bending among the scrub, but by the time he had plunged and scrambled to the bottom of the steep path, bullets were whistling round him. The night, however, was dim, and the riflemen, as they ran, shot at random.

There lay his boat, her prow just touching and swaying in the gravel. If he could push her off, and gain the shelter of the house-deck, he would be safe. Two of the Chinamen, however, who had not slackened their speed in order to shoot, were upon him ; and when he leapt to his bow, and put out the oar to shove off, one of them, and immediately the other, took hold of it. A short struggle ensued. One of the Chinamen, struck by a flying bullet in the nape, relaxed his hold and dropped ; at the same time Hardy's power of grasp failed, and the oar slipped from him ; but so suddenly that the pulling Chinaman slid on his heels, and fell backward into the surf. Hardy was quick to leap upon him, buried his knife in his bosom, regained the oar, and the next moment had the *Taku* afloat.

He hurried astern, trimmed the sail, and half sheltering himself under the deck, contrived to steer, making farther up the harbor, where he now knew the island must be.

In a minute or two the boat became the aim of the three hundred or more additional rifles, now arrived from the plain. They riddled her hull and sail, but she kept on her way, till there came a boom of big cannon from a quite unexpected quarter, and suddenly the splintered *Taku* dipped her bow, and disappeared in five fathoms of water.

The Chinese, apparently, had no heavy guns mounted ready for use at the fort, for they fired none ; but the English had ; and when the sentries reported a daring Chinese junk approaching the island, she was fired at ; and she promptly sank, riddled by her foes, shattered by her friends.

In all the harbor of Kiao-Chau no Chinese craft had dared for weeks to appear.

Happily the outward bulge of the island was discernible at the moment, and not more than 500 yards distant at its nearest point. Hardy began to swim. The Chinese, astonished at the sinking by the white men of a boat containing a white man, ceased firing, though a wanton shot or two dropped about the swimmer.

Panting hard, he reached the near point of the island, where a sparse growth of thin-trunked plane-trees made a wood to the water's edge. And he had hardly trailed his dripping form out of the surf, when two men, springing from nowhere, had him by the throat, and he was on his back with a pistol at his temple.

Hardy said to himself:
"They will do well."
And he added aloud:
"I am an Englishman."

There was a scrutiny of his face, a chuckle, a few exclamations, and he was on his feet.

The search-light apparatus of the fort was out of order. Till he spoke, no one on the island had had the faintest suspicion of the truth.

In ten minutes he was in a lighted room, with nearly all the hundred and fifty gathered round him, hands on knees. There were far more questions than answers. Chatter, chatter went the tongue of Jack.

"But you have not told us, sir, who you are," said Murray.

"My name is John Hardy," he replied, "and I am come to China in search of my ship, the *Powerful*. Can you give me any news of her whereabouts?"

"Oh, Lord!" cried a blue-jacket, named Brassey, "just hark at *that! Powerful*, is it? Why, sir, if you'd as much water in your inside to-night as the *Powerful's* got, it isn't *Powerful's* you would be thinking about, I don't think."

"There has been a battle?"
"That there has, sir."
"Who won?"
"We did."
"By how many ships?"

"The one we came here in, and two the Japs sunk."
"The Japs?"
"Ay."
"They sunk some ships?"
"They did that."
"But they were our allies, were they not?"
"Funny allies at that."
"They gave you no warning of their real intentions, I'll be bound," said John Hardy.
"Not they," some one replied, "it was bash-into-'em, take-me-as-you-find-me-boys, and no mistake. They didn't even carry a flag."
"They have broken the law of nations," said Hardy, looking on the ground. Then, after a few seconds, as if musing, he added: "They have violated the Law of Man."

And the words, taken in conjunction with the most strange, grave face from which they came, had in them something so solemn, and judicial, and meaningful, that, for a minute or two, silence fell upon the men; and they looked at his bent form, somehow expecting him to utter something further of singular and momentous.

But he gazed on the ground and said nothing.

Already this gray-haired youth, this venerable stripling, had produced a profound impression upon them.

Somebody on the outskirts of the crowd whispered to somebody else:

"What a *face* he's got!"

And the whisper went round. And now it was: "Just look at the phiz of him"; and now it was: "I don't think he's all there"; and now it was: "Lor! look at his face."

It was a face in which there was something thrillingly *wild;* the face not merely of a judge and an avenger, but of a judge and an avenger come back from the grave, with just that hint of the Ineffable which makes us shudder.

Yet he sat there simply enough, looking on the ground, with one elbow on his wet knee.

CHAPTER XXI

MURRAY'S DIARY

MR. MURRAY, the nominal head at the fort—though in reality he was only the first among equals—on opening one of the chests brought from the *Iphigenia* in the pinnace, found a quantity of note-paper, and as there were pens and ink in the fort, he bound it in some brown paper, wisely determining to keep a record of the varied days of this strangely-fated crew.

Under date 8*th* June we find as follows :—

8*th* June.—Last night, near twelve, a strange thing happened. We sank a Chinese boat in the harbor with No. 3 south-bastion six-incher, thinking it an enemy. It proved to have contained an Englishman, named John Hardy, ship *Powerful* (as he says). He reports himself as from Pekin in search of ship. That's about all we can get from him at present. No explanation so far as to how he escaped death in long voyage through China. Something strange about him somewhere, and men pass astonished remarks.

Still two sacks of rice left, last of third being used at dinner to-day. Also two hind legs of camel with quarters, three small sacks roots, two jars Chinese spirit from the millet-farm, and about a pound of tobacco. The sow, Joyce says, is near her confinement, and a day or two should bring us great things from her. Harris, Tom Brown, and Daly complain of diarrhœa, and Machen of violent headache. Otherwise all well. Tom Newton to be buried presently.

9*th* June.—Tom Newton buried last night at ten. For last message to his wife see under 6*th* June. This morning noticed a considerable body of Chinese (guessed 500) march past on brow of hill east of island. Big dust-cloud ahead, looking like horse-artillery. Brassey says they mean to give us fight. But I disagree. Their game is to starve us out—if they can.

This noon, Council. Resolved : that at midnight thirty hands swim to mainland at different points, taking Sniders in waterproof bags, and ammunition. To meet near lake to N. E., and make a dash for probable mules on tea-farm N. of lake. Long discussion of ways and means. Resolved : first volunteer to be leader. To surprise of all, the stranger, Hardy, volunteered first. Had listened to discussion without a word, turning from speaker to speaker. Is small, and seems weak in chest. Sow doing well.

10*th June.*—This day cook, to surprise of all, produced pudding made of roots and honey, found, he says, near west stream in valley on island. First we heard of honey here; lads all wild with excitement, and everybody clapping cook on back. Am now smoking last pipe. Tobacco done. Also last of German coffee, and yesterday no more sugar. Lads hope for unlimited supplies of honey, but I rather doubtful. Not the right place even for the wild kind.

Expedition last night very successful. Two mules (all there were on farm), also sack rice (brought over by pinnace), also a skin containing some sort of oil, and no one injured. Joyce says it is good for food, but Brassey denies, and the two came to blows. The men came back speaking well of Hardy, some saying that he means more than he says.

Most of the day spent in washing shirts and sheets by hands. Harris and Brown still bad with diarrhœa, and now also Collins, but Daly better.

He is an original, this man (I mean Hardy). To-day, while washing clothes, great discussion between Brassey and Davis, which nearly came to blows. Says Davis, "Why, the man is fifty-five," he says, "if he's a day." Brassey answers that he will lay to it that he is a lad of twenty-five, and not a day older. Then other hands join in, one saying this, and another that, and the lads getting warm. Hardy sitting a good way off, washing sheets. One says: "Why not ask him, and settle the question?" But no one volunteers to do that. Everybody going to have a look at sow this afternoon, and plenty of bets. But nothing yet to report.

11th June.—Great excitement this morning, and all Chinese liquor finished. Sow littered with four, and beauties all: one pinky-white, two pinky, white and black, and one pure black. Lads all ready for fun, and everybody determined to make a day of it. Hardy alone drank nothing. Brassey very rowdy, but afterwards got to sleep. One of mules refused to eat roots, and was killed in afternoon. A detachment of lads down by sea-shore cutting down trees for firewood with swords, and one hatchet. Not an adze in fort. Very slow business. Hardy recommended blasting, and this tried with success. But fearful anxiety beginning to be felt about powder and shot. Only three rounds of ammunition left to some of big guns, and no possibility apparently of making powder for ourselves. At six o'clock, Council. Resolved: to make a dash in small hours of morning for west fort in order to seize possible stores and ammunition, Hardy leading. Pinnace to take two detachments of twenty-five each. A desperate piece of business, in my opinion not yet necessary, but proposed by Hardy, who has seen fort, and seconded by lads. Search this afternoon for more honey, but without success. Men walking about with hands in pockets, without tobacco.

12th June.—Lovel, William Brown, and Jackson dead, and not less than thirty Chinese. I with bullet-hole in my left hand, very painful. Result: two barrels of powder, and a green tea-box half full of Lee-Metford magazine-rifle cartridges. Half of us, in retreat, swam across harbor-mouth from west fort to east, Hardy among us. Then along east side of harbor by land, pursued by Chinese, and then, swimming again, to island. The toughest job we have done yet. Our guns, ammunition, and some of our clothes, meanwhile, in boat with captured things, and we swimming with swords in our teeth.

But the curious thing is this. As we walked toward our fort, the day began to break, and Hardy having on no shirt, we saw all his body in a queer bruised sort of mess, and two letters, quite distinct, an A and an S, looking as if they had been branded into his right breast. He throws no light upon himself, and not one has the pluck to ask him. It is clear that he is a gentleman, and it is "Sir this" and "Sir that" from all the lads to him.

13*th June.*—Says Brassey to me this noon, "Wasn't there," says he, "something about a John Hardy in the battle of Shoreham that that collier from Perim reported at Hong-Kong before we sailed north?" "Yes," I said, "there was." "Then this," says he, "is the man." "There are many John Hardys," I said. "But this," says he, "is the man." "What makes you think that?" I said. "Everything," says he. And he was so certain of it, that he partly made me so as well. He has gone whispering it, too, to all the lads, and they are talking it over amongst themselves. Nobody asks Hardy, but before this day is out I mean to put the question straight before him. Gun-cleaning pretty nearly all day, and Walters, who has been down to the water's edge on the east side reports that Chinese are heaping a lot of stones on edge of cliff, probably with intention of building. Let them build away. The four piggies doing well, and the old girl as pleased as punch. We shall never have the heart to kill them. Not a scrape of baccy, and no more honey.

14*th June.*—It is to be hoped that this Hardy is not come here to lead us all to the devil, but that is about what I suspect it is going to amount to. Time will show. He has a strong influence over the lads, and is all for wild schemes and adventures. Says he last night, most of us sitting about in the north mess-room, "But what," says he suddenly, "are your ultimate aims?" "Ultimate aims, sir?" says Brassey. "You don't mean to live here always, I suppose?" says

Hardy. "It's enough for us to think of getting food to eat, without looking so far ahead," says Martin Hall. "Don't be a fool, Hall," says Tom Brown; "listen to what the gentleman says." "I have not *said* anything," says Hardy. "I merely ask a question, which I leave to your reflection. If you will think it over, I believe you will be wise. And if you cannot find an answer, come to me, and perhaps I may be able to help you." He very seldom speaks, this Hardy, and when he does, the lads listen wonderfully to him. For quite five or six minutes, I suppose, not one spoke a word after he had said this. And now they are all saying that he's got some fine scheme in his head. This afternoon at five, Council. Resolved: that the Chinese preparations for building on cliff be investigated and destroyed, if necessary, between twelve and one to-night. Hardy proposed as an amendment: that an attack be at once made on Chinese village, three miles to S. E., for purpose of getting in large store of provisions in event of contingencies. But his voice overborne by seventy-five to seventy-three votes. This afternoon Day sent to wind octagonal clock in B bastion, and broke mainspring. Have not asked Hardy anything about battle of Shoreham, or marks on chest, but mean to, sooner or later.

15th June.—This day extraordinary scene at Council. It seems that Brassey, with five or six others, came to Hardy about noon, a sort of deputation, telling him that the men had been thinking over his words of two nights before, and were wanting him to summon a Council and say what was on his mind. Hardy says yes, he would, as they wanted it. So about four, Council. Hardy stands up, the lads sprawling all about, on benches, on the floor, looking at him. Hardy has in his hand one of the three Bibles from the *Iphigenia* third chest. Well, everybody waits, wondering now what is coming, Hardy begins to talk, and keeps on talking for half an hour. All about himself first—his family, where he was born, everything; then about his coming to China to seek *Powerful*, and his capture by the Chinese at Pekin. Suddenly off he tears his shirt, and shows wounds and scars all over body; and he points to the gray patches in his head : Chinese torture, he says ; some of the men wiped their eyes, so movingly he spoke. Sometimes when his face is animated, I declare he looks like a lad of nineteen, and it is hard not to love this man somehow. Then he went on to speak of the Japs and their treachery to the British ships; then he said that all the white men in China had been massacred by the Chinese; and last of all, out he came with the announcement that the Chinese and Japanese combined are about to attack Europe. Every one held his breath at this, and we were all pretty excited by now. "Well, what are we to say of such a race, men ?" says Hardy. "Do you not agree with me that the earth would be well rid of such a people ?" "Yes!" we cry; "yes! yes!" we all shout out. "As for me," he says, "I, here and now, before you all, and before Almighty God, devote my entire life henceforth to their destruction; and I invite you all to take that oath with me." And so saying, he lifts the Book, and kisses it. The men leapt round him at once. One cries out: "You are the John Hardy of the Shoreham battle, aren't you ?" Hardy says "Yes." Then Brassey roars out: "Will you be our leader ?" and every man-jack of us cheers this to the echo; and then Hardy hands Book to each of us, and as we kiss it, each of us grips his hand in token of obedience to his orders. And as the last of us grips his hand (that was Paddy Burke), Hardy, turning away from us, goes leaning out of the window, and Brassey says a tear was rolling down his cheek which he wanted to hide. I suppose there never was such a scene in the world; it was just as if we were all mesmerized by him, some of us wanting to cry, and I as moved by his influence as the rest. The lads are swearing to follow Hardy through thick and thin.

Expedition last night did nothing, and discovered little. There were merely some piles of stone and two carts, but without mules. In one of the carts a hard-backed land-turtle, which the lads brought back. But their climb up that steep hill as good as useless.

From their report it is probable that the regular Chinese force in the neighborhood is being increased. Happily, perhaps, for us, this is a thinly populated part of the country. Something will have to be done for food, and that soon. It remains to be seen what sort of stuff this Hardy is made of. No one can deny that we got on pretty fairly before he came. Heat fearful to-day, but rain now pouring in torrents outside.

16*th June.*—At midday-mess Hardy says to lads; "Don't scatter, men. I wish to talk with you at once." So immediately after meal, Council. Hardy at head of table, I on right, Brassey on left, Tom Brown, Davis and Joyce sitting near. Says Hardy : " You have been good enough," he says, " to choose me for your leader. I hope to prove myself worthy of your favor, but for the present I prefer to consult with you, rather than to give you orders. Here you are, a splendidly trained set of fellows, and Englishmen—148 of us. I believe we might be able to do something more for our country and ourselves than killing a few Chinamen now and then. The thing is to know what we want to do, and to set about it in the right way; and, as a rule, the right way is sure to be the simplest way." " Hear, hear," says Brassey, who is a regular champion of Hardy's, and everybody gives a nod at somebody else. " Well, then," says Hardy, " but no man can work without Tools, and every workman should stick to his own Tool, the carpenter to his chisel, and the blacksmith to his sledge. We, men, are sailors ; and the Tool of a sailor is a Ship. What we have got to do, then, is to get a Ship."

This went straight to the lads—he spoke so sweetly and simply to the understanding of everybody. We cheered, every man, though not a soul could guess where this ship was to come from, or what we were to do with it when we got it. But the mere fact of his saying it made the thing seem possible.

" A Ship, then," goes on Hardy ; " any sort of Ship, so long as we've got our Tool to work with. And you mustn't think that I am child enough to propose to you anything that is impossible for you to do. I have studied you carefully since I have been among you, and I know what each of you can do, and what the whole of you together can do, and what you cannot do. As for ships, they are lying round you in plenty, only waiting for you to go and take one."

Everybody looked at him in surprise at this.

"Ships, sir!" says Brassey, "whereabouts?"

"All round the Chinese coasts," says Hardy. "I told you, didn't I, that the Chinese have seized and massacred in a body all the Europeans they could find in China. Well, at the time of the massacre, there were, of course, merchant-ships of all nations in every Chinese port, and you may be sure that the Chinese took special care to overpower and secure the sailors on board these ships, lest they should escape home and tell what the Chinese were up to. Meanwhile, the ships themselves remain, probably quite empty, or perhaps with a few Chinese on board in charge. I myself saw five in Tientsin harbor when I sailed down the Peiho to come here, and there did not seem to be anybody on board. So you see we have plenty of ships and to spare."

"But," said I, "how are you to get to them?"

"In the pinnace," says Hardy.

"The pinnace can't carry even a quarter of us," said I.

"Then she shall carry half a quarter of us," says he; "and the rest of you will remain here till we come for you in the ship."

"But how are the rest of us to live without the pinnace?" said I. "We can't carry bags of rice on our backs across the harbor, sir."

"I know that very well," says he, "and that is why I proposed to you the day before yesterday to make a raid on a village, instead of going to search into what the Chinese are building, which does not immediately concern us. What we have to do, in the first place, is to get in a good stock of provisions by means of a series of bold and well-planned raids into the thinly-populated country round, first crushing the small Chinese

15

battalion, if necessary; and when we have enough stores, both for us who go, and you who remain, then, and not before, some of us will set off in the pinnace. That seems to me good sense."

"And to me!" cries Brassey, with a wave of the hand. "And to me," goes the cry down the benches.

"But," said I, "when we have got our ship, what do we do with her—go home?"

"No—that is not precisely what we swore to do," says Hardy. "As to what we will do with our ship, I have got a plan which I feel confident you will approve when I lay it before you. But there is a good deal to be done first, and I won't trouble you with that now. The first thing I want every man to set his mind upon is to bring me into the fort here a live Chinaman with two sound legs. Without that nothing can be done."

At this our astonishment knew no bounds. A live Chinaman!

"And may I ask, sir," said I, "what it is you want a live Chinaman for?"

"To send him on a message," says he. "It is the answer which he will bring back which will make our ship of any use to us."

"He won't come back," said I.

"He will," says he.

"Right you are, sir!" cries Brassey.

"I will not keep you any longer now," says Hardy. "But later in the day, I will select a hundred of you to come with me to-night; and I recommend you to look to your swords and your rifles."

And with that we broke up, every one forming part of a group to discuss our new man. The second mule killed to-day, and two more of our men complaining of bowel trouble. Joyce talking of blowing up tortoise with gunpowder, and saying that they are good food in South Seas. Lads conversing about different brands of tobacco, and smelling keg.

CHAPTER XXII

MURRAY'S DIARY (*continued*)

17th June.—Harvey, Lane, Yates, and Tom Joyce dead. Brassey wounded in leg, Harry Jones in leg, Field in shoulder, Burke in forearm, Mackay in forearm, Wright in groin, and I again in left hand near the old place—my bad luck. One or two wounds look ugly, but the rest not much. Bodies of Harvey, Yates, and Joyce with Chinese, but Lane brought back and died in fort. Burial to-day at 3. Not less than fifty Chinese done for, says Brassey. Result: splendid haul of three camels (one killed in battle, and carcass left behind), seven mules, twelve small animals like sheep, two sacks millet, and five rice. Returning loaded from village met Chinese battalion cutting us off. Made quick charge, and thought they would turn tail, but didn't. Sharp fight. Literally forced our way through them. But our powder getting very low. What shall we do? Lads very well pleased with expedition, and speak well of Hardy. He proposes that one of mules be set aside for drawing one of Chinese carts on top of hill, to bring home haul on next expedition. But mules won't eat roots, have to be fed on rice, and grass on island scanty. Hardy says salted mule-meat, but even so, weather very hot. But will be tried. No live Chinamen to be got. They know how to run, these Chinese. At four, Council. Resolved : to repeat raid this night on village, N. W. by N., six miles off, according to report of Fraser and Brassey; Hardy looking far from well.

[Here follows Murray's account of three fresh raids

too minutely described to be reproduced here, and conducted with varying success. In the last of the three Hardy did not join, being ill.]

21st June.—At last, live Chinaman. Captured at high noon. Five lads, among them Hardy, swam one by one to east side, diving most of time. On cliff some Chinamen pouring stones out of carts for building. Men, hiding in scrub, climb up cliff-side, no very easy matter with weapons and other things in hands. Peep over cliff-edge, and decide which Chinaman it is to be. Then rush out. Chinese off in their mule-carts, and a squad of soldiers, some distance off, give fire, but at random, taken unawares. As marked Chinaman turns to gallop off in mule-cart, Brassey, who has lasso, throws; and lasso falls clean over Chinaman's head, dragging him from cart, which gallops off alone. Splendid feat for Brassey, for Chinaman was not near, and Brassey has wounded leg. Chinaman quickly bound, and hustled down hillside. Pinnace waiting at shore to bring lads and Chinaman, and Chinamen atop still banging away. But no one hurt. Lads say that Hardy gripped Brassey's hand, and gave it a squeeze. This like Hardy's decent way. Chinaman being very kindly treated, by Hardy's orders. A brawny raw-boned brute, and seems not to know what to make of treatment.

22d June.—To-day at one, Council. Resolved: that sufficient stores now in fort to last all two weeks, and that pinnace starts as soon as Chinaman is sent on message. Resolved: that Chinaman be sent to-morrow, Hardy wishing him to grow accustomed to kind treatment before starting. Hardy has chosen to accompany him on voyage the following:—Brassey, Tom Brown, Fraser, Burke, Knollys, Leaf, Pawsons, John Jones, Maitland, Samuels, Clayton, Rogers, Machen, Gibbs, John Pound, Maunder, Chapman, and Glyn. I remain in charge. Practically no powder will be left when lads set out. To-day overhauling of pinnace, and preparations. Lads found some opium on Chinaman, which they smoked, and some of them still very queer.

23d June.—To-day great fun, and lads talking of sagacity of Hardy. But no one understands meaning of message. Chinaman brought before Hardy after midday meal. Hardy at table, with pen, ink, and paper. We all standing round, Chinaman looking queer. Hardy looks at him and says, "You talkee English?" Chinaman makes no sign. "Can you talkee English?" No sign. Up jumps Hardy on a sudden, a razor in his hand, and he seizes hold of Chinaman's pigtail, as if to cut it off. "Oh, save, savee," cries Chinaman. "Very good," says Hardy, "you talk English, then." Hardy had guessed beforehand that he could, because Chinaman, on day of capture, had on European felt hat like those some of Chinese boatmen wear at Shanghai; that was why Hardy singled out this particular Chinaman. Well, Hardy says, "You poor man?" "Me very poor," says Chinaman. "How much you give for one silk pigtail?" says Hardy. "Fifty tael," says Chinaman. "You got fifty tael to buy one pigtail?" says Hardy. Chinaman looks scared. "Fifty tael?" says he, "no, no." "All right," says Hardy, "me going to cut off your pigtail, and me going to give you letter to carry Pekin. You carry letter well, and bring back true answer soon, me promise to give you back pigtail, and no do you any harm. You understand?" Chinaman trembling like a sail in the wind. But he says, "Yes." Hardy says, "Very good." Then he turns round to paper, tears half a sheet, and begins to write, lads looking over his shoulder. He writes:

"To Ni-ching-tang, Imperial City, Pekin.

"You tell me quick where Japanese navy is, or me very likely get caught, and then me tell Yen How who set me free. If you can write, you write name of place where navy is on this paper, and also name of your nephew at Tung-chow, so that me may be sure the answer comes from you. If you no can write, you tell this man name of place, and name of nephew. Be quick, or me get caught, and tell Yen How about you.—JOHN HARDY."

When Hardy had finished his letter, he read it aloud

to Chinaman, and gave it to Chinaman. He said, "If you no be back in nine days from now, me burn your pigtail in fire, and you no have pigtail no more." And with that, up he jumped to his feet, and wrapping pigtail round left hand, with two sweeps of razor he had it off about three inches from the root, leaving just enough for the man to plait it on to again. Chinaman curled and shivered, as though razor was in his flesh, and a fine long pigtail it is, too. Hardy then wrote name of Ni-ching-tang's nephew, by which I am to verify that Chinaman really has been to Ni-ching-tang, and handed paper to me to keep. Nephew's name is Li-kien. If Ni-ching-tang cannot read, Chinaman will deliver message verbally. It is clear that this man Ni-ching-tang has some strong motive for telling real truth to Hardy, but we none of us know what motive is, nor why Hardy is anxious about station of Japanese fleet. However, we have much confidence in his views. Chinaman was let free, and taken to mainland, and much fun we all had. Pinnace now ready, and the nineteen men to start at midnight. Nearest treaty-port, according to map, is Chefoo. And to Chefoo they mean to go. Pinnace loaded with last coal in fort. Compass sextant, chronometer, stores, and everything we can think of on board. Weather stifling hot, but lads in good spirits.

24th June.—Lads, apparently, got out of harbor all right last night. For us here the game is a waiting one. After to-morrow, by Hardy's orders, a man to be always on the lookout near the east fort during night. If lads get a ship, she will show three lights in a triangle to let us know when she comes. They will send boats ashore to east headland, to take us off, we swimming to east side of harbor, and taking all live stock still left. If Chinaman not come back by the time Hardy returns, nothing to be done, and red light to be shown by sentry to ship. This day killed the sow. The lads yawning, and spoiling for a fight."

[Six days of the diary follow, containing nothing but trivial details of the life of the fort, and the account of a massing of some two thousand Chinese in the locality. The next entry of importance is on the 1st July.]

1st July.—This day at noon, Chinaman spied on east shore of mainland making signals. Great excitement among lads, who have been dull. Sent two men to fetch Chinaman over, and the fuss that beggar made about coming into water lasted nearly an hour. At last lads managed to bring him over between them. Chinaman handed me Hardy's note to Ni-ching-tang, and underneath in English letters, just legible, the words "Nagasaki" and "Li-kien." It is clear, then, that Chinaman did his work well, and the only thing open to doubt is whether Ni-ching-tang has told the truth in saying that Jap navy is at Nagasaki. Chinaman trembling with eagerness to get back pigtail, doubting apparently that we would keep our word, and the lads having great sport in making him think that we wouldn't. Pigtail produced at last, and lads lashing one another with it all over the place, to Chinaman's agony. Then pigtail given to Chinaman, to his great joy. But I don't think it prudent to let him go free, and am keeping him prisoner for some time yet.

2d July.—Some lads sent out to scout, report continued massing of Chinese tents on plain to S.W., 500 counted, and we here without the power of firing three rounds of shot. Heaven only grant that Hardy turns up trumps. The men seem to take him with perfect confidence, and the lapse of time makes no difference to them. It is wonderful to me how thoroughly Hardy has got over them. I never saw anything like it. The two hind-quarters of sow completely spoiled owing to heat, and the men all saying it is head cook's fault, and he very sulky.

[On 3d July there is no entry.]

4th July.—Here we are, every man-jack of us, on board a very smart and spanking little German barque called the *Conrad*, a thing of about 400 tons, and we making straight for Nagasaki, God only knows what for. However, everybody in the best of spirits, and the lads ready for any game. This man Hardy is, in my opinion, as wild a creature as ever drew the breath of life, and yet it would be a lie if I say that I have not every confidence in his leadership, for I have. The *Conrad* is very high out of the water, and is scudding along with a good stiff breeze, the foam singing past the level of her bulwarks, and her deck too steep to walk on without gripping hold of things. She's got nothing in but her ballast, and not too much of that. So away we fly, under all plain sail and courses—a tidy spread of canvas for this light thing—but toward what? I am surprised at the lads: they don't seem to be asking themselves that question. The nineteen who went to Chefoo have got a fine old tale to tell of the capture of the *Conrad*, which they accomplished at about ten at night, without the least trouble. There was nobody aboard of her but an old Chinese woman, and one of those frizzy dogs that the Chinese eat. Not content with the ship and her three boats, Hardy boarded two other ships in the port, and seized three more boats, so that, counting the pinnace, we have got seven boats in all, which is not bad for a little nipper like this. What is troubling me is the thought of provisions; we have not enough to last us another three days at the present rate of going on. The ship is packed with men, and very far from packed with food. It is true, we should be in sight of Nagasaki by sundown to-morrow, if this breeze lasts. But how in the name of Providence we are to get provisions at Nagasaki, even if we are not blown to the devil by some little Japanese gunboat, is what I don't see. It isn't that I mistrust Hardy; there can be no doubt that he has a head-piece, and can lead. But I am a prudent man, and this looks to me like the wildest and maddest voyage that ever was made by any crew which ever put to sea.

5th July, 1 P. M.—Breeze continued good during night and all morning. *Conrad* splendid, and twice did twelve knots. Lads looking out confidently for coast before sunset. Hardy having long private talks with Richardson and Lovel, both of whom have been Eastern traders, and say they know Nagasaki harbor well. Everybody getting pretty excited, and some saying Hardy ought to speak. I with great weight of fear at my heart, which I can't get rid of.

5th July, 6 P. M.—Good for Hardy! I believe it will work! though as wild a thing, I suppose, as ever entered into the brain of a man! This day at five, Council. Resolved : that in the event——

[Here Murray's diary abruptly ends, and is not resumed till some weeks later. But the account which follows is also due to Murray, though given in a different form.]

Some little time after one bell in the second dog-watch on the 5th July, the *Conrad's* crew sighted the blue coast of Kiûsiu, they at that time being in a very high-wrought state, on account of the announcement made to them by Hardy in the "Council" at five, of which Murray speaks. It may be said, by the way, that Murray (a homely well-meaning man, more cautious than enterprising by temperament) fails to give in his diary anything like a fair idea of the enthusiasm with which John Hardy by this time seems to have inspired this crew. As a matter of fact they now followed him blindly, adoring his audacity, believing in his success, entranced by his personality. Hardy was for them a dazzling Angel sent to lead them to vague glories and to indefinite conquests, the precise nature of which did not, for the present, trouble their sailor-brains. When he unfolded his plans at the "Council" on the 5th, they discussed nothing, but hailed with rapture his proposals, eager to use their magnificent training for him, to do and die for him. Even Murray was infected. And at eight o'clock they lay-to behind a small island outside Nagasaki harbor, and waited there.

The moon rose. And everybody looked at her. For in all the creation there was nothing half so interesting to this crew this night as the earth's satellite.

She was at her full, and gravid with light. Up she climbed from the East in peerless, cloudy majesty. At midnight she was nearly overhead, and had then wheeled about her a light fleecy cloud, prismic with rainbow hues, like Miss Löie Fuller in her serpentine dance. The night was full of shining, and shining was on the calm water.

The crew of the *Conrad* looked at her, and swore. John Hardy, sitting among the main-sheet ropes behind the wheel, looked questioningly at her, and muttered; but the moon did not hear.

It was better to be out at sea among the brisk breezes and the spray. At one o'clock Hardy gave the order to let go the sheet of the main-jib, and put the helm to lee. The *Conrad* swung round, and went snorting once more to Mother Carey and the central sea.

At ten on the following night she was back at the same spot behind the island, and there she lay-to again. And the sailors watched the moon arise, and saw her climb to her noon, gravid with light, and saw her wheel about her a light cloud *à la* Löie Fuller. And they swore more than ever.

But this time there was no turning back. It was now or never. Their stores were at an end.

John Hardy said to two men leaning over the bulwarks near him:

"Well, by moonlight, then, lads. It may not turn out to be so bad as we think."

And at about two o'clock in the morning, six boats put off from the *Conrad* and rowed away. Two contained nineteen men each, one twenty, one twenty-two, one twenty-three, and one thirty-three. On board the *Conrad* eight men were left.

At this hour the moon was westering far down the steep slope of her setting course, and all the smooth sea was branded with trails of crushed and tremulous silver. The old and drowsing Night, heavy with vigil, was all enkindled now and aglow, instinct with the glamour of the moonbeams absorbed through many a long hour, like an old toper who has imbibed in solitary orgy all the night, and towards morning he rises gorged for bed, drunken, and sighing with surfeit. A flush of pallid gold suffused the fainting air. Yonder, like a lamp which has burned through all the slow period of the dark, and in the small hours it fumes and smolders red, and gives an odor in the room, so down with troubled visage went the moon. Hardly a breath sighed through the slumbering harbor, and about its dark and silent islets.

The narrow inlet of sea which forms Nagasaki port lies nearly north and south, and is about twelve *go* (three miles) in length. At its mouth it is only a quarter of a mile broad, and though it spreads out within, it is nowhere of very great breadth. All along its length, however, on both sides, the land opens up into numerous bays of some capacity. On the east side the land is mostly flat, and here used to be the "foreign settlement," with a water-frontage of some 700 yards, backed by picturesque slopes on which stood the villa-residences of the rich merchants. On the west side, however, where the moon went down, rose wooded mountain and steep crag. The whole is thoroughly sheltered, and affords anchorage for the biggest ships.

The six boats, furrowing their silent, silvery way, entered the harbor-mouth at the northwest, the largest boat (which contained Hardy, Richardson, and Brassey) leading. Any one looking at this little fleet would have said that each of the boats contained no more than two men. The rest of their crowding crews were stowed away in the bottoms, and lined the sides, lying mostly at full length, and covered with strips of tarpaulin. Under the tarpaulins, too, were lanterns. The cross-seats, except those used by the rowers, had been removed.

The course lay among a number of islets, with the navigation of which Richardson seemed quite familiar. They passed Kami-no-Shima, the site of a disused gun-battery; and they crossed a stretch of sea, all white and encrusted with moonlight, to Takabok.

From the cliffs of Takabok, two centuries before, thousands of Christians were flung by the Japanese into the sea, because they refused to trample upon the cross. And after two centuries Hardy came to Takabok.

Yonder, a little inland, was the burning light of the Iwoshima lighthouse, and, farther still, the less brilliant beam of the Kage-no-Shima pharos. Farther still lay Pappenberg, and then Nezumi-Shima, which, in old quiet days was so often used as a picnic-place by the white residents of Nagasaki.

One by one the islands receded, and the file of daring boats stole nearer and nearer upon the interior of the harbor, now in shadow, now adventuring swiftly across a patch of sea gloating in the dream of moonshine. And now, behind them is the last island, and before them the open basin, and ponderous in black slumber on the basin—the great navy of Japan.

But where are the eyes of the watchmen, that they cannot pierce those dark coverings, and divine that there, beneath them, is creeping nearer and nearer an insidious death, a strange retribution ? The watchmen, if they see, cannot divine. The riddle of destiny is far beyond them. All droops and faints in slumber, the sea, and the old night, and the moon musing in her far western couch, and the divining of the watchmen.

Only the best-trained crew in the world, led by the best leader, are awake : and they have sworn an oath.

And, suddenly, a miracle of luck is revealed to them. For yonder all the western half of the harbor is seen to be lying in absolute shadow, while the eastern half is still glittering in aspen coruscations of white light. And the main part of the fleet, it is clear, is lying within that western gloom.

The boats, by signal, separate. Each knows its work —each has its instructions.

They are, in general, to aim at the stars, they are to fly at big game, they are to make for battle-ships.

But each has separate recommendations to fulfil. And to every man is given his place, and his work, according to his powers. The company is organized into captains, commanders, lieutenants, as in the big navy at home. Hardy has been minute.

The biggest boat of all, containing thirty-three men, cruises at zigzag for three or four minutes; and then Hardy sees, and decides. He whispers an order ; and the boat—the long-boat of some European four-master

—turns directly westward, and enters the recess in the coast-wall which lies north of the Tetegami dock. Here the water is hardly ruffled by a ripple; and here the blackness of shadow is complete. Few points of light are visible within that gloom—only the white harbor-lights of a great ship.

Her massive hull is just discernible, disparting the water with its outward-bulging girth. She conveys a suggestion of such ponderousness, that it looks as though no power on earth could ever move that squat mass an inch through the water. She is the bran-new giant of the Japanese navy, the terrible *Hirosaki*, and she has a crew of 576 men.

But they sleep, and the thirty-three wake; and yonder to the far eastward, in the broad brand of shimmering and weltering moonshine, is a boat in which some harbor-police are lolling on their oars, chatting, seeing nothing. And the bull's-eyes of the lighthouses glare steadily, and the watch-lights of the ships glare steadily, and they see nothing.

The oars are muffled, and the boat glides through shadow beneath the poop of the *Hirosaki*, and when a grappling iron steals upward and fixes in a beading of the stern, we may very well say that the British lion is crouching to spring.

Up wriggles Brassey by the pole and gains the cornice, and, immediately afterwards, up wriggles Hardy. And when Hardy gains the cornice, he coughs a little; and Brassey whispers in his ear a long "Sh-h-h-h."

Yonder, eight yards from them, is the officer of the watch, walking to and fro, between the mainmast and the aft twelve-incher.

The two lie on their faces, and are hidden by a ridge of bulwark above the cornice. Within reach is a coil of rope, and Brassey's hand steals between an interspace of the taffrail, and with absolute noiselessness draws forth the coil, makes a knot round one rail, and lowers a rope-end to the boat.

And now the men arrive rapidly. There is plenty of room to receive them. They are like flies climbing an **overhanging rampart by a spider's** *fil de toile*.

Before the last man is up, three of them have run stooping forward, and the officer drops without a groan. Just then, from for'ard, a man climbs the stair to report to the officer that the lights are duly burning: it is his half hourly duty. And as he reaches the topmost rung, the sword of Brassey is in his breast and he drops.

The upper deck of the *Hirosaki* is a village, nearly five hundred feet long, but an almost deserted village. Just for'ard of the foremost funnel, two men are talking, one leaning against the foremast, one with his hand resting on a boat-davit; and a moment before the sword pierces him, the latter gives a light laugh at a jest of the other; and the other utters a feeble cry, and dies. The upper deck of the *Hirosaki* is an English village.

They descend to the main-deck, to the fo'cas'les, to the cabins, to the engine-rooms, down to the turtle-back armor-deck, at the water-line, and everywhere, with the silence and the thoroughness of the Angel of the Passover, they smite, they slay. As a man cries out, he dies; he opens his eyes, and they are sightless. The ship flows with blood.

At a door for'ard, Hardy lifts a lantern and looks into an apartment in which sleeps fifteen men. He shuts the door upon them, secures it, and does not kill. They are the remnant,—the only men left alive,—and he will have need of them.

In the bunkers of the *Hirosaki* are 700 tons of coal. The Englishmen are soon crowding in the engine-room.

Five other ships, besides the *Hirosaki*, are already in their hands. But their work is not over. Massacre for massacre—John Hardy's for Yen How's! Each has his Sabbath, and his Passover-night.

Once more the six boats put off from the six captured ships, each containing from five to nine men, all carefully picked and mixed, according to their special knowledge of ship-work; and these six meet at an agreed spot opposite the patent slip of the Dock Company. Then three of the boats' crews abandon their boats, stepping over into the other three boats, and these three row away, each containing sixteen men.

And each glides beneath the stern of a Japanese warship, and the men climb, and kill, and hurry to the engine-rooms.

Down in smoky disaster and eclipse sets the red moon, and the deep dark which precedes the morning covers the silent tragedy.

Three pistol-shots altogether, two in one ship, one in another, have been fired by the Japanese. These shots represent all the struggle which has taken place.

But the darkness which has supervened, almost as suddenly as the flickering-out of an out-worn lamp, cannot prevent the watches on other ships from perceiving that some of the fleet are pouring out an unaccountable smoke from their funnels. They must be lost in amazement, unless they conclude that the ships have received secret orders from the Admiral to sail. But they look on, and do nothing but look—for the Admiral is with the fleet, borne in the *Hirosaki*, and all, they think, is under his eyes.

There is a rattle of chains, and the steam-windlasses are a-clank, and as the first faint hint of day tinges the East, the solid-looking bulk of the *Hirosaki*— moves. And one after another the nine bulks move, wending northwards in file.

Nine—they are few in number, but they represent a good quarter of Japan's weight in war-ships. And with that quarter, Hardy would then and there attack the other three-quarters, were it not that he lacks one thing—men. The crew of a six-inch quick-firer is five; and five men represent the third part of a complete ship's-crew in this sparsely-manned fleet.

But the sound of cannon is good to the ear of Hardy, and in mere self-indulgence, as the *Hirosaki* steams past the island of Takabok, he sends a wire-gun shell among the still slumbering fleet. And the startled hills of Nagasaki awake, and cry aloud with many a voice of surprise, and the shell bursts in the engine-room of a cruiser.

The shot is not answered. There is an amazement

so profound as to resemble coma. While it lasts action is impossible.

But the amazement of the Japanese navy at being shelled by their own Admiral-ship was, if possible, surpassed by the crews of the three new Chinese cruisers, the *Hi-Chi*, *Hi-tien*, and *Hai-Shen*, when, three days later, at noon, a fleet of nine Japanese ships proceeded without warning to sink them as they lay at anchor at Shanghai. They made no resistance to this overwhelming assault; they simply sank.

In each of the nine were a few Japanese who, by Hardy's orders, had been spared to do forced labor on the ships. Being unarmed, they behaved well, and from them was learned the probable station of the three Chinese cruisers.

The "Hundred and eighty" (so called) then proceeded southward, and touched at Hong-Kong, intending to take on board whatever men they could find there. But there were no longer any white men at Hong-Kong, though there was coal.

They then turned their bows toward the West, among them being the *Conrad*, with her crew of eight.

CHAPTER XXIII

THE FROWN OF ENGLAND

By the end of July, one thing at least had been clearly hinted to the whole of Europe: that if those English could not write music, they could work; if they could not make pretty things, they certainly could fight; if they were not "*élégants*," they at least possessed the knack, and the secret, and the sword of the Conqueror.

"*La morgue Britannique!*" "*la raideur Britannique!*"—it was not then, after all, a mere insolence of semi-savages, but a pride based on a genuine supremacy of racial value and valor.

The Continental nations were not quick in learning this fact: a lingering unbelief persisted in them; and in learning it, they perished; and in teaching it to them, Britain herself all but perished.

The numerous campaigns had now occupied not quite five months; and at the end of this time Europe was in a state of collapse and exhaustion far exceeding that which existed at the close of the Thirty Years' War.

About a league to the southwest of Liège, in a pinewood, there stands a small, old-fashioned inn with overhanging gables, whose frontage looks directly upon the brown waters of the Meuse. Here the Emperor Wilhelm, Duke Paul, representing the Romanoffs, and M. Hanotaux met by appointment.

The first was chiefly a soldier, the second chiefly a diplomat, the third chiefly a man of business.

They sat in one of those vast bedrooms of old Belgian inns, on the first floor, grouped near a window which overlooked the river.

The deliberation was conducted, as usual, in French.

"The situation," said M. Hanotaux, "has—developed. And developments generally demand new plans. The facts we know : by means of a single *contretemps* to our fleet, France finds herself with two invading armies in her territories, Germany with three, and Russia with three. And in no case has any one of these eight armies been unsuccessful."

"The defensive," said the Emperor, "has always been intensely repugnant to the genius of the German army. It is an army of conquest and aggression. The smallness of its victories in this war has been due to the fact that it fought on German soil."

Duke Paul and M. Hanotaux smiled at each other with their eyes.

"But the question is one of means, rather than of causes," said M. Hanotaux. "Let us face this fact boldly : that our great enemy is aided by the geography of the earth. We should have beaten England— we none of us doubted that we should. But we have not. To me there seems to have been two chief reasons for this failure, which may now be more or less removed : First, the diversions caused by the hostilities entered upon against us by other nations ; and secondly, the sea."

"But both reasons remain ?" said Duke Paul interrogatively.

"The sea does," broke in Wilhelm, "but, candidly, it is my opinion that France should long ago have made peace with Italy, and Russia with Austria."

"Your Majesty is perhaps a little sanguine in this view," answered M. Hanotaux, "for Italy was the aggressor, and perhaps one might say the same of Austria. On the other hand, Germany seems to have no real cause for a bloody war with Sweden and Denmark."

"But was not Sweden, then, the aggressor, monsieur, as far as Germany was concerned ?" asked Wilhelm. "Did she not wantonly attack my coasts for no other valid reason than that Germany was the ally of Russia? And since Denmark has joined Sweden in this attack, what would you have? This, be sure, is not a matter for the peace-maker, monsieur, but for the unsparing and implacable sword!"

"Still," said M. Hanotaux, and he stroked his straggling *barbiche de bourgeois*, "our conference, conducted in a spirit of unyielding insistence upon rights, will hardly result in good fruit. The fact is, that we each of us have to fight one great, and at least one smaller foe. I have inaugurated this meeting for the purpose of asking in the most definite terms this question : Since the resources of Europe are visibly nearing their end, do we prefer to conquer the great foe or the small? Is it wisdom to persist in both attempts?"

"I agree with you in principle," said Wilhelm.

"The principle is obvious," said Duke Paul.

"And to me the details also seem obvious," said M. Hanotaux quietly. "England triumphant over Europe means, of course, the wiping out of the empires of the world—it means a Cockney earth. When I say 'a Cockney earth,' I shudder, your Majesty—I shudder, M. le Duc Paul,—and you shudder, too. The thought, you will say, is not pretty (*Ce n'est pas bien jolie ce que j'ai pensé-là!*). And the nations will not permit that? Let us make peace with our brothers, that we may crush the stranger!"

"A League of Europe?" said the Duke.

"A League of Europe," answered M. Hanotaux, and bowed.

Wilhelm flushed with enthusiasm, and he said :

"I agree!—in principle."

"The principle is obvious," put in the Duke.

"And the details, I think!" cried M. Hanotaux.

"Who will make a beginning?"

"If we say—Germany."

"Not Germany!" said the Kaiser.

"Then Russia," said M. Hanotaux.

"Hardly Russia perhaps," mused Duke Paul. "The

heart of the Tsar is set upon the crushing of Sweden, at least——"

"Then France!" exclaimed M. Hanotaux, "since, you leave to France this glory."

"You mean that you will accept the conditions demanded by Italy, monsieur?"

"Yes, your Majesty!"

"At once?"

"No—not precisely—but soon."

"When?"

"After the next great battle."

"Whatever the result?"

"Yes, M. le Duc Paul."

"But after the next great battle the southern resources of France will, as I understand it, be at an end," said Wilhelm bluntly. "You will be compelled to do what you offer to do."

"Not 'compelled,' perhaps, your Majesty; for the territorial resources of Italy will be practically at an end also. There remains, however, her—Navy. We have need of it."

As the inwardness of M. Hanotaux's scheme unfolded with these words, it won the whole interest of his interlocutors. In both the royal and the ducal brains ripened as the same instant this thought: "A Second Invasion of England."

"I follow you with the closest attention, monsieur," said Wilhelm.

"And I also find your reflections of the profoundest interest, monsieur," added the Duke.

"France," proceeded M. Hanotaux, "will adopt that line of conduct under the following conditions: first, she will satisfy the claims of Italy on the understanding between her and Italy, that Italy becomes the ally of the Allies; and secondly, France demands that the two Allies follow her example, by generally granting the demands of Sweden, Denmark, and Austria, on the understanding that they also become the allies of the Allies against the common foe of Europe."

Wilhelm leapt up.

"The thing is done, monsieur!" he exclaimed.

"It is a question of *when*," said Duke Paul.

"Precisely," said the Kaiser, "it becomes a question of when."

"*When* the next great battle between France and Italy has been fought," answered M. Hanotaux.

"No!" leapt from the mouth of Wilhelm, in a half-suppressed start, and then there was pause. The fact was, that each desired to fight yet one battle with the enemy with whom it was proposed to make terms, in the hope and belief that the victory would be his, and the terms of peace therefore more advantageous for him.

Duke Paul spoke meditatively; and he said:

"I agree, on the condition that Russia will make no terms with Sweden and Austria until after the next considerable battle with each of these, whether the battle of France with Italy has then occurred or not."

"And the conditions of Germany are identical," said the Kaiser.

"Then there is nothing for it but to shake hands on the compact, your Majesty, and M. le Duc Paul. It may be observed, however, that your condition, and mine, insures a certain and very considerable reduction of the not large territorial forces now at our disposal. Is there no departure possible from this determination?"

There was no departure. The three men spoke on for an hour; and as the darkness gathered, they rode away toward Liège, and took train in different directions.

The agreement, often repeated, was this: five battles, one by France, two by Germany, two by Russia; then, if possible, a European peace and League.

Russia would be prepared to hand over to Austria the doubtful legacy of the still warring Balkan States, and all that stretch of fair land from the Golden Horn to Cape Matapan; and she would yield Finland, with an indemnity, to the victorious arms of Sweden; Germany would buy off Sweden and Denmark; France would yield to Italy the Haute Savoy, Avoie, the Alpes Hautes, Basses, and Maritimes, and Var.

For all this large generosity there was a cause, bitterly near home, awfully pressing. The one thing now that could save Europe from England was the imposition upon England of the necessity to recall her armies to defend her own territory.

For, at last, 100,000 British soldiers occupied all the Seine valley between St. Germain and Argenteuil, and, the headquarters of Lord Roberts and his staff was the Taverne St. Roch near the great *escalier* of St. Germain. A hundred thousand men—a small army when the war began; an immense war-host now. There was no intention of attacking Paris, which required an investing circuit of 125 miles;—but Paris was not France. Normandy already was once more British; the rest of France lay open; and Italy had crossed the Isère.

Germany's plight was hardly less extreme. Her splendid legions had thrown themselves northward in three continuous streams to meet three branches of the same Teutonic race of which she was part. To the west, occupying Schleswig-Holstein and the upper reaches of the Elbe as far as Domitz, Denmark lay encamped; to the east, Sweden had drawn lines of circumvallation by a ring of earthwork forts and Schumann gun-turrets round Breslau, having captured the Breslau-Posen railway; and midway between these two was that brazen-browed, nimble, ever-intruding enemy, who alone had made possible to the others their victories. Northern Germany, from Hamburg to Tilsit, had been the scene of the most unparalleled series of massacres—carnage after carnage—ever witnessed in history; Royal Saxon Corps, famed in military history, Bismarck Cuirassiers, gallant Silesian and West Prussian Corps—paragons of the soldier's hope of attainment—all had been flung, and flung in vain, into the devouring maw of war; still the British came, though in ever-lessening numbers; and still from farther and farther south marched the precious levies of the Fatherland. Seven of the twenty corps of the Imperial host remained; and of these, two Bavarian brigades were marching upon Naumberg, whence a nondescript army of Socialists, Nihilists, and malcontents had issued from its headquarters a manifesto to the nation, announcing the day of Liberty, and inviting support.

As for Russia, she turned a fourfold face south, southwest, northwest and inward, and everywhere saw doom. The Army of India, having waited in vain for invasion, crossed the Helmund, annihilated at Merv the still-unrecalled remnants of the Russian army of Turkestan, and had now, after a great victory at Novo Tcherkask, reached Kharkov by road, with the Kremlin for its *objectif*. Odessa, Sebastopol, and the Black Sea littoral were British. Of the two divisions of the Austrian army, one had in a single day disappeared; but another quickly sprang in its place; and this, with its sister army, adopting Moltke's principle of marching separately and fighting together, had, after a strenuous campaign, only surpassed for carnage by the great drama of blood transacting itself in Northern Germany, made Poland an Austrian province, and crossed the sources of the Niemen. Russia was doing doubtful battle in Bulgaria, Turkey, and Asia Minor. The battleships of Sweden were at the mouth of the Neva; and in the heart of Russia itself a deep subterranean muttering, like a presage of universal earthquake and overthrow, was suggested by the mere word "Nihilist."

This, in briefest outline, was the situation on the Continent at the moment of the conference in the wood at Liège. The three nations which had primarily been made the tools of Yen How, regretted now their rashness. They had miscalculated the Lion.

But, suddenly—as if it needed only the conference in the wood to bring them luck—their sky cleared. In the darkest hour of their extremity they found a hope, their last.

On two days following, about two weeks after the meeting in the wood, two considerable victories attended the arms of the Allies.

One of these was French: the 14th (or Lyons) Army Corps of 40,000 men met the advancing Italian Army between Bourgoin and the left bank of the Rhone, and though outnumbered by ten thousand, gave to Italy an emphatic, and indeed final, negative to her long-fought attempt at conquest. And at once the Aurillas brigade of the 13th (Clermont-Ferrand) Corps, which was all that was left of it, was ordered southward to cross the Alps and carry the threat of war into the enemy's country, prior to the proposition to Italy of the terms agreed between the Allies.

The second victory was Russian, and was gained in a far more momentous conflict over the magnificent British-Indian troops, which had gallantly won its way from Quetta almost to the walls of Moscow. Upon this battle General Dragomiroff, in a great, final bid for victory, had concentrated almost the whole remaining forces of his master. It was a mixed combat in which Ural, Orenburg and Transcaspian Cossacks fought with Bengal Lancers, and Turkestan Infantry Brigades with Royal Fusiliers. The battle, from the commencement of which the 90,000 British were greatly outnumbered, was, after five hours' massacre, won by a flanking movement of Don Cossacks. The number of the slain was 160,000.

Great as was the exhaustion in which this dear victory left Russia, the immediate result was a sudden and enormous increase of her prestige. And two things at once happened: first, Sweden, no longer acting in concert with the great arm of England, which was the incentive to her audacity, became anxious to secure by peace her conquests in Northern Russia; and secondly, the Kaiser, knowing that terms would now be offered to Sweden by Russia, became anxious to make terms with Sweden before her hands were freed to direct upon Germany the entire remnant of her forces. In this way it happened that nearly every one of the contending nations were, owing to the results of these two battles, strongly motived toward peace. Nor could Austria resist the pressure of her allies, Italy and Germany, nor the large amenities of Russia south of the Balkans; and in the many-sided treaty signed at Vienna on the 23d of August, Denmark, too, compelled by the pressure of events, was one of the signatories.

It was now that the long expected had come at last.

Led by the rigor of events, and led by the general tendency of long-maturing sentiment, an exhausted Europe had inaugurated a League—as the first preliminary to a renewal of her life—having for its object the destruction of an exhausted Britain.

For Britain, too, was exhausted; and already had lost semblance to that land of free-handed opulence which her sons remembered with sighs. Bull's girth had thinned.

Yet if photographs at this hour could have been taken of all her people, and the traits of these agglomerated into the expression of a single face, that face would have been the wild and wan and gaunt visage of a Man, on whose brow brooded a fatal frown of indignation and resolve, not to be softened but by death.

The idea of Europe was to hurl itself in its whole banded strength upon this diminished force. And it would be strange if, this time, the island could withstand the continent.

England's navy had, on the whole, done well. Up to the moment of the new League, she still might be said to command the seas. But with the League, even without the practically intact navy of Italy, her supremacy was gone. *With* the navy of Italy, it was twice and thrice obliterated.

The new Allies, indeed, looked forward with certainty to another great naval battle before they could effect their design; but their ultimate passage to England was practically assured.

And Sweden, flushed with victory, contributed an Army Corps; and Russia, freed from invaders, contributed two; and Germany one; and France one; and Austria three; and Denmark two brigades; and Italy two brigades.

Mobil!

The port of debarkation was fixed at Antwerp, whose neutrality thus suffered willing violation, and in the last days of August 360,000 troops, troop-ships, and war-ships were hasting over sea and land to rendezvous upon Antwerp.

England, warned both from the Continent and

America, was not in the dark. On the 5th of September, when the great Armada set sail from the Belgian port, her whole available force in ships of war was massed in Portsmouth Harbor, all but ready to sail.

It was on this very day, towards two in the afternoon, that a singular species of duel was taking place between two men at Worthing. It was war *in extremis*, as bitter as, and more breathless in its mad intensity than, the great war going forward around them.

One of these men was called Richardson, and the other Atkins. Atkins was excise, with a salary of thirty shillings; Richardson was municipal, and acquainted with rates. His *locale* was the Town Hall, and he earned forty shillings. Both were fairly active young men of twenty-five.

Apart from their steady and respectable employments, each had a species of less reputable avocation, which, however, he pursued with extreme zeal, and, for some reason or other, was proud of. Richardson said that he was "on the staff" of the *Evening News*; and Atkins that he was "on the staff" of the *Sun*.

This only meant that they had agreed to send any local news that might be of interest to those papers.

Now, on this 5th of September, a bit of local news of considerable interest did, in fact, occur. For a strange-looking little craft, which was nothing else than a Maltese *speronare*, had arrived at the pier; and from her had landed a man of uncertain age, who slowly walked up the pier with his eyes on the ground, made his way to Dixon's Commercial Hotel half-way up the Pier Street, and there disappeared. The rest of the *speronare's* occupants had at once put to sea again. But it was quite an hour afterwards, before either Atkins or Richardson, being employed on their Jekyll affairs, got the least scent of this Hyde matter.

It was Atkins who, at the dinner-hour, first entered Dixon's commercial-room. In the front of Dixon's was announced a "Daily——Ordinary," the two words being separated by a great gap where the word "Shilling," now painted out, had once stood.

As Atkins entered the room, he saw the back of the

stranger, who was leaving it by a door which led to the bedrooms above, and he started.

The whole interest of his life was instantly centered upon this man; there was something in his appearance, his dress, which aroused the instinct of the reporter. About the man was the brine and odor of the sea.

At this time, a bit of news was to the people of Britain like rain to the desert. Men often spent their very last half-penny in buying a paper, which they knew could tell them little more than they already knew.

We have said that Atkins was interested at sight of the stranger.; but this interest became a passion the moment that, approaching a spread side-table, he saw beside a soiled plate a piece of paper; and on the paper; a certain name written at the bottom of a promise-to-pay, together with a London address.

It had happened that the stranger had, to begin with, informed Dixon that he was without a copper in his pockets; and Dixon, after some demur, on the security of a gold ring, an honest face, and a written promise-to-pay, had not only trusted the stranger with a meal and a bed, but had lent him twelve shillings to pay his fare to London that night. The promise-to-pay he had in a moment of bustle left on the table, and Atkins saw it, and turned to run.

And as he turned to run, lo, Richardson was at the door. And Atkins let his flat hand fall upon the paper, and stood leaning with careless grace.

Richardson, on his way to Dixon's, had heard of the arrival of the stranger, and there was a breath of haste at his lips. He said:

"Hullo! Anything up?"

"Not as I know of. You heard anything?"

"No. Seen the article in to-day's *D. T.*——?"

"No. Why are you so late to-day? I have had dinner ten minutes——"

"What, are you off? It's only——"

"I've got to be. Beastly job on hand—gauging business for Hatley's. See you to-night at the club——"

Atkins' diplomacy was bad, for his walk toward the

door, for one thing, was too rapid to be natural ; and Richardson had noted his statuesque pose, his rather pale face, and his unmoving hand on the paper. So he had no sooner passed through the door, than Richardson, too, had read ; and at once he, too, rushed to the door. But it was locked on the outside.

The thought of summoning slow Mr. Dixon by the bell never even entered his head ; he simply flew to the window, dashed up the sash, dropped into the area, and climbed up to the rails on the opposite side by the help of a swinging coal-cellar door.

Yonder, half-way down the street, was Atkins, running with all his legs. Richardson, as though life lay before, and death behind, was after him.

Atkins, however, was considerably taller and fleeter, Richardson being inclined to fat ; and the race was clearly the foremost man's, when, suddenly, there appeared from a bye-street, with callous saunter, a policeman about ten yards ahead of Atkins.

And at once Richardson sent forth the impassioned shout of "Stop thief! Stop thief!" many times repeated.

And an instant later Atkins was firmly gripped in the arms of the officer.

"Let me go, Jones, you infernal idiot!" screamed Atkins, "you ought to know better, you damned *fool!* Can't you *guess*—Jones, you silly ass——"

But Jones, with zealous sense of duty, maintained his grip on the frantic man, till he saw the accuser mysteriously rush onward past the accused. And he tossed his head with a smile, as he relaxed his hold of Atkins ; and he said :

"Oh, well, I suppose it's only one of their little newspaper squabbles——"

So Richardson only reached the telegraph-office about ten seconds before Atkins ; and the telegraph man was engaged to Atkins' sister.

And therefore the *Sun* got its message some five minutes before the *News ;* but by some sleight-of-hand, or extra energy, the *News* was not outdone. It reached Piccadilly Circus some fifteen seconds before the *Sun*, though the *Sun* was first at Holborn ; and it was never quite determined to which of the two Finsbury and Tooting owed their gratitude for the news. On the placards of each the words were the same :

JOHN HARDY

ARRIVED

IN ENGLAND.

CHAPTER XXIV

BEFORE THE BATTLE

DURING all that afternoon and night England, Scotland, Wales, and Ireland uttered its voice.

For the 5th-6th of September the usual 5,000,000 letters and post-cards delivered by the Post Office leapt to 14,500,000. This meant that the whole nation had taken busily to pen-and-ink, to paper and card-board. It meant that it was profoundly stirred about something, that it wanted something with its whole heart.

These extra millions of letters were directed to London, some to the Government offices, the majority to the London daily papers. Not a thousandth part of them were ever opened. The Circulation Office of the London Postal Service Department was kept in a flurry of business all through the night. St. Martin's in the morning got postmen where it could ; and the bags of the carriers bulged.

When any vast collection of animals acts in this spontaneous way, all doing the same thing, it is that they are stirred by some instinct which is in unison with the soul of the world. The Universal Voice is, in truth, the voice of God. Democracy is thus a kind of Holy Scripture. Its will is the Decalogue.

The nation, having eagerly drunk the news that John Hardy had suddenly reappeared in England as mysteriously as he had disappeared from it, demanded his presence at the impending battle. It insisted that no nonsense about formality or convention should deprive it of his possible help. Most of the people demanded his appointment as Admiral of the Fleet.

Before the Battle

And why? He had only been instrumental in winning a single battle for England. If they had reasoned, their ardor of persuasion could not have been so intense. But the fact is, that their cry proceeded from that divine instinct for truth which, in hours of extremity, often inspires nations and sometimes individuals. That Hardy was the right man, just then, just there, they felt intuitively; and they did not mince matters in proclaiming it.

The only person in Europe to whom the coming battle, or his own possible share in it, did not seem of direct momentous importance, was Hardy.

For the immediate motive of the Allies was to compel the withdrawal of the British troops from the Continent; but supposing they effected a landing in England, there impended an enemy upon them, as Hardy knew, far more terrible than all the combined armies of several Europes; and this enemy would at once compel them to do the very thing they sought to force upon Britain.

And it was near—it was not far off. As he stepped into the train at Worthing that night, he bought a paper; and in a small-type paragraph, unmarked perhaps but by him, he saw this quaint item of news:

"A train containing 500 Chinese has arrived at St. Petersburg from Vladivostok. They seem poor, and the object of their journey is unknown. It is the intention of the Russian authorities to send them back to their own country."

Hardy muttered to himself:

"So soon, Yen How?"

But in the eyes of England, of Britain, of Europe, the coming battle was the Greater Waterloo of world-history; the final shock of this annihilating war; the crowning Armageddon before a probable thousand years of Peace.

If Britain failed now, she failed; and if Europe, then Europe failed, too. There could be little further struggle: for who would be there to make it? There would be no fight left in the limp nations.

Hardy reached London at eleven P. M. It was

partly expecting him, for as soon as the two Worthing reporters had got off their news, Worthing had pricked its ears and heard. Dixon's became the center of the town, and a moving crowd surveyed the house for hours. Long before Hardy appeared, all his immediate plans were known from Dixon; he was then cheered by the full street; only those near enough to see him well being mostly silent, impressed with something of that strangeness of expression which made the sailors at Kiao-Chau whisper: "What a face!"

London, therefore, expected him, without certainty as to the hour. A considerable crowd waited at Victoria; but when at last it saw him, made no sign. They looked for a very young man, with swift glance and free air. They saw a man with stooping shoulders and gray in his long hair; and decided that this was hardly he.

But one pair of eyes knew him under his disguise. Old Bobbie Mason had been waiting all the evening at the station, wondering why his boy had forgotten him, had sent him no line or word. When at last he saw, he started with horror; but he knew his own.

Outside, instead of the crowd of busy cabs, Hardy saw a meager muster; and his musing eye noted the raw-boned look of the horses. As his carriage passed through Buckingham Palace Road, a baked-potato apparatus stood before the Palace, and he noted with a pang the largeness of the crowd around it. The streets were almost deserted. Even the policemen seemed fewer. In a bye-street, near Oxford Circus, an old woman walked, and behind her a cat, with little halts and runs, followed persistently, sending out piteous feeble cries to the night.

Old Bobbie, sitting there by his side, waited for a caress of the once affectionate hand. But no caress came. They drove onward in absolute silence. The only words which John had spoken were the two: "Well, Bobbie," at the station-platform. The old man was frightened.

Once only, as John was moving off to bed, the old butler broke out; and he cried, with clasped hand:

"Master John—what—what—have they done to you!"

And John answered:

"They have tortured me to death, Bobbie, if you want to know."

And that was all. The rose-leaf lips were pressed pretty tight now.

Early in the morning the Government knew what it had to do, if it meant to keep its place. In a thousand startling ways it learned that the nation's will, this time, had got to be done.

But the thing was officially impossible. Hardy was nobody, officially. The ships' crews were complete; and it was anticipated that the main portion of the fleet still at anchor would sail at noon. The Government could not exactly telegraph to a Captain or a Vice-Admiral, and say: "You must give up your place to John Hardy, because he is a better man than you." They were absolutely at their wits' end.

But the chief characteristic of the British race is its nimble way. It actually does manage in the end. At nine o'clock Captain MacLeod, once of the *Jupiter*, now of the *Royal Sovereign*, was seized by "a sudden illness"; at half-past nine, Admiral Sir Nowell Salmon, principal Naval Aide-de-Camp to the Queen, was at 11A Cavendish Square; at ten, Lord Charles Beresford, upon whom, in the hour of peril, the supreme command had been imposed, telegraphed to the Committee of National Safety, and also to the Admiralty, offering to Hardy a joint command of the squadron: at half-past ten Hardy was hasting in a special train toward Portsmouth.

But he went under compulsion, not knowing why. He had no theory of naval war. He had, indeed, won a battle, but—he shrank a little from this prominence. The truth was, he was more or less unconscious of the clearness of his own eyes and the valor of his own heart. It needed that the actual hard facts of a situation should be before him before he could assume the aggressiveness and the self-assurance of the hero.

When on the point of setting out from Cavendish

Square, he had cut from the newspaper bought at Worthing the paragraph about the 500 Chinese. And he had written the two following letters, the first to Mr. Goschen at his private address:

"DEAR SIR,—I am just about to set out to fight in the battle which you kindly allow me to attend. In case I should get killed, I am writing this letter to ask you if you will kindly send a ship, flying the English White Ensign at her mast-head, under that the Blue Peter, and under that the Union Jack, to the island of Monte Christo, with orders to bring home what she will find there. I believe you will find that this will come in useful to you in a few weeks' time.—I am, sir, your obedient servant,

"JOHN HARDY."

The second letter was to the Prime Minister. It ran:

"MY LORD,—I take the liberty to inclose you a slip from a newspaper about some Chinamen who have come to St. Petersburg, because I believe it is well worth your attention. In my opinion, within three or four weeks from now there will be some four hundred millions of yellow men in Europe, and perhaps in England, too. I have just come from China myself, so I ought to know what I am saying. A very great man, named Yen How, is the cause of all this. In my opinion, the very best thing England could do would be to withdraw at once from the Continent the armies she has there.—I am, my lord, your obedient servant,

"JOHN HARDY."

If ever man was shocked with fright, or started at the keen spur of terror, it was the Prime Minister on reading this note.

Now he understood some things which had puzzled him.

News had reached England that some American cruisers in Chinese waters had mysteriously ceased to

Before the Battle

report themselves. Later had come the news that no intelligence could be obtained of some Italian and Austrian ships of war sent out to China during the "Eastern craze." Merchant ships from Europe had sailed round the Cape to the Far East, and their long-delayed return was still awaited. It was known that China and Europe were telegraphically disconnected.

These things, at another time, might have given to Europe some hint of the actual facts. But during the preoccupation of the war, not the remotest inkling of the truth occurred to any one. China was a forgotten land. The result of the great battle in the Hwang-hai was still unknown in England—all was unknown. Hardy was the first messenger from that silent, but busy, Eastern world who had appeared for many a month.

At the Hard a boat awaited him. He was taken on board the *Anson*, which carried the Admiral's flag at the main, and was received by Lord Charles Beresford in his private cabin.

The cheery sailor took the hand of the grave-faced one, and said:

"I congratulate you heartily, Mr. Hardy, on the merited enthusiasm and confidence which you have aroused in your countrymen, and I shall feel myself honored by your collaboration."

And Hardy said:

"Thank you, my lord."

And, after some few words, they sat together, and Beresford said:

"The facts, since you are ignorant of them, are roughly these: the navy of Italy is practically intact. Of her first-class battleships, two were sunk by Riviera forts, but about 130,000 tons of her 150,000 odd tons in this line remain, with say 16 guns over 13 inches, and, counting the whole fleet, 44 over 10. With the names, tonnage, and armaments of the various ships you are familiar, the two lost ships being the *Re Umberto* and the *Ruggiero di Lauria*. France, on the other hand, has lost heavily in the war; her Toulon squadron of eighteen armored ships, which she had reduced by those sent to the first invasion of England, was destroyed in the Bay of Algeciras, during an attempt to pass through the Straits. A few antiquated wooden things like the *Colbret* and the *Suffren*, as well as that rather lame duck, the *Richelieu*, still remain.

"Her Levant squadron, however, is mostly good for fight ; there was a brush with our East Mediterranean force, but the French turned tail, and were lost in a mist after some mutual injuries. The majority of the fifteen coast-defense iron-clads, moreover, are intact, and I have no doubt will be dragged into this final effort. Altogether we have, I think, to reckon with a contribution from France of, say 96,000 tons, and this will include, I think I may say, the *Brennus*, the *Sfax*, the *Trident*, the two three-masted *contre-torpilleurs*, *Voutour* and *Cosmao*, the *Amiral Duperré*, the *Levrier*, the cruiser *Troude*, the *Marceau*, and the *Magenta*. Those, I think, are all I can be sure of.

"In the Baltic there have been four battles, one British-German, one British-Russian-German, one Swedish-Danish-German, and the last Swedish-Russian.

"On the state of affairs with regard to Baltic ships I am unfortunately not so well informed. I very much doubt if there remains to Sweden a single effective ship of war ; but, if I am not wrong, we may expect to to have do with a contribution from Russia and Germany combined of, say, 100,000 tons, one-half of which, I calculate, will be battleship weight, and the rest cruisers and torpedo flotillas. Austria will send her single battleship and her 32,000 ton-weight in cruisers, making altogether, with torpedo-boats, say, 40,000 tons. Putting all these together, I have calculated, Mr. Hardy, an opposition of 456,000 tons.

"Very well, now. Let us turn nearer home, and see what force we have to oppose to this great armada. Britain, I assure you, has had a hard and up-hill fight of it. There lie around you ships recalled from every quarter of the globe, except China, where, I hear that you say, our squadron has gone to Davy Jones. If an invading army were to descend from, let us say, the planet Jupiter, they would find all our colonies undefended. Happily our enemies are in the same plight. Altogether we have at our command, including available coast-defense ships, 156,000 tons, just about one-third of the enemy's force ; and if these figures do not fill you with a certain gravity, it is because you are a Briton and Mr. Hardy."

Beresford smiled as he concluded, leaning back his chair ; Hardy, looking upon the ground, did not smile.

After a minute Hardy said .

" I take it, my lord, that after this battle there won't be any ships of war left anywhere ? "

" There will be the Japanese, Chinese, and American navies," said Beresford, " and some things of Spain, with some inconsiderable Portuguese and Dutch ships. Europe will then have to fight with her Atlantic greyhounds."

Still Hardy did not smile.

" And what are our best ships, my lord ? " he said.

" Our best ships are good," replied Lord Charles Beresford. " We have the *Illustrious*, the *Hood*, the *Anson*, the *Trafalgar*, the *Royal Sovereign*, on board of which you will bear the joint direction of the battle, though, I am sorry to say, without a flag-captain ! also the *Centurion*, the *Nile*, the *Benbow*, the *Hero*. You will see in a few minutes for yourself. Not all the most modern of the modern, perhaps—but all good ships and true."

" There won't be much of them left after the battle, my lord," remarked Hardy.

This was obvious. Lord Charles Beresford coughed. And he said :

" I suppose not. But now—the case being as I have explained to you, what are your ideas as to a plan of battle, and so on ? "

For some time Hardy was silent, perusing the ground. Afterwards he said :

" To be candid, my lord, I have no idea, not a single one. Or rather, I have *One*."

" Very good, Mr. Hardy ; let me hear it, and we will then confer together upon it."

"My idea is this, sir," said Hardy, "to ask you to let me take a cruiser, or a pinnace, or something, and go to the foreign fleet with a flag of truce to try and persuade them, by hook or by crook, to go back again to their own country."

"My good Mr. Hardy!" broke from Lord Charles Beresford's lips.

"You are astonished, my lord," said Hardy. "You guess that I am as fond of a fight as any one, and you did not quite expect to hear that sort of proposal from me. But I make it seriously to you, and in doing so I forget my own inclination, and even I forget the glory of England. I am thinking of the good of the whole world. The fact is, sir, I happen to know more of the actual conditions of the present and the near future than you do, and therefore see things in different proportions. I say to you, Lord Charles Beresford, that mankind is at this moment in by far the greatest fix in which it has ever been since the first man stepped; and how it is going to get out of it, God only knows. You think you have been having a great war in Europe, and so you have. But this little great war of yours is not anything compared with what is coming upon you, sir. Believe me, for I know, or I would not say it. It has been man fighting with man all the time, has it not? But how if all the devils in hell, myriads of them, my lord, suddenly break loose upon you? It would be an easy thing for four millions of yellow men, with a proper leader, to conquer Europe in its present state. But it is not four millions which are coming; it is four hundred millions; and every single one of them a devil, as I say, vomited from hell. I have just come from China, and that is what I have to tell you, sir."

As Hardy ceased, he lifted his hitherto careless eyes, and now there was a flash in them; in the face of the other was horror, query, incredulity.

There was a dead silence. Lord Charles Beresford had of old been himself one of the preachers of "The Yellow Danger"; but he had preached it as a theory, afar off. When he was told that it was here—

had come—it shocked and appalled him as though he had never once heard of such a thing.

In the midst of the silence there was a knock, and the Admiral's Flag-Lieutenant entered the room. He said :

"The *Indefatigable* has steamed in, sir, and signals that the enemy are now passing the Straits."

A chain of four British cruisers, going and coming within signaling distance, the remotest keeping watch upon the enemy, the nearest in touch with Portsmouth, had been told off for this duty two days previously.

"We must be looking alive, then," said Lord Charles. "The words you have spoken, Mr. Hardy, are terrible ; and the course you suggest seems to me one almost requiring the authority of the civil powers. But now, you see, there is no time. I suppose I must take upon myself the responsibility of acceding to your views."

"I believe that England will approve our conduct, sir."

"Good. At the same time I can't say that I have much faith in the success of your expedition."

"I *hope* it will succeed, my lord. If it does not——"

"Well ? "

"Then it will serve another end."

"What end ? "

" I shall have a good look at the enemy's formation, forces, and disposition."

And at these words the eyes of the two men met.

And Lord Charles Beresford smiled.

And John Hardy, for the first time, smiled.

CHAPTER XXV

THE GREATER WATERLOO

THE ships lay in harbor with fires banked and steam at a quarter of an hour's notice.

The single signal "Weigh!" went up from the *Anson*, and ten thousand sailor-hearts went fluttering, as the fat chain-links, like processions of slow-footed sea-tortoises, came waddling clumsily in-board.

It was arranged between Hardy and Beresford that the plan of advance which the latter had long since determined upon should be put into execution and maintained, up to the time of Hardy's visit to the allied fleet. If, after the visit, Hardy desired to take over the sole command, he would signal that fact throughout the fleet.

At noon exactly the ships steamed out. At once the news was flashed over all Britain, and an hour later the churches of the land, in hamlet, town, and city, were thronged with worshipers imploring the Almighty to protect His Witness in the earth, and not to forsake in the hour of her extremity that chosen Nation, His Servant, which had proclaimed the greatness of goodness, and, as far as her poor striving eyes could see, had loved Righteousness, and had hated Iniquity.

The ships passed Spithead massed in four columns in line ahead, flag and senior officers leading their columns, Hardy at the head of the starboard line in the *Royal Sovereign* and Beresford at the head of the extreme port. Ships had stringent instructions to keep their speed, and maintain an exact formation. Six knots, eight knots, ten knots were signaled; and it was evident from the position of the steam-cones that every ship had steam in plenty.

It was a bright early-September day ; but as often happens on such days, a bluish mist, which was half a mist and half a luminosity, delicately veiled the distance.

Off Selsey Bill the second link of the chain of look-outs joined the fleet, an hour afterwards the third, and half an hour afterwards the fourth. The last, having come in at the rate of twenty-one knots, reported the enemy off Winchelsea, steering W. by S. in four lines abreast, the last line consisting mainly of troop-ships, and the whole occupying a vast breadth of sea midway between the French coast at Dieppe and the English at Winchelsea. In half an hour everybody of any rank in either fleet had a glass at his eyes.

It was the head signalman of the *Royal Sovereign* who first sent a thrill through his ship by reporting that he could make out something to eastward ; and five minutes later every glass could detect the enemy, faint and toy-like in the vague haze as mirage, or the other-world hues of soap-bubbles. The fleets were then twenty miles apart, and it was just after four, the day being as bright and hot as ever.

Hardy, the glass at his eyes, said to a signal midshipman, an old *Britannia* shipmate of his own age :

"I want No. 98. Have her signaled alongside at once."

No. 98 was a quite new first-class torpedo-boat, the fastest thing in the British navy, and the first of her build. Only 130 tons in displacement, she yet had a length of 160 feet, and an I.H.P. of 2800. She steamed, or rushed, at the rate of thirty-three knots, and while she was doing it her crew were not comfortable, and the sea in all her neighborhood changed color. Hardy, before he stepped aboard her, took the precaution to drape himself from head to foot in oil-skins.

Away, then, in a few minutes, drove No. 98 at full speed, swaying through a horrible vibratory heave of her flanks, like a charger which has galloped all day, and at nightfall he sprawls with drooped neck at the inn-gate, the sweat recking on his rocking ribs; so drove No. 98, groaning for speed, seeming far too frail for the power that pumped and travailed within her rocking ribs.

Eastward she flew, a mere white specter of hurrying foam; and within this shroud of spray, Hardy, in his oil-skins, lay flat on his face, his left arm round an upright at the extreme bow, a double spy-glass at his eyes. From the masthead amidships floated a large white flag.

As soon as No. 98 was seen to shoot ahead of the fleet, Lord Charles Beresford signalled slow speed, and the fleet proceeded at a mere crawl through the water, this having been previously agreed upon. It was Hardy's idea that the enemy were probably ignorant of our exact forces, and that something might possibly be gained, when the facts of the battle unfolded themselves, by maintaining this ignorance as long as might be. Hence a nearer approach was for the present avoided.

In thirty-five minutes Hardy was on the deck of the allied Admiral-ship, the ship being the *Andrea Doria*, and the Admiral, in virtue of seniority, Admiral Prémesnil, the Grand Duke Alexis being second in command.

He was led, his face half enveloped in the throat-flap of the oilskin, and the water streaming to his feet, into the Admiral's quarters. Prémesnil, a tall man, with gray hair, and a stately courteousness of manner, sat opposite Hardy, supporting a thoughtful brow on thumb and finger.

"May I ask, sir," said Hardy, "are you fairly well acquainted with English?"

"Fairly well, sir," answered Prémesnil; "and that is not a confession, but a boast."

He bowed. Hardy bowed.

"Well, sir," said Hardy, "I come to you to make a proposal of peace. But before I can say anything, I must ask you to slacken your speed, so as not to approach too near to my fleet during our talk. Our fleet is almost stationary. I ask the same of you."

"It shall be done, sir. But first let us understand who we are. I, as you guess, am the Admiral-in-Chief here: Admiral Prémesnil. Who are you?"

"I have the joint-command of the British fleet," said Hardy, "in collaboration with Lord Charles Beresford. My name is John Hardy. I speak for myself and my colleague."

"Might I ask—Hardy of Shoreham fame?"

"Yes, sir."

"Good. Then I shall at once comply with your request as to speed, and order you a glass of wine. You have had a good drenching, I see."

The Admiral touched a button, and gave an order as to speed. But Hardy declined the wine.

He put his brow on his hand, and he began to talk slowly and gravely in his plain, strong Saxon, unfolding to the Admiral why he was there, going into the minutiæ of the Chinese character, prophesying in simple English, but with the conviction and effusion of a Hebrew Seer, the doom of Europe.

He spoke for half an hour without interruption. And when he was finished the Admiral sighed, for he was weary, and was wondering what this all was about, and when it would end. He did not believe a word of the matter.

The thought occurred to him: "Can this be a ruse to keep back the battle till darkness comes on?"

His manner stiffened. He was narrow and technical; he lacked both sight and insight.

"And what are your proposals, sir?" he said.

"I have made them!" said Hardy.

"But not seriously—come now."

Hardy leapt to his feet, flushing.

"Do you reject them, then?"

"In my own name, and in the name of my colleagues, without consulting them, most decidedly—yes."

"Then, sir, we will fight you."

"Since nothing else remains, Mr. Hardy."

"I say you *bon jour*, monsieur."

"Good-day, Mr. Hardy."

They bowed. Hardy passed through the door, his brow very pink, the Admiral following.

Again they bowed as Hardy passed down the ship's side, and never met again.

Back tore No. 98 to her own fleet, Hardy lying at her stern with the glass held steadily to his musing eyes.

To the surprise of the British, the torpedo-boat, instead of returning to the starboard column, made for the extreme port, steering for the *Anson*.

At this time Hardy, stung by the French Admiral, and excited at the near approach of battle, was flushed in face, and about him was something of his natural look of youth. His blood was up. He had come into contact with the realities of the case—the very realities to which his own inner nature was akin. Here he was at home, among native things, which he could manipulate without fail. His nature, as it were, rose and buckled on its sword, feeling its force, not doubting its dowry. He was prepared now for any responsibility. His soul recognized and acknowledged itself, and his eyes were bright. He was a Hero.

As other men discover theories and apply them to facts, so he, on contact with facts, evolved theories. He had formed a plan of the battle.

He ran up to the *Anson's* side with alacrity. And as he was hurriedly met by Beresford, he hurriedly said:

"These people will have nothing to do with peace, my lord. The thing now is to beat them.

"I heartily agree, Mr. Hardy. Am I to understand that, having seen their disposition, you are prepared to take over the sole command?"

"I am willing, my lord."

"Good! And have you come to tell me that?"

"No. I came to save you a journey to my ship, as I was already abroad from mine. What I want is a meeting of all captains and commanders in your wardroom at once. But it must be at once."

Beresford instantly turned, and sent a middy packing with the order; the flags climbed up, and a flotilla of forty-three hurried boats came converging over a wide space of sea.

The Greater Waterloo

They were soon on board, and gathered in the wardroom. Beresford, half-rising from his chair, said: "Mr. Hardy will speak on my behalf and on his own, gentlemen," and sat down again.

Every one of those assembled eyes rested critically upon Hardy as he rose, he in his oil-skins, they all in uniform, prepared to pass judgment upon him as seaman, as general, as man.

Would he not hesitate, or blush, or strut, or stammer? Would he not show himself blatant, or timorous, or crude, or uninitiated?

They none of them felt absolutely sure of him. Only Hardy felt absolutely sure of himself, standing on fact. He rose with the self-assurance and the self-unconsciousness of Cromwell, four-square to his place and his hour.

This is what he said:

"We have not much time for talk, gentlemen, as the enemy must now be approaching us at the rate of eight or ten knots, and I do not want them to come too near before I tell you what I think. Lord Charles Beresford has calculated that they outweigh us by three to one, and that is just about the truth. Now I am not at all sure that you will all absolutely agree with what I am going to say about that; but, personally, I am quite certain of my ground. They are three, I say, and we are one. Well, suppose three men attack me in the street, what would be the best thing, and what would be the worst, which I could do? The best thing I could do would be to set my back against a wall, face them, and try to drive away at them; the worst thing, would be to get in the middle of a triangle formed by them. We agree, of course, as to that; and hence the horror which all military people have of the phrase 'between two fires.' But surely, gentlemen, with a ship it is different! On land you must not be too bold, for then you become rash; but on board a ship, I give it as my opinion that the rasher you are, the better the chance you have! *Why*, let me ask you, ought I to try to get my back against a wall, if three men attack me in the street? There is no other reason than this : that I have only got one face and two hands. If I had three faces, and six hands, the best thing I could do would be to get in the middle of them, and try to finish them all off, before any two could attack me in one quarter. Now a ship has four faces—a bow, a stern, and two sides—and under each of these a gallant number of hands. I believe now, whatever the books on naval tactics may say, that you will be on my side in this matter; for one, of course, must not go by books, where so much is at stake.

"But I do wish to convince you quite fully. Let me point out to you, then, what you know, that the modern battleship, as distinct from the old-time ones, is a far more potent thing as an attacking than as a self-defensive machine. The *Camperdown* rammed the *Victoria* as they were playing about together, and down, with hardly a sigh, went the *Victoria*, like lead. If you were to armor a battleship to resist the attack of a 111-ton gun, that ship would sink without troubling any one to fire the gun off. And what does this prove? It proves that if three ships attack one, the best thing which that one can do is to turn three faces simultaneously to those three ships, and batter away at them with her hundred hands, making sure that, not one, but four ships will have disappeared when the smoke clears. In other words, the one ship must get in the middle of the three. It is a question of time.

"Of course, gentlemen, if a ship could float with only one side, then it would be of great importance for her to avoid getting 'between two fires.' But when one side is broken, both sides sink, and it is of no consequence whether or not the other side is broken too; while it *is* of consequence that that other side should, before it sinks, be sinking an enemy's ship. It is a question of time.

"I hope I make myself clear. I am led to express these thoughts to you, because they have just been passing most vividly through my own head; and they have been doing so in consequence of the sight I have had of the enemy's fleet.

"The arrangement of that fleet you already partly know. The important point is this: that their first and second lines abreast consist of two rows of battleships, the first numbering ten, and the second nine. Now these are arranged in echelon; so that you get a series of nine triangles with their bases toward us, and their apex away from us, as you see in this drawing which I have made, marking the names of ships as far as I could determine, or guess, them."

A paper with a diagram was handed round.

"Now, gentlemen, since we have just nine battleships, we have it in our power to make a dash into these nine triangles, and fire away; but in that case, every second allied battleship in the front line would be attacked by two, instead of one, British ship; and we really have not the material to spare for these luxuries. No: what I propose is that we spread ourselves out, so that six of our battleships shall occupy the whole length of the French line abreast; and in that case, as the diagram shows us, our extreme starboard ship will find herself running into a foreign triangle, base facing; our second ship into a quite distinct foreign triangle, apex facing; our third ship into a third foreign triangle, base facing; and so for the six ships, base facing and apex facing, alternately. Thus our six ships will engage eighteen distinct foreign ships; and the foreigners will have one ship left: and we shall have—three.

"Now that one left ship of the foreigners I wish to have attacked by torpedo-boats No. 47, No. 53, and No. 98 at the same moment, the instant the battle commences. They are to do nothing else till that one ship is in the air.

"Well, with regard to our three battleships left, it is chiefly to tell you what I think should be done with them that I have called this hurried meeting. Gentlemen, it seems to me, really, that a perfectly whole and sound ship, suddenly and unexpectedly entering a battle when it is more than half over, must be not only a tremendous weapon in herself, but must necessarily be the cause of a tremendous demoralization in the minds of her enemies. Hence it is that I grudge the time taken up by every word that I am now speaking. The enemy cannot be quite certain of our numbers—they do not know that we have these three ships. I therefore want these three, at once, to retreat westward under forced draught till they see the smoke of the battle, and then, making a detour, to get behind the enemy's troop-ships, and dash among them from the east. I have very good reasons for knowing that this time, it is not a matter of supreme national importance whether the foreigners land upon English soil or not ; but still, we do not want the people of Britain to be saying that they had a fleet, and it was not good enough to clear the seas of foreigners. The three ships will therefore worry among the troop-ships, sinking all they can—on this clear understanding, that they be not careful to destroy straggling ships, that they waste little time, that they dash as soon as may be into the general battle, and finish the destruction of the enemy.

"The three ships which I tell off for this duty are the *Centurion*, the *Benbow*, and the *Hero*.

"With regard to the method to be adopted by the Six, the three which enter a triangle-base will, after as much fight as possible without lowering speed in the middle, pass through and ram the apex; then if possible, and if need be, reform, return, and fight. The three which enter their triangles by an apex, will ram the apex, enter, and fight.

"One of the greatest horrors of modern sea-battles I believe to be the danger we are all in of doing injury to our own ships. But this time we shall be so spread out, that nothing of that sort is likely to happen—to battleships at least. But to captains and commanders of cruisers and composite vessels I commend that reflection. For they, passing into the second line of the enemy, will have a thicker fight, which, I hope, will be conducted on the same principles as those I have enunciated for battleships.

"That is all I had to say, and now we must look sharp, I think, especially those Three. I wish you success and good-bye. After all, ships are dead things; it is not ships that fight a battle, but men; and every one knows that we have the right men. Nice steering, dash, and plenty of quick thunder: that, I think, is much. We ought to be able to destroy this foreign fleet. I have seen their Admiral-in-Chief, gentlemen, and he certainly did not look to me as if he knew much about ships and fighting."

A low noise of laughter ran round the room. Already the magic of Hardy's plain but dashing and fascinating personality had caught and won his colleagues. It was impossible not to see by the faces around him that he was approved. He possessed the faculty of making men work with enthusiasm for him.

"What about the battle-word?" said a captain, as they turned to troop way.

"Suppose we say *Trafalgar?*" said Hardy.

"*Trafalgar* has been already used three times during the war," said Lord Charles Beresford. "I had decided upon another, Mr. Hardy."

"What, my lord?"

"*Shoreham,*" answered Lord Charles Beresford.

And a murmur of "Hear, hear," as the officers busily shook hands, spread half-way up the stairway; and Jack, a short while afterwards, knowing who now led him, received the signaled word with high enthusiasm.

By the time Hardy reached his own ship in No. 98, the three appointed battleships were off to the west.

It was just three bells, first dog-watch; and the day, as if lingering to see, showed hardly a tendency to darken. The allied fleet was now much more distinctly marked on the horizon. The British had quite a stripped appearance, prepared, to its mast-heads, for battle.

As soon as Hardy reached his deck he ordered ten knots to be signaled. And at once the two masses of power began to approach rapidly, growing up upon each other, marching over the insubstantial deep, to meet.

It is impossible for even the coolest heart to be present at the impending of a contest so august, without a quickened beat, a thump of awe. Even to contemplate the thing from afar is horror. The weak flesh shrinks. The forces that rush to horrid combat are hardly of man—they stride out into the infinite, they reach the supernatural, they become *ghostly*. Commonplace Jack suddenly finds himself face to face with ineffable Hell.

They are ten miles apart—they are eight—they are six. The heart seems jammed in the dry throat, and the hands shake like reeds through which the huntsman's dog has flitted. The anticipation of the thing is, if possible, a greater horror than the reality.

The five ships have pricked their course off, debouching to port, and the three appointed torpedo-boats are rushing like sword-fish still farther to port upon the single doomed ship designated by Hardy. Only the *Royal Sovereign* in the far starboard limb maintains her straight course to eastward. Hardy is in her conning-tower, and his eyes, alight with awe and joy, are everywhere.

Signal after signal goes up from the *Royal Sovereign*. The speeds on both sides intensify. She is five miles from the two ships between which she means to run, and she is the foremost of her own fleet. In two minutes she is four miles; in two more three. How frightful is her Silence. . . . ! If the earth's foot should slip upon its course, and she were perceived to be sailing slowly, yet with ever swifter and madder joy, toward her native sun, just so the wild heart would beat, and the blanched face be pinched. . . .

The ships are no longer mere toys one to the other. They are two miles apart. Hardy waits, grandly patient. They are two thousand yards apart. . . . And then the *Royal Sovereign* talks.

talks—and is answered. It is a single savage bark of Cerberus, the hell-dog, answered by two single savage Cerberus barks—the talk of heavy guns. But before the sounds have passed in pallid flight over the sea, there breaks forth a continued rolling row, like that solemn roar of doom and deep-throated jabber of bubbering and thundering Etna, the mere intolerable tumult of which throws the three crews into a sort of crazy daze. It is the lighter guns which jabber.

John Hardy forgets Yen How and his tortures. He is a youth again. A wild hilarity lights his gallant eyes.

But now he is passing midway between the two ships, and straight before him is the third. Not an instant of that precious period passes unmarked by him. Though his face, like all faces there, is a face of ecstasy, the back of his brain is cool as ice.

"Plenty of quick thunder," he had said—in his robust, Cromwellian way! And as he passed by her, the great *Brennus* reeled and plunged, with a sort of tragic haste, from sight.

But now all the battle, over many a mile of troubled sea, is rolled in smoke; and nimble-treading clouds pass in mysterious haste to and fro across the water. From fifteen miles away to northward there comes a great detonation, and the *Italia* is "in the air." The three torpedo-boats detailed to attack her have been sunk, but the sixth steel-needle waits half a minute swinging between her screws, and bursts, and sends her—flying.

Near by, Lord Charles Beresford on the *Anson* has rammed the *Lepanto* at a triangle-apex, and run on with sinking bows toward the *Amiral Duperré* and the *Oldenburg*; and these two he passes with such a rain of wrath that not a single crew is left alive at their unprotected guns.

Now, if never before, is proved the truth of Hardy's saying, that the modern battleship is a destructive, rather than a self-protective, engine. Even as he gasps the sharp, short order "Ram!" the two masses of white cloud, within which are the *Royal Sovereign* and the *Francisco Morosimi*, coalesce ; they are both tearing along at fifteen knots in nearly opposite directions ; they close—they meet ; and there is nothing on earth to which to liken the shocking jar with which those armored powers crash.

On both ships every living brain spins and faints ; and before any one has recovered consciousness, the *Francisco Morosimi* is wheeling furiously in a hollow basin of sea, whose waters shoot and gurgle in cataracts above her leaning hull.

All along the line of fifteen miles, from the *Italia* "in the air" to the *Francisco Morosimi*, in the deep, the tale of tragedy has accumulated ; and in three minutes the charge is over, and the ships are firing stern-guns.

Only three minutes—and at the end of that time, one British battleship, the *Illustrious*, and four foreign battleships, the *Italia* the *Francisco Morosimi*, the *Lepanto*, and the Admiral-ship, are no longer there ; seven minutes later, and nine more foreign battleships, with three more British, sink, without receiving further injuries. Some of the crews of these last are afloat in boats.

Two of the six British ships in tatters, and six of the enemy in tatters, still float. Hardy slowly opens his eyes, leaps to his feet, looks around, and orders his helm to starboard ; for there is a wide clear space about him. He is told, in reply, that it is impossible to keep steam, as the water is rising in the stokeholds.

This only means that he cannot ram again, not that the fight is quite over for him. The *Royal Sovereign* creeps wearily round ; yonder to the northwest is a still reeking ship, the *Sfax*, hardly moving ; and like a dying lion, intent upon dealing a last rent to his enemy, the *Royal Sovereign*, trailing her wounded stern, drags herself painfully forward upon the *Sfax*.

The ships are alone, and the combat, dreadful because almost stationary, lasts five minutes. Neither is fit for fight, yet neither will strike colors. The rain of shells clash midway in the air, and burst in unison, as if with clapping hands, and grand hurrahs of flame

The Greater Waterloo

and sound. The ships are near ; and suddenly cries Hardy : "Helm hard to port—hands prepare to board !" And as the *Sfax* discharges a last broadside at nothingness, the high bow of the *Royal Sovereign* creeps forward upon her quarter ; there is a small crash and mutual shudder of the meeting ships ; and the next moment, Jack, with Hardy at his head, is swarming, cutlass in hand, with nimble impetuosity, into the enemy's aft upper-deck. The feat is unexpected ; the Frenchmen wince and die ; in a moment the British tar is everywhere, and his touch is rough. A white-faced commodore rushes past Hardy on the main-deck, crying : "We yield ! we yield !"

The stern of the *Sfax* sways and wobbles a little : she feels the suction of the *Royal Sovereign* which has quietly sunk beside her.

Hardy stills the tumult, orders the French flag to be pulled down, and leaps to the conning-tower. He looks abroad with keenly curious eyes over the sea. Around him is a great dull roar, and the air is all of thin smoke. No human brains can now altogether divine, much less direct, the vast drama that is still progressing. Far away, beyond the ken of vision, the battle is raging between meeting cruisers, between torpedoes and contre-torpilleurs, between shot and shell, ram and barbette, in incalculable hurly-burly. But through all this confusion there has run, and runs, a thread of plan, on at least one side. Hardy, as far as he can see, is well content. He waits and waits, with wildly throbbing heart, for the appearance of his three battle-ships.

As for himself, he is a prisoner. The *Sfax* has neither screw, nor rudder, nor boat.

At last they come, hurrying from the eastward, where they have been delayed by sinking the greater part of the enemy's troop-ships—in line abreast. Hardy's signalman has been busy among the French flags, and when they approach within a thousand yards of the *Sfax*, summoned by steam-siren, he signals them to destroy, or capture, first the five dismantled battleships which remain.

And with this order the battle is nearly over: the mere apparition of the fresh ships has all but won it. There is a renewed energy of firing which lasts from four to five minutes. And then a gradual, and finally deathly, silence grows upon the dun air and the callous green sea-surface; and night at last descends.

CHAPTER XXVI

THE YELLOW DANGER

WE, writing the history, have gone into detail, and explained the means employed by Hardy in the winning of this great battle. But the mass of the British public, not looking narrowly into means, looking only at the astonishing result, hailed the victory as a perplexing miracle of genius.

That even one of the British ships should return to harbor was marvelous. But that three should return, having in tow two Italian and one French ship, after destroying the overwhelming remainder of the invading force, this seemed to approach the incredible.

The three ships arrived at Portsmouth at eleven in the night. They were the *Nile*, the *Hero*, and a sloop, the *Pelican*. (The *Benbow*, the third of the ships kept by Hardy in reserve, had been torpedoed at the last moment.) They had on board, besides their own crews, Lord Charles Beresford, Hardy, and a number of boat-loads of British and foreign sailors which they had picked up. The three captured ships—the *Sfax* and two Italian gunboats,—all disabled, were towed to Newhaven and left. The three British, almost intact (the *Hero* had some central-battery guns unshipped), proceeded to Portsmouth.

At midnight there was a sound of jubilee bells in London, in Liverpool, and in every considerable town in Britain. Watch-night processions, which showed no intention of going to bed, filled the streets; and penniless Hodge at the door of the village ale-house heard a rumor, and was glad.

Better times would come now; hard Scarcity and dreary outlook would be no more; the great war was over; and the True Blue had won it.

But the real case was fearfully different. The war just practically ended was a preliminary: it was the first-piece comedietta before the tragedy, and it was put upon the stage by a great actor in order the better to set off his own grandiose strutting and storming. It was the streak of foam which foreruns the tidal-wave.

If ever a man had a day of strain and toil it was John Hardy that day; with every breath his chest wheezed in labor; when he landed at Portsmouth at eleven, his hands hung so heavy that he could hardly stir them. His voice was gone. The sound of thunder still sang in his ears.

Yet, even while preparations were being made for a train to conduct him to London, he wrote, and had sent off, a telegram. It was to the editor of the *Times*. It said:

"Kindly reserve two columns for letter from me for to-morrow. Will let you have manuscript by three A. M.

"JOHN HARDY."

At this message Printing-House Square rubbed its tickled hands, and was prone to dance. The editorial head grew dizzy with big anticipation. For copy at that moment from John Hardy, two columns of it, was copy indeed—and gratis! It seemed too exquisite a thing to be true.

"But what can it be all about?" wondered the editor.

"A thrilling description of the battle!" suggested an inspired sub.

"Hardly that, perhaps," doubted the Chief.

One of the staff waited in Cavendish Square, which, till far into the morning, was filled by an upper-class crowd. A little before three the Times man drove from Hardy's door with the precious copy written in pencil; and not till then did Hardy's head drop asleep on the table where he sat; part of the copy he had scribbled in the train with half-closed eyes.

The letter contained no thrilling description of the battle; though it was thrilling enough, too, and made the *Times* editor rub his eyes in a somewhat unusual way.

Was the letter a stupendous hoax? Or was it a letter the publication of which would lift the *Times* to a greater pitch of glory than was ever dreamed by human editor in this world before.

The *Times* man was questioned narrowly. From whom had he received the letter? From Hardy's old butler himself. There could be no mistake.

It appeared next morning, side by side with the detailed description of the battle. And England rubbed its eyes, too, as the *Times* editor had rubbed his.

Hardy had spoken out clearly, careless, in his belief in the British character, whether he threw the nation into a state of panic or not. He told what was coming; he explained the motive with which the European war had been brought about by Yen How; he told of the massacre, of the action of the Japanese fleet; he showed how there was not even the least possible chance for Europe; how England alone, for a time at least, was sheltered by her sea; and how this was the chance of England to come forward and prove her patriarchal heart, her imperial clemency, her motherhood of the world. He gave his reasons for thinking that the fulfilment of his prophecy was near, impending, about to happen. And he wound up with a series of numbered skeleton recommendations. They were:

1. That the tiny remainder of the British fleet be utilized to seize all the merchant-ships in European ports; and that these ships, together with all the available ships in the British mercantile marine, be employed, with or without the consent of foreign governments or individual owners, in bringing over to England, and in taking to America, and to Africa, such of

the inhabitants of Europe as could and would seek shelter in those countries.

2. That America be invited to a League with Britain, having for its object the salvation of the white races, and the extermination of the yellow.

3. That the armies of Britain be at once recalled from the Continent.

4. That the government at once begin to make all possible provision for the huge increase of population in Britain which would result on the appearance in Europe of the yellow men.

Such were the *Times'* two-columns, and under the last was the name, John Hardy.

Of the sensation which this letter caused it is impossible to give a real idea, for there is nothing else to which to compare it. By noon copies of the paper were being bought and sold for ten guineas.

At this hour thanksgiving hymns were being sung; and the name of Hardy was being made the text of a thousand sermons.

After the battle of Shoreham, he had been instinctively adopted by the race as its "darling"; the battle of the Channel made him definitely its hero; his letter made him its Leader.

He was at once elected a member of the Permanent Committee of National Safety.

Not that there was no searching of heart, no doubting, as to this extraordinary letter. To many people it seemed as wild as possible. The proof which Hardy adduced to show that the Yellow Wave was near (*if* it was coming at all) was his contention that Yen How, having destroyed Europe by the European war, would not be sufficiently silly to wait for Europe to recover herself before his invasion. The argument was sound, if the hypothesis was sound. But where were the signs of his coming? There was an "if."

On the whole, however, the nation had learnt to trust him; and trusting him, it stood aghast at his awful message.

At this time, the people of Britain, if they had never been so before, was genuinely a nation, as distinct from a mob. They had suffered keenly together, resolved and acted nobly together : and they had been welded in the furnace-heat. By a Nation we mean a multifold Man. It was remarkable, about this period, how large an amount of attention was attracted by certain badly-spelled letters written to the papers. Each man felt himself verily part of the whole, and " the government was upon his shoulder." It was no longer a nation of shopkeepers—it was a nation of Councillors. " To be made perfect by suffering " is even more true of communities than of individuals. " Happy," it is said, " is the nation which has no history "—but " nation " in that phrase should be spelled "crowd." It is the Marathons and Trafalgars which knit and nationalize. At all events, Britain, now, with her largely decreased population, was certainly knit and nationalized. She could proceed from thought to action almost with the spontaneity of a single brain and arm. In her hand was the sword—but upon her brow sat Deliberation, and the grave air of the Statesman.

This was all the more, and not the less, reason why Hardy's announcements were followed by the wildest dismay, the most unalloyed panic. For Britain, and every Briton, felt that it was England, in the end, who would have to dam the yellow wave, or sink beneath it ; that it was she, and she alone, who must needs take up the cross of the world, and, like the Christ of the nations, with many an agony and bloody sweat, redeem mankind.

Whatever else was true or false in Hardy's letter, this, it was clear, was true : that, in the event of the yellow wave, Continental Europe was powerless.

When there would be no eye to pity, and no arm to save, it must, then, be the arm of England which should bring salvation. And *was it able* . . . ?

There was the fleet of Japan, the fleet of China. And if even there were not the fleet of Japan, neither was there any longer a British fleet at all capable of opposing the landing, even in open boats, of an endless succession of innumerable armies on various parts of the coast.

These reflections at once occurred to every one. And they had the same effect upon the mind, as if it had been scientifically announced that some fatal change was about to occur in the composition of the atmosphere of the earth.

It was felt, of course, that the yellow conquest could not be an ordinary conquest, if it happened at all. There was no question of conqueror and conquered living together afterwards, and fraternizing, like Norman and Saxon. The yellow conquest meant, naturally, that wherever it passed, the very memory of the white races it encountered would disappear forever.

At this dark thought the heart quailed; and there was Panic.

And at five o'clock of the day of the *Times*' two-columns, the *Pall Mall Gazette* came out with the following:

(From our own correspondent.)

By Anglo-American Cable Co.

NEW YORK.—The *New York Evening Post* publishes to-day the report that a body of Thibetans (?) has seized the Russian railway between Kokand and Krasnovodsk, together with the partially-dismantled fortress at Samarkand, and have finally appeared at the east bank of the Caspian. Their number, probably amounting to ten or fifteen thousand, has not been definitely ascertained. The rumor originates, I understand, from an *Evening Post* correspondent at Astrakhan, and comes *via* Odessa and Paris.

This item of news, meager as it was, was enough for Britain. At once every one jumped at the right conclusion. Here, it was agreed, were "the signs of his coming"—the first!

As when a sudden comet lowers near the earth, terrifying the heart of kings, prophesying Change to the nations, and shaking pestilence from her "horrid lair"—so, with its growing certainty, did the British nation cower at the drear future. Some one rediscovered the telegram about the 500 Chinese at St. Petersburg, and noised it abroad afresh. The bleak and dismal sky lowered darkling.

At twilight the Prime Minister was sitting by John Hardy's bedside, which two physicians had just left.

CHAPTER XXVII

THE THREE GOSPELS

ABOUT the time when the three important personages met at the inn, in the wood near Liège, Dr. Yen How was deep in study from morning to night. On the table before him, all round his feet, overflowing every article of furniture in the apartment, were maps, general maps, local maps, special maps, survey maps. He had a goodly wide brain, and every village in Europe, its position, its name, its population, and every stream, and fort, and railway, and town, was climbing into that brain, one after the other, with the intention of staying there. And when he was finished he knew how God had made Europe, and how man had made it, and what was in it.

He knew also Asia.

While he was still pondering his maps, China was already far on its march. The seizure of the railway-line by "Thibetans" (?), reported in the *Pall Mall Gazette*, had taken place four weeks before the news reached New York. The British army of India, afterwards annihilated in Russia, had passed that way, and left an easy task for the yellow pioneers.

Even before this China had begun to flow westward. Yen How had found her a frozen stream; and like a frozen stream when the sun shines strongly, she had moved at last under her steady heat, slowly, in trickling rivulets, long before the crash of the dripping ice and the billowing broad rush of the torrent.

Having waked China by the methods we have described, how did he effect this irresistible Western tendency, so mighty in its impulse at last, that an arm a million times stronger than Yen How's could not have checked it, had he willed ?

He did it by preaching, with the inspiration of Confucius, only with a far greater success than Confucius, his three Gospels of Greed, of Race, and of Cruelty.

And in doing so, he remembered the density of the skull which he had to inspire with ideas; he was not preaching even to Russian moujiks, but to men still slower of understanding. To plow a fact into their brains he knew that he must plow hard. But he was quite equal to this. With his usual thoroughness he said : " A hundred ways : and of these *one* will not fail." At all events he had chosen the doctrines which the Chinese were most apt to learn, and had, in fact, already been taught by nature. And herein lay his chief wisdom.

Just when the pressure of the new taxation crushed heaviest upon the penurious poor of China, he collected an army of 400,000, composed of men taken from each of the regiments into which all the land of the Mongols was now divided; and this force he hurled into two divisions across the Si-Kiang against Annam, the ancient antagonist of China, and Burma. The horrors perpetrated in these atrocious and totally unexpected raids could not be described; a great massacre resulted, and the army amassed hoards of spoil, gathered from many a Buddist *vihára* and jeweled palace-gate. And immediately on its return, the individuals who composed it were redrafted, laden with booty, to their former districts, to spread through every village in China fairy-tales of gore and gold in foreign lands.

There was not, moreover, a drill-sergeant of the remotest squad of conscripts who did not become a missionary of Yen How, preaching for him the three glad tidings of hell.

Many Chinese did not know that there was any other land than China, nor had, till the Massacre, seen a white man, nor known that there were such things as white men.

Now they heard ; and the astonished ear was charmed.

Could it be that beyond that land of pinched scarcity which they knew, there was *Another,* in which feeble, pretty creatures, resembling real men, lived in rose-beds, and threw to one another balls of gold, and made love on couches of eider-down and ivory? And if not, what was this rumor, these tidings of good, coming strangely from afar, this new talk? And this new holiday of blood, and this new drilling, after four thousand years? And this new Movement, and this new stirring of sap in the old, dead tree-trunk after the long long changeless winter? Surely the seasons return! and *by wondrous miracle* leaves are again on the branches, and all is new! There *is,* then, Spring and joy in the world? and not utter, ugly woe—four thousand years of age? Gold?—and frail, white limbs to be torn apart?—and the blood of luxurious kings to be quaffed by thirsty Chinamen in carved goblets of alabaster?—and cushions of embroidered silk hanging in plenty for all among the lazy, rotting melons on the far-off trees?

Far into the dreamiest wilds of savage China, Mongolia, Thibet, came this message of blessedness, this New Religion of lust. And every citizen became a convert, and every convert a zealot, and every zealot an apostle.

And the more intolerable Yen How made China for them with burden, and drill, and tax, the louder and deeper swelled their cry to be led forthwith into this promised land of plenty afar.

In the Commentaries of Cæsar we read of whole communities packing, as it were, their trunks, leaving their own land, and migrating in a body to some new territory. It was this strange, wandering tendency which now possessed the Mongolian race; but instead of a tribe or community on the march, the stars were to look down and behold a nomad Empire.

This weird and, indeed, awful spectacle destiny had held concealed in her womb; for this, too, was to be one of the acts in the drama of Man; and in the fulness of time it was evolved, and seen.

But no one knew better than Dr. Yen How that the

Mongolian race in its passage across the old world
would meet with obstacle and pain—the weariness of
the march, the day's hunger, the fight in the street,
the rain of shot and shell at Metz, and Königsberg,
and Paris, and Dover ; as for the Japanese section of
the race, he knew that Greed and Cruelty alone were
incentives sufficient to provide a steady impulse to
their native firmness and valor ; but as for the Continental section of it, he decided to hurl them forward
by an added impulse—the excitation of the instinct of
Race.

In China this instinct took always a religious form.
And hence Yen How had skilfully contrived to invest
his Massacre with something of the solemnity of a
Rite. In the cities round the coast, where the white
man had long been known and abominated, the massacre gave an impetus to racial animus, which perhaps
was capable of no further fury ; but, in addition, he
planned for China on the whole a religious mania in
connection with this very race-instinct, which he
counted upon to inspire it in the direction he willed
with the frenzy of the Crusader.

The religion of China consisted in the worship of
the dead ; and this worship took the form also of the
worship of the living, whenever the living happened to
be a reincarnation of the dead. On the belief in reincarnation, Buddhism and Confucianism were at one.

The living were reincarnations of the dead when
they were either proclaimed to be so by the priests, or
when they were proclaimed to be so by the Emperor,
or—when they could work miracles.

Now Yen How could work the most astounding
miracles ; and he was proclaimed by the Emperor, and
he was proclaimed all over China by the priests, to be
the reincarnation of a dead man. And the dead man
of whom he was proclaimed to be the reincarnation was
—Confucius.

To begin with, he was made a Saint.

Then (at about the time when John Hardy joined the
Englishmen at Kiao-chau) began a remarkable triumphant passage through China of this great man and his

enormous Court of dignitaries. In a grand religious festival lasting by Imperial Decree through a month, Yen How was presented and hailed in temple and at praying-mill, from Pekin to Lhassa, as the Heaven-descended Leader of the Only Race, come back, according to old promise, to lead them to the conquest and fruition of the world. His progress was attended with more than Imperial pomp ; he was raised high on a throne of royal splendor, and exhibited to the muttering and kneeling people : the dazzled eye admitted him a god.

If in some mountain-dell of remotest China there dwelt some benighted peasant who had never yet heard the name of Yen How, the ruler, the driller, the oppressor, there was certainly not one now who did not know of Yen How, the Reincarnate, the bringer of glad tidings, the Head of his People.

Confucius was China ; and Yen How was Confucius. He stood for the Race.

Thus did he center in his own Person the whole race-instinct and race-religion of the land. He associated the new creed of lust with the old of superstition ; and of both he was the embodiment and Prophet.

He knew that principles must center in a Person before they can lead nations by the nose, and fire them to heroism and martyrdom. No stirring Mahomedanism without Mahomet, and no strong Christianity without Christ. But in thus making himself the sole guide and motive-power to the whole people, the one center of adoration and trust, he went a step too far ; he committed an error in tactics ; he did not take into account every contingency.

For if the shepherd chance to perish what will become of the sheep ?

CHAPTER XXVIII

THE YELLOW TERROR

THIS was the very question which John Hardy, with his sure eye for the main fact among ten thousand, asked himself—

"If the shepherd chance to perish . . . ?"

At all events, it was the shepherd with which he, personally, had to do. Between him and Yen How was the tug of war; and he knew it.

So, a week after the battle in the Channel as he lay among his pillows, almost as white as they, he called old Bobbie to him, and said:

"Bobbie, do you know anything about British regiments and the dress they wear?"

"Not much, I'm afraid, Master John," answered Bobbie.

"Well, then, you will find out, please, and as soon as possible—to-day. I want to know what regiment it is whose privates wear——" and he frowned in an effort of recollection—"wear a scarlet uniform with white facings, and have somewhere about them a Prince of Wales' plume and a coronet. Yes, that is it. Please find out; and whether they are still in existence, and all about them."

The old servant bowed and went away. In his eyes now was a perpetual wonder and reproach. The color and taste of the world were changed to him; some one had meddled with his heart's delight; Hardy had come back, but the dazed old fellow could not find him.

Hardy was now recovering from an attack of asthma which had brought him near to death. When he opened his eyes to renewed care and thought, he had lost a week. The Chinese were in Europe.

He put out his thin hand and languidly lifted a *Times*, and he saw the words "The Yellow Terror," and his hand fell helplessly; and presently he lifted the paper again, and he glanced at another place, and saw the words—" It is *this scream of the Chinese* which seems to inspire their victims with some indefinable new species of terror, never before . . ."; and his hand fell again.

But already, by the next morning, he could sit up in bed to drink his cordial, and then he began to study the week's events. His vitality was in reality intense and tough, and the thread by which he clung to life a strong one. He set to work to gather facts, and he could work stoutly.

While the pile of papers was about him, old Bobbie hobbled into the chamber.

"This, I think, Master John, is the name of the regiment you want," said the old man, handing a slip of paper.

On the paper was written—

"The Duke of Cambridge's Own (Middlesex Regiment). Regimental Dist.: No. 57—Hounslow."

"Well, Bobbie, and what about them?" asked Hardy.

"The depot of the regiment is Hounslow, Master John; and their late history is this: the first line battalion was in India at the beginning of the year, and the second line battalion was drafted from South Africa to join them a month after the commencement of the war. Both of these, as far as is known, have been destroyed in Russia. The 3d and 4th (militia) battalions have been fighting in North Germany, and seem to be no longer in existence, except for some few now in hospital at Chelsea, sir."

"And have you found out the names of those?"

"No, Master John."

"Then do so at once."

He went on reading. The details had about them a certain indefiniteness, and they were not voluminous;

but he was quickly able to determine that the Chinese avalanche was pouring in four main streams.

The 500 " Chinese" who had come to St. Petersburg " seeming poor," and were to be " sent back to their own country," were not Chinese at all, but Japanese; and before they could be " sent back " they had mysteriously scattered, and disappeared in the general mass of Europeans. They were intended to report to Yen How when the moment had come for him, personally, to move forward toward Europe.

The Jehu of that wild four-horse chariot still sat far back in his seat, the reins taut in his hands. The fourfold van of his army was upon Europe, while its rear was still upon Pekin. It stretched across the world.

Between those two mighty masses of mountains which, like the ramparts of the New Jerusalem, have locked in the Celestial Empire from contact, or knowledge, or suspicion, of the vague world beyond, they came. The Dead-sea lake, after old ages, was amove, aflow. Through that mysterious land, which the race-venom of the Mongol race has made a third unknown Pole in the midst of the earth, crawled the weird procession, the unbounded caravan. The wild elephant and the mild-eyed zebu saw them with wonder, and the summer monsoon went gadding with the marvelous tidings toward the plain, and over the sea to Africa, gossiping that there above, on the high flat land, was a New Thing moving under the sun. The sources of the Me-Kong, the Saluen, and the Irrawady, which only the eye of the couchant tigress and of the yellow man had seen, beheld their week-long passage, and heard the creak of the cart, and the cry of the camel, and the muling of a child at the breast.

They heard also the sudden scream with which the Chinese laughed.

Never was so sloven and pell-mell an army; never so straggling, and lumbering, and clumsy an array; but never a power more eager, and more certain, to reach its goal.

The Friant Division of the French Army, going from Presburg to Austerlitz, once marched forty-five miles a day for two consecutive days. But never a day which did not see this far-spread host sixteen leagues farther toward its aim. They could not be called infantry, though millions, during great part of the way, went on foot; for the armored carts which Yen How had provisioned, the presence of which spread out the host from continent to continent, were the chief means of locomotion, and continually changed their occupants. There was, moreover, no care for life; if a man was ill, if he dropped out of the march like a bird from the flight, he was left to perish, or to return.

The length of all the units of a single army-corps in column of route was so unlike anything with which we are familiar, that the figures are incapable of conveying any idea of its vastness. If the corps could have marched on a single road its length would have been 1200 miles, that is to say, the length of three Englands; and the entire corps would have taken thirteen days to pass a given point.

This inconceivable worm of humanity contained among its two millions of individuals women incapable of walking a thousand yards, children born since the march began, old men, boys and girls of ten.

Each of these pilgrimaging masses of men was in itself a nation, such as those of which Cæsar writes, only probably far vaster. Its members came, nearly all from the same province, spoke the same dialect, had been impelled forward by the same set of influences, had been drilled by the same captains. Only its officers were, in the main, Japanese; and into the rank and file of each corps had also been drafted thirty thousand Japanese, all men.

At the time when the five hundred scattered at St. Petersburg, and Yen How, immediately afterwards, received from them through Vladivostok and Nagasaki the news that all Europe was ready to receive him—there were already of these nomad nations a hundred and forty on the march.

Some of these hosts (particularly those that passed by the depression of the Jungarie Mountains, along the course of the Irtish, where the central plateau of Asia finds its Western gate) had need to traverse tracts of desert country, bare of flocks, bare even of forage for mule and camel. Even by these, however, no widespread difficulty as to food and forage was felt. Whole districts of China had been left bare, as though eaten up by human locusts, by the successive corps which, as it were, bore the country away with them.

Already, on the march, the soldiers of Yen How—men who have lived upon skeleton scarcity from birth, at the rate of some fraction of a penny per week—began to taste the luxury of life. Not merely dried vegetables, rice, salt and tea, he saw squandered around him, but sausages, pressed meats, fresh meats. The administrative convoys and regimental trains, intended for the distribution of supplies to the troops covered many a mile; the administrative convoys being in four echelons, two half-a-day's march in the rear of the regimental trains, and the other two intended to bring up possible additional supplies from the rear. Auxiliary convoys, also in four echelons, and containing many hundred of vehicles, took up deposits of rice, biscuits, and hay, made long before the commencement of operations at cantonments which extended to the farthest bounds of Chinese and Thibetan territory. They also carried supplies of preserved meats and forage, and followed the army-corps at a distance of two days' march.

Each individual of an army-corps, besides, was compelled to carry seven pounds of food in some utensil corresponding to a mess-tin or haversack; this to form a reserve not to be touched, except when every other means of supply should fail.

During the process of mobilization, each division of infantry, and each army-corps headquarters, had already vast collections of requisitioned herds of animals, from dogs to camels, sufficient for four days' meat, but intended by the help of other provisions to last for months. On the march, the cattle marched between the advanced column and the main body of the column.

It was grand with what smoothness the immeasurable machine slid into motion as China began to flow in earnest; there was no confusion; western army-corps marched first, and then the next in order took up the minuet of nomadism, all converging and diverging in rhythmic involution and evolution, like the harmoniously intertwining currents of a stream. In the week, on the day, at the hour that Yen How designed, they moved, they passed away,

Through all that breadth of Thibet between the Himalayas and the Kuen-luns, on a level equal to the height of Mont Blanc, they came pouring and blundering ponderously, fifty army-corps of them, some abreast, separated only by short intervals of twenty or thirty miles, a hundred millions of them,—and behind each man a pigtail wriggling in haste.

Towards what do they press? What vague blessedness? They do not know. They do not ask. When the Pied Piper played his tune, all the rats of all the cities went gaily in haste after him, entranced, they, too, with wriggling tail, and whiskers cocked, and vaguest prospect. Yen How is the Piper of these prone, purblind, forward-shouldering multitudes of nations—he himself a dancer to another piping.

Then, again, along the sources of the Irtish they poured, and, one night, all round the inhospitable steppe-like slopes which surround the lower level of Lake Balkash, there camped another fifty army-corps, some within sight of others, making by far the largest collection of human beings covering a similar area which the stars had yet seen. And the next morning, and during all that day and the next, army-corps after army-corps, they moved, they passed away.

The first (Thibetan) fifty are southern and western tribesmen, used to hard industry, short of stature, their skin a clear yellow, almost of lemon. They are from farthest Taiwan, from Fo-kien to Yun-nan, and from Kwang-tung to Ho-nan; and they pass between the sources of the Yang-tse-kiang and the Mekong, and between the Hwang-ho and the source of the Kia-ling, climbing to the flat roof of the world through colossal forests bordering on everlasting snows, where glaciers and masses of angry water tear and pierce the mountains, forming natural routes through the impassable. By the time they reach the high table-land of many rains and rushing rivers and abounding lakes, they find silent villages and deserted groves of the mulberry. The Thibetans have already passed away. And on through the stripped and empty land they go, shouldering and trundling—a hundred millions—and behind each man wriggles a pigtail in haste.

Then, by the caravan-route which passes from Pekin through the Gobi desert north of the Southern Altais, pass the second (Balkash) fifty. They are Kobdoans, Northwestern Mongolians (so-called), and tribesmen of the Chinese provinces north of the Hwang-ho (except those of Kan-su, Shen-si, and Pechili); men of a duskier yellow, as of weak-tea-and-milk, tall, and nomads already by instinct and habit, not averse to a further house-flitting—in plenty of company! And these pass the sources of the Irtish to Balkash, and thence go swarming down into the lowlands and desert places round the Aral Sea, where Russia had so sweated and striven in vain. Across the Caspian they will follow at the right hour the pioneering (Thibetan) fifty.

Then there are ten corps (the smallest of the four great branches), which, one by one, take the caravan-route passing from Pekin north of the bleak and bare Kuen-luns through all that rich agricultural region— an oasis in a land of barrenness—which is traversed by the Tarim river, beginning at Lob Nor, and ending beyond Kashgar. They are from the teeming provinces of Kan-su and Shen-si—twenty millions—behind each man wriggles a pigtail in haste.

But the fourth main branch—Pechili, Korea, Kirin, Manchuria, Eastern Mongolia—tarry long behind; for these are to travel swiftly, and in luxury—in Western-civilization railway-trains! Not till the last moment before mobilization is the Russian garrison at Vladivostok shelled by Japanese ships, and Vladivostok itself seized from land by Chinese soldiers. From

Vladivostok runs a railway to St. Petersburg; and outside Vladivostok harbor, while the shelling of the forts is proceeding, waits a fleet of merchant-ships crowded with many thousands of large-grade railway-carriages, such as are required by the Russian lines, all manufactured at Nagasaki. And so to Vladivostok come the thirty Western corps, the sixty millions, the fourth great torrent of that disemboguing Nile. And as the crowded trains move out westward from the station, a shocking shrill scream of glee and terror from two thousand throats—the shrill glee and terror of a child in its first swing—fills all the air. It is "the Chinese scream."

But how great a general is that little doctor! This large matter of his, which would have bewildered, and abashed the genius of Cæsar, is all clearly perceived and calculated in his intellect of ice. When he thinks of the world-magnitude of it all, he says "Poh!" To God the world is a grain of dust; to Yen How it is a geographical globe: he metes it with a compass; in a moment he walks about it. With what ease and thoroughness has his first thought—that thought which could have occurred only to genius—been realized! By a few scratches of his pen Europe has been prepared to receive him. "*There will be no more Maxims there,*" he had said to the Marquis Ito with screwed-up eyes; and there *are* no more Maxims there, or none worth mentioning. To lead one's troops "along the line of least resistance"—that being the first maxim of the general, how great a general is this Yen in the first of all creating a line of no resistance at all!

But to guide that restive, rearing four-horse chariot even over the levelest plain,—how iron-strong must be the wrist of its Jehu, and how sublime his gallant callousness.

This was his general plan: to connect himself telegraphically with his armies, and personally to direct their actions even in minute particulars. For the peculiarity of these monstrous hosts was this: that by means of their unimaginable numbers they could, almost without effort, carry out works in a day which no other army could dream of ever accomplishing at all. Thus, the fifty Thibetan corps crossed the Caspian from Krasnovodsk to Baku, with its carts, transports, and stores, on huge towed rafts constructed *within two days* from materials which they carried with them. So, also, wherever the first three great branches passed, they were followed by as many lines of telegraph as there were corps, just as the spider is followed by the thread it spins. And in the center of this web sat Yen How at Pekin.

Such was the general plan. His particular plan was this: that the first line of Europe's defense should be Germany; for with exact foresight he calculated, some months before the battle in the Channel that, in almost any case, Germany would still have left some of her army-corps. Russia he meant to take by surprise; the Balkan Peninsula by surprise; and both, he calculated, would be incapable of serious opposition.

Into Russia he would pour the sixty millions who went screaming along the Vladivostok railway; into the Balkan Peninsula sixteen millions of the first (Thibetan) hundred millions. The remaining eighty-four millions of these were to be German, Swiss, and Austrian. The two other branches, numbering altogether a hundred and twenty millions, were to be divided into thirty French, twenty Italian, ten Norwegian and Swedish; and because Holland and Belgium had not been directly ravaged by the war, and Spain only by the American war, he designed for Spain the large number of thirty millions, and for Holland, Belgium, and Denmark thirty millions.

And at Pekin Yen How might very well have remained, and directed all this with absolute exactness and success, were it not that, at the back of the man's brain, there lay this singular thought: that none of the women of England must be killed!—till he gave the word. And he knew well that no earthly power save his own strong, present, personal grip, could restrain his wild hordes, fresh from the gleeful slaughter of Europe, from washing their hands in the blood of every human female in Britain.

Therefore he took train at Vladivostok.

The difference between him and Hardy was chiefly this: that with the race-instinct and race-hatred and race-ambition of the Chinaman was mixed a personal, private motive, stronger even than the race-motive. Hardy, *like the very greatest*, was concerned only for the world.

It is written in the Book of the Law of the Universe that selfishness shall sooner or later be a source of weakness. Whoever denies this has not gone deep.

The difference between Hardy and Yen How was the difference between Wellington and Napoleon. The latter, being more richly endowed, should have been the stronger—and was not.

At the time when Yen How took train there was no longer any country corresponding to what was meant when one said "Russia."

As soon as the first contingent of the first army-corps passed through the Urals north of Mount Iremel, its first care was to destroy all telegraphic communication between the locality and western centers. Up to this moment not even a suspicion of what was coming had occurred to any one on the Continent, for it was not till the day after the first arrival of Chinese that the two British forces in France and Germany received homeward orders.

On the very day of their arrival, the final battle had been fought in France near Bar-sur-Seine with a French loss of eighteen thousand; and on the same day the Emperor Wilhelm, rashly advancing with his staff and an insignificant reconnoitering party too near the British lines at Landsberg, was surprised by a troop of mounted vedettes, and taken prisoner.

But when, on the next day, Lord Roberts invited General Daubisson to a conference, and Sir Evelyn Wood invited the freely-liberated Kaiser, the announcements by the two British generals of their intention of immediate withdrawal, and of its cause, was received with mere amazed incredulity. The blow of the thunderbolt was stupefying. The Continental leaders did not fall to their knees and beseech the aid of their

British invaders; there are tidings too large to find room in the brain.

But even while the two conferences were proceeding, what was to become known as the "Yellow Terror" was already abroad—and fifty thousand Chinese had settled in fifteen or twenty Ural villages, whose streets were strewn with disembowelled dead.

And almost as fast as the news could spread westward the Chinese spread westward also.

It was the strangest army of occupation. As soon as an army-corps entered upon Russian territory it scattered and vanished; it split up into divisions, and one division went one way and one another; and divisions split up into brigades, and one brigade went one way and one another; and so the subdivision went on, every regiment, every company, having its town or village allotted to it by long-previous design. By the time the first contingents of the second corps had crossed the Volga at Syzran, there were probably not a thousand Russians left alive anywhere between Perm and Astrakhan.

There was no fighting. Those that could fly or hide, fled or hid. The rest heard the "Chinese scream," and died. For every one that died two screams went to Heaven—the scream of the victim and the scream of his slayer.

Then spread "the yellow terror"—at first slowly, then with the wings of the lightning.

In old Saxon times mothers frightened their crying babes with the swiftly-whispered words: "The Danes are coming!" But the panic horror with which Europe in a few days learned to receive the simple announcement: "*The Chinese are coming!*" had no resemblance in its unutterable awesomeness, in its supernatural affright, to any previous terror experienced by men.

The Black Death of the Middle Ages, which nearly altogether emptied Europe, inspired no doubt an equal tragic *suggestion ;* but it probably failed in something of that staring, pallid, dry-throated *panic* characteristic of the Yellow Terror, chiefly on account of the element of the unknown and wholly novel in the Chinese cataclysm,—on account, also, of the *certainty* of his doom which pierced the heart of each European,—and on account, thirdly, of certain hints of unutterable horror which accompanied the rumors of the onward sweep of the yellow wave.

The reign of hell which had followed upon some Japanese victories during the Chino-Japanese war was well known in Europe. If China had fared so at the hand of Japan, how would Europe fare at the hand of China led by Japan . . . ?

Lamentation and a voice in Ramah, and a widening, running shriek, swelling into a cry of such volume and intensity as had never yet risen from earth to Heaven, marked the middle of the month of September in Europe.

Then came to pass, even to the utmost, that vision in the Apocalypse " Woe, woe to the inhabitants of the earth . . . "

Among the millions that rushed westward in plague-stricken panic and frenzied selfishness was the famous duellist Edrapol, who then happened to be at Cracow.

He made straight for Paris; and on arriving at the hotel in the Avenue Wagram where he always stayed, he found awaiting him this letter:—

"SIR,—As I promised you, I am writing to seek you out for the purpose of the little duel to which you challenged me, the European war being now at an end. I confess to you that this duel of yours and mine seems to me a very absurd thing; but still, a bargain is a bargain. I am in a low state of health at present, and quite unable to come to you, even if I knew where you are to be found. But I write instead, so as to be able to say I did not altogether break my word, and am getting the letter to you at considerable personal trouble. I hope you will receive it, and send me, when you can, a reply.

" I am, sir,
" Your servant,
" JOHN HARDY."

CHAPTER XXIX

THE WEAK POINT

DURING the first part of that memorable Week of accountable, yet strange, Night, when the darkened sun and the quaking crust of the earth seemed to the affrighted imagination of men surely to portend the coming of the great and dreadful day of the wrath of God, John Hardy's agents were hot on the trail of the young woman whom he sought.

Three weeks previously, the old butler had brought him a list of the men left in hospital of the Duke of Cambridge's Own regiment, and as Hardy's eye ran down the list, be saw a name which he had heard, which was on the tip of his memory, yet which he had been unable to remember. His eye lit up at the sight of it. It was the name of the soldier John Brabant.

There was nothing miraculous in the fact that Brabant still lived ; yet to Hardy it seemed nothing less than a genuine miracle. Faith in the Divine formed the groundwork and rock-bed of his simple nature: and his eye continually searched for, and assumed, the stealthy, busy Finger.

A day afterwards he was able to leave his bed, and at once he hurried, muffled up, in a close carriage, to the Chelsea Hospital, and the bedside of Brabant.

Brabant, as it happened, was dying from exhaustion as the result of an amputation, and did, in fact, die a few days later. He was, however, able to give the address of the villa at which the girl Seward had been, or was still (for he was not sure), a servant.

To Hardy, the one thing of paramount interest in

the world seemed to be to have this girl, whose initials he bore branded on his breast, secure in his own keeping. He had the instinct to lock her away in some castle of absolute safety, and feed her every hour with his own hands, lest chance or change should befall her.

That, at a time when the earth was travailing in deathbirth, all should depend, one way or the other, upon a London servant girl, was wondrously like the way of Life. Things happen so—not " with vigor and rigor," as Mr. Matthew Arnold very well says, but in that fast-and-loose fashion. When fate is not freakish, she is unlike herself. The unprecedented is the natural, and may be counted upon. Destiny is full of novelties.

That a nerve in this particular girl should set a nerve in Yen How a-tingling, and that Yen How's tingling, spreading out beyond all limit into transcendental rapture, should infect a whole planet with tingling,—this was nothing more than the launching of a battleship by the pressure of an electric button, or the loosening of an avalanche by the rolling of a pebble. In such surprises both Fate and Nature abound.

But Ada Seward was no longer at the Pattison Villa; all the information which could be gathered there was the fact that she had a brother, a bicycle-smith, residing in Church Road, Chelsea, to whom she may have gone after suddenly leaving the Pattisons. But the brother declared that she was not there; and either he could not, or would not, give any further details about Ada to the agents employed by Hardy.

It became clear that about the girl and her movements hung some sort of mystery; that something was being concealed with regard to her.

Hardy commenced to seek her throughout England, advertising in every paper, and setting to work the best detectives.

If she were abroad ? If she were dead ? And if Yen How knew it—had secret means of knowing it ? In that case Hardy had no hope.

He remained in a state of brooding, morbid pensiveness. At night he sat long at table after dinner, drinking much too freely, his right hand on the mouth of the decanter, his left hanging heavy, his head sunk. In this way three weeks passed; and still the girl remained hidden.

Then came the memorable Week of Darkness.

At this time the wild flood of migration from the Continent was in full sweep. England had risen nobly to Hardy's summons to offer herself as the City of Refuge to the ill-fated peoples of Europe, and had opened to them a large and pitying bosom, as a mother folds her terrified child.

The merchant marines of all the still unswamped nations, with the whole available merchant marine of Britain, were engaged in the continual task of deportation.

But like "the pious pelican" which feeds her young with the blood of her own torn breast, England fed the stranger with her life.

The famine grew sore in the land, even though the self-governing colonies, at the first warning of the facts, set stoutly to work to meet the demands upon their feeding powers.

In Britain itself, quite suddenly, there sprang into being the visible germs of a real Socialism. The necessities of the human race no longer admitted of quibbling and compromise with the root facts of life, and the root laws of God. It had been the custom before the war to say, in a phrase so generally accepted that it had passed into an axiom, that England "*could not feed herself.*" The wild fancifulness of this assertion (which might bring a smile to the lips of even a child who seriously thinks of it) may be seen from the arithmetical fact that England (or any ordinary piece of land of similar size) can feed, not only herself, but almost the entire population of the globe—under right and natural conditions of life. For if a man, or a child, unhampered by artificial customs, will set to work with a spade and a hoe upon the ground, it is a fact that a very small piece of fertile land—something like a tenth of an acre—will supply him not only with food to keep him continually munching, but with so much more than he can eat himself, that he shall have enough left over to give in exchange to some one else who has spent his time in making boots and clothes, and wishes to sell these in exchange for the surplus corn and carrots grown by the first man. Now, on the broad bosom of Britain, which is not niggardly, but rich in alimentary bounty, there are 790,000,000 of such pieces of land ; and 790,000,000 is much the larger portion of the population of the earth.

England, therefore, if she be properly governed, can quite surely feed not only herself, but the rest of mankind as well.

This had been the "open secret" of social life, preached through many a century by the singled-eyed great ones—with their simple and discerning wit ! But it needed nothing less than the inexorable compulsion of Destiny to teach it clearly, once and for all, to the whole race.

Meantime, in the absence of regulations, which involve time for their accomplishment, the rich men, and the not-poor men, of Britain came nobly forward with proffered purse to the perishing millions.

American gold, too, streamed into England. Here came the news that the immigrants from Europe were being received with pitying effusions in that land of hospitality. The terms of the league proposed by Hardy were occupying the attention of the two Governments, and nearing completion.

Meanwhile the only possible defensive measure against the Yellow Wave on the part of England was an intense activity at Chiswick, at Jarrow, at Chatham, at Birkenhead, at Sheerness, at Portsmouth, at Paisley, at Glasgow, at Newcastle, at Pembroke, at Sunderland, in every Government, in every private dockyard. Thousands of men were requisitioned from remotely allied trades to aid in the agonized work of building, building, building. But Hardy, for· one, smiled at the idea that Yen How was going to be simple enough to allow Britain time to build ships to beat him.

He, for his part, had set going another activity, equally eager, and more to the point.

By direct suggestion to the First Lord of the Admiralty, he had singled out the men of the Royal Naval Artillery Volunteers as the nucleus of force which must now become the hope of Britain.

Though there was hardly any longer a Royal Naval body of men, there still remained a considerable Royal Naval Reserve, when therefore Hardy designated the Artillery Volunteers, Mr. Goschen, who alone was in the secret of his plans, expressed surprise.

Hardy, however, persisted; and the next day, by proclamation, the members of the force were requisitioned for service. At the same time a large additional number of volunteers sent in their names, to be the commanding officers of the stationary drill-ships.

The members of this force, which had always, since its formation by special Act in 1873, formed one of the most exclusive clubs in the world, consisted only of professional and business men,—doctors, bank-clerks, solicitors, stockbrokers, authors,—who had regularly left the desk, or the consulting-room, or the office, to attend at least twice a month at gun, rifle, pistol, and cutlass drill, until they attained the standard of "efficients,"—men who had cast off the orchided frock-coat, completely sinking their social position, to put on the blue working-dress of the simple blue-jacket on the yearly cruises in the gunboat, or the Saturday-to-Monday cruise in the seamanship-practise schooner. These men, belonging exclusively to the great middle class, represented the very essence of the mood of England. And it was with them that Hardy proposed to set up the first dam to the Yellow Wave.

He wanted 4000 of them; and he got them.

The various drill-ships of the local brigades were assembled at Portsmouth with tenders, and the work of drilling and instruction went forward with unremitting zeal, the 4000 and odd gentlemen who composed this strange force subjecting themselves to the most grinding discipline, sleeping in hammocks, swabbing decks, cooking food, and cleaning guns; opening, above all, their already trained minds to the art of fighting on moving water.

But when they asked one another *why* they were doing all this, there was no forthcoming answer. They certainly were the men, but where were the ships?

Hardy, in his jealousy lest his ships might be used for purposes at all other than those for which he designed them had kept his secret well. They were to him like buried gold to the miser. He gloated over the thought of them, over the loud bad language he would make them talk, when that great hour came.

Meantime, he sat brooding often, sometimes desperately ill, sometimes with his hand resting for hours on the mouth of the decanter, his sunken head crowded with the busy fumes of wine.

And as he sat so one night—it was the Tuesday of the Week of Darkness—something spurred within him, and he sprang to his feet, and took his cap, and went out into the stifling dark air.

His once gentle heart, though embittered and desperate, was not wholly dead. Under this sudden impulse, wine-inspired, he jumped into a cab and drove to Hampstead.

He stopped at the door of Miss Jay. He had now been several weeks in England, yet had not seen her. Why he now went he did not ask himself: some vague motive worked in him to insult, or press, or smite her in the face,—such was the tragic desperation of his empty and callous heart. Love, tenderness, were far from him now; yet in the depths of his nature some ungovernable cry in the dark, some fierce yearning perhaps, spurred him toward the sister of his soul: such subterranean throes occur in the dim places of the hearts of men.

Her carriage drove up to the door as he entered it, and he found her in evening dress in the drawing-room, cutting the leaves of a book. War, and eclipse, and the overthrow of the world, seemed to leave untouched the reposeful tenor of this very modern young lady's life.

Here was the "*morgue britannique*" in its very ultimate demonstration.

"You are well again, then, Mr. Hardy?" she said, giving her hand, "I am so glad!"

"Well or not, I am come to see you, you see."

He threw his cap one way and himself another, and looked gloomily at her.

She, for her part, was shocked—at his aged eyes, his wild aspect, the quite visible gray in his hair. Now, at least, she recognized a grown man, and a master of men.

For minutes of inward reflection there was silence between them. He said:

"I told you I would come again, and come I am."

Her heart bounded. She answered:

"Yes."

"Have you got over all that about Art?" This he asked with a momentary gentle smile.

"No—not got over it"—the irony in her leaping up, and smothering the pity: "not yet. A weakness of that sort clings so to one. In the absence of a sun, one works by lamp-light—which is all that remains."

"Well, I see you are still a mocker. But one cannot always go on mocking."

"No, no. I do not mean, really, to mock at anything. In reality, I am very sorry, and sad, at everything."

"Is that so?"

"Yes."

"Well, I believe that, too. At bottom you are good and kind."

"I hope so."

"That was why I came to see you, now. God only knows why I came. You ought to have married me when I told you."

"Oh, as to *that*——" she said.

"No, no, do not begin that again!" he retorted fretfully. "Can't you guess that I am changed in mood, and everything? All that is not for me any more."

Somehow her heart sank; and the sadness of autumnal winds sighing among dead leaves smote its chords. So wild a pity is in the world, and so bitter a sob.

She said:

"I can see that you are changed, yes; and I divine

that you are far from happy. What has been the matter?"

"Why should I tell *you?*"

"There is no reason in the world, Mr. Hardy."

"You see, that is the way you talk to me!" he said, regarding her fixedly under his eyes: "soon, when I am gone, you will be saying to yourself, 'Well, it was bitter of me not to love and comfort poor John Hardy in his misery.'"

"Gone?" she questioned,—"gone where to?"

"Gone to God"—and in a lower tone—"gone to Hell."

And now she rose, and in haste went to sit beside him. And the pity of ministering angels was in her voice.

"Tell me," she said, "for you have come to me feeling that I am your good friend, and you should tell me."

"Ah, it is nothing," he said, and he flung himself backward on the sofa where he sat.

"It must be very much since it has affected you so. I heard something . . . but did not quite realize it. You should—you should have come before."

"Come for what? I tell you it is no good at all any more!"

"But you are too—too despondent. See—you say you want my love and comfort—there is my hand in yours, my friend. If you do not tell me your trouble, that will mean to me that you do not—really —care for me."

"Ah, I did, though! I did!"

"And do—or you would not come. Can't you see that? You do still. So you must open your heart to your friend."

He looked into her eyes, and they swam in tears. His head lying back on the sofa-back rolled from side to side.

"You are a good, kind girl," he said, "and I knew that long ago. I had a kind of power to guess everything that was in you. Why did you not—but it is useless talking now. Let me go away."

"No, no—do not say that."

"Well, now, I call you wondrously good."

"Of course I am—*of course.* Can't you divine I—*naturally*—do not wish you to go. You look so sad—so worn with suffering. Why is that? How is it? Ah! I am so—I could not tell you. But you—tell *me*, for I beg you, all your trouble."

"Well, well . . . But to what end?"

"Because *I* ask you; and because I feel that it will do you good to tell me."

She ought to have said, "Because it will redeem you, and save you to tell me"; for that was the truth.

And indeed, an impulse did then rise in John Hardy to tell to *her* at least that history which he was hoarding and hugging venomously in his breast, which he had breathed to no living soul, save in one short sentence, to old Bobbie Mason; the history of those long tortures—how the scream of a cat had been rent from his twisting and beastialized soul—how he had cursed the deaf ears of God—how, now, his poor nerves, tingling in a chaos of jangling dissonance, like the wires of some shattered instrument of music, represented all the universe to him as a mere black nightmare crowded with sighing winds and unutterable, dismal shapes of woe—how, above all, his passion for vengeance had settled within him into the cruel and wicked malice of a fiend.

He had the impulse to tell it all out, and save his soul; and he said:

"Well—I will tell you—if your ears can bear it. You know, do you not, that I went to China—but no, no, no! I am not a child, Miss Jay! do let me get away——!"

And suddenly he had snatched his hand, had sprung up, and was gone almost before the cry had leapt her lips.

And she, for a long time, sat staring vacantly at the floor, and did not go out that evening.

During that (Tuesday) night, the Japanese fleet, just arrived in Europe, appeared in twos and threes along the southeast coast. On Wednesday morning, England heard the news that Hastings, Brighton, Worthing, and so on to Bognor, had been reduced to heaps of broken stone, some seven hundred people having been killed. None of the muzzle-loading district coast-defense ironclads had been left afloat.

That was on the Tuesday. On the Wednesday evening Hardy received a small wooden box, bearing the direction: "John Hardy, England." It bore no stamps, and had evidently been brought from its origin "by hand."

On opening it, he found a quantity of paper stuffing; and, this being removed, a dry and shriveled, but still evil-smelling, object, upon which had been stuck a small oblong piece of paper. On the paper were three lines of tiny, neat writing; and the words written were these:

"From Yen How to John Hardy."

"Heart of His Royal Highness Prince Heinrich of Hesse."

Prince Heinrich of Hesse, as Hardy knew, was a young child of eight.

Even while Hardy sat contemplating this object, a private detective was ushered into his presence. He came to say that, at last, by means of a confession of her brother, he had been able to trace the whereabouts of the girl Seward.

CHAPTER XXX

THE CHINESE SCREAM

THE French invasion was twofold, one-quarter of the Italian Chinese crossing into the Gulf of Lyons to Cette by towed floats, and so along the canal from Cette, across the narrow part of France, to where the canal meets the Garonne near La Reole, and thence to the Gironde and the Biscay coast. This horde, with half the French horde proper, making altogether twenty millions, were to be British.

So it happened that, while the French horde proper were pouring through Belgium by Verviers, Liège, Namur, and Charleroi, pressing towards the practically unfortified northern frontier of France between Maubeuge and Rocroy, at Hirson, five million Italian Chinese had already decimated the western sea-board, and had been organized into stores-collecting, and barge, raft, lighter, and tug-collecting and constructing brigades.

All behind these two invading hordes, what resistance there had been was over, with the exception of some half-dozen detached strongholds, whose garrisons were gradually yielding to famine; and everywhere to the east and north of France, again with some exceptions, was the unsparing pigtail. These exceptions were Hungary, Turkey, Lapland, Finland. For in Europe the Mongolian invaders found some twenty-seven millions of Mongolian inhabitants already there, and it was one of the purposes of that great inventor and consummate statesman, Yen How, that these should be left alive to form (the Hungarians especially) the nucleus of a new civilization, which was to be neither like the old Western, nor like the old Eastern, and like nothing in the world save something which *he*, Yen, had quite definitely mapped out in his own wide space of brain.

The western sweep of the Yellow Wave had, in fact, been slightly swelled by some hundreds of thousands of European Turks and Magyars.

Near Charleroi was made what was practically the last battle-field stand of Continental Europe. The Elysée, with rash pride, had issued a manifesto to the people of France, inviting all who could not fly to give in their names as fighters at *bureaux* established in various quarters of various cities. To this call 200,000 French youths and old men responded, an untrained army, of which the last residues of the Reserve of the Territorial Army formed the nucleus, set forth to hurl themselves upon the infinite.

It was computed that each fighting European destroyed, one way and another, thirty yellow men. But could the arm of each, dead-weary of slaughter, have destroyed three hundred, or three thousand, still the effort would have been wasted. Over the carcases of a thousand dead straggled a million living. To shoot the vagabond Atlantic with cannon is a mockery of one's self.

The garrison of Paris remained; but the occupation of the French capital, supposed to be impossible to any other army, was, though bloody in its accomplishment, not extremely difficult to this.

A corps and a half, making nearly twice the number which, in its palmiest days, had inhabited the city of light and joy, sat down along the northern valley of the Seine, their lines occupying a length from the Achères-Poissy railway-line to the Forêt de Bondy, well beyond that outer *ceinture* of fortifications composed of great strongholds such as Cormeilles, Franconville, Cotillons, Montmorency, Domon.

The first care of the besiegers was to isolate the city; and in every direction, during one night, all the lines of railway radiating from the center were blown up along a distance of some score of yards.

The Chinese Scream 315

Then at once, with light siege train, a brigade was thrown forward, and an attack begun upon St. Germain-en-Laye.

Precisely what was the thought of the French general, what his ultimate hope, in making his determined resistance is not known. But a determined resistance he did make. Such had always been the splendid desperation, the tragic pride, of France.

The Chinese, on their part, might very well have drawn lines round the entire outer *ceinture*, and waited there till all the cats and dogs of Paris and its villages had been eaten; but this no longer suited their mood. The yellow man in his senses, is, indeed, afraid of cannon. But the entire race was by this time no longer in its senses; here was a people dancing mad, gorged with gore, flushed with victory, greedy of agonies. Fear they no longer knew. To celebrate forever a jubilee of devils in a scarlet world—to raise ever higher monuments built of human corpses, and shriek and dance around them—to live, to roll, to die in red—this was their sole remaining instinct.

General Saussier, sitting at St. Cloud with his staff, received telephonic message from St. Germain:

"Chinese are being mown down by thousands, but still they come."

And half an hour later by telegraphic click-clack from the mighty seven-battery Fort de Marly:

"Strong assault by Chinese. No. 2 redoubt carried by gangways and scaling-ladders in teeth of guns. Loss of enemy immeasurable."

And an hour later from St. Cyr:

"Chinese now swarming over glacis. Battery in rear carried. Ammunition cannot, I fear——"

No more. So southward and eastward spread the tale of huge carnage, of steady, rapid advance. By nightfall of the first day of siege, St. Germain, Marly, St. Cyr, Versailles, Châtillon, had fallen.

It was on the next morning, at the hour when the sun should have been seen to rise, that men were first startled by a continuance of the darkness of the night. The secret of this phenomenon was, of course, unknown at the time. In England, presently, it was given out by the scientists that some monstrous thing had happened, probably in some region of the South Sea—some unparalleled passion of Nature—which had poured over the earth in inconceivable mass its scoriæ and tufaceous particles and multiform volcanic ashes, darkening the day. That some new properties were present in the atmosphere could not be doubted; for at the same time an intolerable oppression settled upon the chest, and, perhaps by reflex action, down sank the spirits of men; the minds of the children assumed the garb of crape and sackcloth which the Mother had put on; and an awe, and a charnel horror, and a *fear*, such as the heart had never yet known, gripped it now.

In England, it may be presumed, this unutterable pall of gloom lay much less heavily upon the imagination; for here the Chinese and their reign of terror were a mere inconceivable nightmare, not a present fact. But in England, too, the universal nerve felt the strangeness and the thrill of that ghastly obscurity.

It was ghastly because it was not complete. Utter gloom would have been more tolerable. Towards noon, during all the week, the sun was not wholly hidden, but appeared as a garish blotch of leprous lavender, giving nothing that could be called light, making only the darkness visible; while, as if to vie in chromatic hideousness, the moon appeared one night for an hour as a black eye-socket, with a rim of pallid green; and then disappeared.

The sickly gloom of the daytime was just sufficiently relieved to enable near objects to be discerned by the troubled eyes, while distances were lost in unrelieved blackness.

The event at Timor, by which the entire island was destroyed, was of so extraordinary a character that positively the whole planet, with the exception of some parts of America, may be said to have been infected by the catastrophe. Nagasaki disappeared, with many of the inland towns of Japan; a tidal wave inundated a large tract of the Kimberley district of Australia; Vesuvius plumed her cones with a rufous fume of lurider red; and old Ætna, purring and stuttering her thunders, broke into strange and gruff garrulity. Over Europe, from the Mull of Oe to the Urals, there was an almost continuous, just perceptible quaking of the ground, which nowhere broke into violence, nowhere did damage, yet was remarkable for its menacing continuity, its unparalleled universality.

Not a breath stirred the air.

If beneath such a sky and upon such a quaking earth we could really conceive "the Chinese scream," we should then really understand the speedy delirious deaths of the few successful fugitives from Europe during that week of apocalyptic woes.

At Auxonne, in the Place d'Armes, where there stands a statue of Napoleon I., the whole remaining population assembled on the irruption of the yellow man, almost filling the open space, and fell to their knees with clasped hands, waiting. They only knew the nearness of the Chinese (who always, and everywhere ran noiselessly, barefooted, or in soft shoes), when the sudden Chinese scream at the glimpse of the crowded victims burst upon their ears.

One of the terrors of this massacre, and of others, was the uncertainty as to which sort of death any given victim might die; one of the horrors was, that whatever death a Chinaman inflicted, he loudly imitated with his lips, in an instinctive way, the nature of the death. They came pelting in their swinging run, into the *Place* at Auxonne, and as one lifted a club to smite a head, he screamed inarticulately; and as the club fell, he cried "Shrash!" And as another caught a flying child by the heels, he screamed inarticulately; and as he swung the frail skull against the base of the statue, he cried, "Pop!" And as another aimed his pistol at a near man, he screamed inarticulately; and as the pistol went off, he cried "Bam!" And as another seized a woman from behind by her hair, he screamed inarticulately: and as he danced and jumped upon her spouting abdomen, he cried "Wash!"

A very large proportion of the populations of Europe had been absolutely unable to fly: many had not had time, when the Chinese were upon them ; many, with infinite effort, had reached the coast to find no craft there to bear them away. Roughly speaking, about one-half, calling upon the rocks and hills to cover them, remained ; many, as at Auxonne, shut up in fortified towns. For a time the darkness of day and night enabled many to hide about the country ; but it is doubtful if any considerable number could have owed a final escape to this means.

At Epernay, half a regiment having entered the town toward night—though between day and night there was small distinction now—went marauding with flaring torches into every house, searching for victims and finding few. The streets were empty—the inhabitants had vanished. In this surprising famine of blood the baulked hordes poked furiously about, like tigresses robbed of their young. At last, a party ferreting around the entrance of M. Moët's cellars, discovered the subterranean excavation which extends in vast vaults some nine miles through the chalky rock of this region. Hither for the most part the doomed people, in unreflecting panic, had rushed, as into the last hole left on earth to cover them ; and here like rats in a trap they were caught. With thrilling screams the Chinese, at the signal, ran swinging from their scattered search about the town, toward Moët's in the main street. It had been drizzling all the day, and their feet were dabbled to the knees with the soft clay of the neighboring hill of Montigny, of which was made the Epernay earthenware ; so that within an hour the long ramification of the ransacked excavations were a mere filth of dabbled gore and mud. The vaults, moreover, contained several millions of bottles with from four to five thousand pipes of the best champagne ; and here at this depth of forty feet below the streets, in the midst of this gloom relieved by rare lurid flares, there was transacted so red an orgy of massacre, screaming lust, and sighing drunkenness, so mixed a drama of filthy infamy and sabbatic Satanism, as earth, and perhaps hell, never saw. In the manner of crime the yellow man is ingenious ; what w cannot conceive, he can do; so that where we end he begins, his natural talent being for the grotesque and the *macabre*. And when the orgy grew still for very surfeit, when there welled from him the sigh of perfect peace, down dropped his head upon its pillow of flesh, and his snoring breath fanned the hair of the naked dead.

Simultaneously, the other wine-vaults of Epernay were invaded; and, above, too, the streets were strewn with dead and drunken. The town was burned down before the night was over, some thousands of Chinamen perishing in the flames.

As for the Parisian corps and a half, fort after fort of the outer *ceinture* glutted their monstrous batteries with carnage, and yielded. At Meudon two gallant companies of *chasseurs à pied* flung themselves down an escarpment to hurl back an assault with scaling-ladders; they hurled back the assault, and were literally trampled under foot by the swarm of on-coming multitudes. Then it was the turn of Mont Valerien. Bouviers fell, de Buc, Bois d'Arcis. At Satory every siege-gun of the Japanese was uncarriaged, and the fort was only taken by the sheer powerlessness of the great guns any longer to keep range with their mangled rifling. Issy fell. At Châtillon the whole stock of ammunition was exhausted in slaughter. Vanves fell, Ivry fell, Montrouge fell. Nearer and nearer closed in the inevitable crowding circle. The Chinese were at St. Cloud, at Putoux, at Suresnes, and at Sèvres.

Even while the war was raging round southern forts they came screaming through the Porte de St. Cloud, and went swarming into the Bois up the allée de Longchamp, making for the Porte Maillot which gives direct access to the cities. The iron-barred gate was closed, and the foremost, pressed forward by the now disorganized mob behind, fainted and perished in the block. Still onward surged the crowd, trampling itself in frantic, blind rage into a ghastliness of heaped-up death, while the *gendarmerie* which lined the walls sent whistling gusts of lead through the trees upon the ever advancing hosts. Then a stream of Chinese extricated themselves sideways, and with a half-run to the right sought to make through the trees for the fosse, and so for the "*fortification.*" And as they turned, they fell; and others following, turned and fell. And now, the whole current began to tend in the way of those pioneers. Forward they are pressed, and press, and fall; but they fall ever nearer to the fosse; and now they are falling *into* it; and down through the wide, ever-filling ditch they press, treading upon a carpet of dead flesh only; and now there is no more a fosse, but a level floor of bodies; and across this they rush, and attempt to climb, and fall; and the level floor is no more level, but slants upward to the parapet; and along this sure gangway of soft and sinking luxury, this vast snake-nest of intermixing pigtails, they press; they run now they cannot fail: they gain the parapet; they screamed; and Paris is Gomorrah.

The mystery of license to which, during all that week of black horror, the chief of the cities of men was a prey, can only be hinted here. It was well understood that Paris was to be the capital of the new Chinese world; and it was therefore with a certain feeling of old proprietorship that the Chinese entered it. They dealt with the inhabitants as a man, returning from a long journey, makes short work of an accumulation of rats in his chief cellar.

They stormed in a solid body up the wide Avenue de la Grande Armée, and also in two solid bodies, right and left, just within the fortifications. Near l'Etoile, stretching right across the breadth of the avenue, and also across the Boulevard de Berthier, there were barricades of the Garde Municipale, and street-fighting, and massacre, and mounds of trampled yellow corpses. But the flood behind swept onward the flood before with the inevitableness of the ocean-tide. Within a few hours all that length of thoroughfare which the Parisians called the "*boulevards extérieurs*" was occupied; and the inhabitants were driven inward like wild horses within a ring of prairie-fire.

Another host had entered south by the Porte d'Ivry into the 13th arrondissement, another from Montrouge by the Porte d'Orléans into the 14th ; and now, swarming in their millions, they infested the ways and byways of the city, its squares and its bedrooms, its stables and its public buildings, with glad rage, with prying Bacchic stare, with gaping mouth.

Here was the New Pekin.

The bony visage of the yellow man, in moments of unbridled lust and mad excitement, is a brutal spectacle. The countenance is a travesty; the divine image becomes a mask of hellish farce. It is as though a panting skeleton played a comedy. There all is seen —the nakedness of the passions, the bare, rampart hideousness: the face becomes an indecency. What added to the frenzy of these riots was the fact that among the invaders were sweating women, crazy with heat and dust, and the instinct of blood, and the ultimate wantonness of crime.

On the night of the entry, on each of the iron railings in the wide space of the Place de la Concorde glared an impaled head. At the Invalides, in the circular pit where lies the tomb of Napoleon, there lay a compact mass of bodies reaching to the level of the railings ; and on this bed of mortality lay a score of Chinese men and women in exhausted sleep.

Here, too, was subterranean massacre in catacomb and *égout*. On the Quai St. Michel a body of fifty Quartier Latin students stood waiting in proud, pale, silent patience, holding hands, and died smiling.

While the city from La Villette to Boulogne was still one shrieking Sodom, Yen How arrived in Paris. Though eager to be away to the coast, he had come hither to inaugurate a ceremony, which was to be memorable. This was on the Tuesday of the sunless week.

He lost no time. He summoned to him at the Elysée captains and generals of brigades, and commanded them to make ready the people for the long-predetermined Ritual.

To-day he was no more Yen How the General, he was Yen How the Prophet-Priest.

He had with him the Chiam, the hereditary high

priest, counting an Aaronic ancestry of a thousand years; he had with him a gorgeous retinue of bouzis; he had with him the idol of Quanheim, the Chinese Virgin, sitting among cushions in rich robes—the idol of Matsoa, who swam from a far country to China through many seas in one night—the idol of Quonin, Virgin of the North—the idol of Fe, the eagle-headed joss—the idol of Minifo—the idol of many-handed Puffa—many idols; he had with him the books of Confucius, and the books of Tansin; and he draped himself in the robes and solemn gauds of the Arch-Priest, that he might inaugurate and set up in one central Temple of the West the religion of the East.

He chose Nôtre Dame.

And the work of torture, and infamy, and slaughter, now nearly over, ceased; and on that day the people flocked toward the Cité, and the ancient church of Christ.

Never was assembled such a multitude within a city. To lend the last impressiveness to the ceremony, Yen How had ordained that these should be the sole public idols, for the time being, brought over from China. A Chinaman without idols is like an opium-smoker without opium. This gorgeous ritual, therefore, was in itself quite sufficient, once for all, to fix and establish Paris as the center of the new Empire. In the earlier hours of the day messages were everywhere flashed over the Continent, and to China, stating the exact hour of the Inauguration; and at that hour, account having been taken of differences of longitude, by far the greater portion of the yellow race bowed its muttering head, prostrated itself, and turned a jaundiced eye to Heaven.

Yen How, with thick ivory ring on thumb, arrayed in a blaze of color, was borne in open palanquin of gold all along the Rue de Rivoli and by the Pont de l'Arcole through the kneeling throng, preceded by thousands of bouzis, bearing the majestic god Fo, and the huge-bellied, broad-faced Gan.

The line of route was illuminated with the myriad variegation of lanterns, as was also the interior of

Nôtre Dame. While everywhere, from Montmartre to Montrouge, a noise of jangling bells rang through the somber air. At the hour of the sacrifice, steaming human heads were offered to Matsoa, as a variation on the usual boiled heads of the pig.

In the tiny shrines which, on three sides, surround the nave, where pricket-candlesticks and rich, religious *decor* had long represented the rather foppish religiosity of the Parisian "*dévote,*" were set up the statues of grotesque and grinning josses. The Crucified gave place to Fo, and the Immaculate to Quanheim.

The studied pomp of this memorable Hegira was overwhelming in its effect. The prostrate multitudes groaned in inward agonies of veneration; and the God of their veneration was, in reality, Yen How.

When the sacred books were opened and solemnly presented, it was not forgotten that Confucius, who wrote them, was mysteriously *there*, in carnal presence, before their favored eyes.

He, for his part, the little doctor—even in that grandiose hour of his triumph—smiled inwardly, as usual. In all the sun and earth there was hardly heat to melt that ice.

Only where the focussed rays of self touched the secret spot, he warmed, and flowed, and felt.

The pageant of Inauguration was at two. By four the broken Paris-Calais railway was repaired, and Yen How with his retinue set off westward.

Already Paris presented a strange sight, apart from the heaps of dead in the streets, and the bodiless heads and arms with which the screaming Chinese played ball. She looked Chinese. The Mongolian race, like the English, can adapt itself readily.. All the winding length of the Rue du Faubourg St. Honoré was, in two days, bright with gauds and hues. Shops had been appropriated by individuals, who made haste to find pigments to daub the legend in characters which seemed to grin. Lanterns were hung out. The gay city assumed another tone of gaiety: vermilion on her houses, and vermilion in her streets.

The work of blood recommenced.

At battered Marseilles, the Chinese, entering by the Boulevard de la Madeleine, found a deserted city, filled with the roar of the famishing animals at the Zoological Gardens. Their only prey was the very aged, and a number of nuns, medical men, and invalids, collected chiefly at the New Hospital. In their squeeze to get at these a number of Chinese were crushed to death.

At Lyons an incredible *mêlée*, made up of the madmen of the hospital of Antiquaille, of Chinese, and of Sœurs de la Charité, raged for an hour through the vast, straggling building. Beneath the Pont de la Mulatière there occurred a block of corpses which spread gradually upward between the banks of the Saône ; and this, within two days, aided by the stifling heat of the stagnant and sunless air, resulted in a pestilence among the invaders. At once the dying men were seized with the instinct to rush northward toward Paris, the home of the gods ; and it was only the promptness of Yen How, who ordered the clearage of the river, and the instant shooting of every sick Chinaman, which prevented more widespread disaster.

At old Valence, where some failure of commissariat —caused by the deportation southward of provisions, and the voluntary destruction of the vineyards—had occurred, there was scarcity for a day, and food in plenty the next. The low hedge that divides the yellow man from omnivorousness was in Europe found to be very low indeed—where the flesh of men is not yellow, but pink, like the new-born mouse. At the first spur of hunger, the hedge was leapt with an easy bound.

For a day hard scarcity ; the next, flesh in plenty— roast and sodden, bake and stew.

Meanwhile, if there was a man in Europe who had a strong will neither to be eaten when dead, nor tortured alive at slow fires, nor shot with arrows, nor pierced with bullets, nor pulped with the clubs which the Chinese use for pounding rice—that man was the duellist Edrapol.

Thrice had he been caught, and thrice he had escaped.

He reached Dieppe, and for the second time within

two days, he had no sooner reached his point of aim than the irruption came.

He ran at the first breathless news down to the basins; and, with a crowd of hunted men and women, saw the last little boat making her way, thronged with people, out of the mouth of the outer basin.

He had forgotten, in his mad haste, both sword and pistols; and as he saw hope cut off by way of the sea, his first instinct was to rush back, and get what was like life to him—a weapon in his hand.

Even as he ran through the street, along which men and women were rushing in wild-eyed distraction, he heard *the scream*. It had reached Dieppe.

Edrapol stopped, and gazed crazily about. His big soft felt hat was pressed back hard on his head; the long hanging ends of his white mustache shook. It was not a mustache—it was a drapery.

Here was a stern end to an existence of pleasure; here an absence of all punctilio intruding itself upon a life which had made punctilio its bride. The Chinese slew without "seconds," or ceremony; though the aggressors, they chose their own weapons. The trifler's heart sank within him.

Round he leered, standing a moment in the third position, as if to parry the *tierce* thrust—his hat pressed hard back on his head.

The scream came from a side-street; it was very near: his inn was before him; he flew forward.

He reached the deserted house, rushed up the stairs to a room, and dropped to his knees before a portmanteau. From his arsenal of weapons he chose a six-chambered revolver and a dainty rapier. With these in his hand he felt better.

He stood and listened, his beard, his whole body, shaking.

In about a minute the place was filled with noise, shouted gibberish, shrill laugh. Edrapol bolted his door.

But it was soon discovered, and battered in with clubs. About ten Chinese, hot, crazy, bent upon blood, rushed in upon him, screaming.

But this time they reckoned without their host. A man does not acquire a European reputation for nothing.

Edrapol put his legs into the exact pose of elegance suited to the occasion, and with the revolver in his left hand and the rapier in his right, he began to kill scientifically. Every shot entered the middle of a heart or brain, and every stroke failed not to sever the intended artery. The last pigtail dropped upon the writhing corpses of his fellows, and Edrapol leant a little on the handle of his dripping rapier, the model of grace.

It was near sunset then, about two weeks before the dark time.

He crept from the chamber. The house was empty. He found a recess in a wine-cellar, in which he hid till three the next morning.

The house was then full of other Chinese, and the corpses of white women; but the living were as unconscious as the dead, drunk with the orgy of the day. Edrapol passed through them, and made his escape from the town eastwards and southwards.

For a week he lurked in a little empty farmhouse between Dieppe and St. Valéry; and then some Chinese came to the farmhouse; but Edrapol escaped.

For another week he seems to have dodged and lurked about in that neighborhood, near the shore, in the vain hope of somehow getting away in a ship. But no ship came.

He was carrying about with him a piece of cheese which he found at the farmhouse, and this, with occasional autumn hedge-fruit, appeased his hunger. He remembered the bonbons of Moissier with regret.

Unexpectedly, one midnight, walking along the beach, he came upon a broken hut, and near it a small seamy skiff, containing half an oar. He was just able to move her; and after three hours' work, got her to the water's edge.

He put off in her, and as the water oozed in, he baled it with his voluminous hat. When he was not baling, he paddled.

His notion of reaching England in this fashion was

hopeless; but the old duellist, the luxurious *boulevardier*, clung to life with the desperation of a pampered woman. And he fell upon his feet where another would have failed.

On the third morning, he was picked up, half dead, by a small barque, almost in mid-channel. She was the *Conrad*, which had borne Hardy to Nagasaki; she was then, for the first time, on her way to England. So that, late that night, Edrapol's glittering fingers pulled the patriarchal tassels of his mustache on Newhaven's broken wharf. And there he examined the edge of his rusted rapier.

CHAPTER XXXI.

THE MEETING.

As for the girl Seward, Hardy was told by his agent that she occupied a flat in Bloomsbury, a flat rather well furnished, where, with a servant of her own, she lived alone. And, without five minutes' delay, Hardy was in a carriage hurrying to the address given.

He doubted if this could be the girl he wanted. She lived, certainly, under another name. And how came Ada, the nurse-maid, to be flourishing in such a style? Morbidly anxious as he was to have her safe and sure in his own keeping, it hardly occurred to him that this very opulence accounted for the reticences and hesitations of her brother with regard to her.

But in twenty minutes he was sure. On a third floor a servant led him into a smug drawing-room, and there, on the wall, he saw an oval colored photograph: and he recognized the slim bust, and the little Chinese eyes, and the piquant Geisha-girl face, warm-yellow in tint.

At the door, the servant, a narrow-browed, mean-looking creature, had told him that Miss Seward was away; and as he wished to speak further, she had asked him within.

Where, then, was Miss Seward?
She had gone away.
When?
Four hours before.
Where to?
To Dover.
Was that certain?
Quite certain.

The Meeting

But whatever had she gone to Dover for?
That the servant could not say, or would not say.
But was Miss Seward coming back soon?
The servant did not think so. Miss Seward had left her sufficient money to keep her for some time.

Did the servant know much of Miss Seward's private affairs?

She knew something. She and Miss Seward were very good friends indeed. Miss Seward sometimes spoke of things to her. But, of course, she did not know everything.

What did "*everything*" mean?

It meant nothing.

Then Hardy began to woo, to implore; then to speak of big matters; to say that all this was important to more than he could name. But the girl smirked, and did not follow that flight. The last thing that occurred to him was a bribe; only in the final moment of his despair did the thought flash through his mind. He hinted at hazard a hundred pounds, and the promptness of the response surprised him.

It was a large sum for a poor girl.

Yes; and all he wanted to know was *why* Miss Seward had gone to Dover.

She had gone in order to go over to France to the little Chinaman who was in love with her.

And now it was the turn of the servant to be surprised—at the swift energy with which Hardy vanished from her eyesight.

He bore on his breast the initials of this girl, Seward; she was *his*, his very own.

But he was in this dilemma: that things far more momentous on their surface demanded his personal presence where he was. It needed all the acumen of his shrewd eye to determine which was the main fact which must influence his conduct.

He drove to the nearest post-office, and telegraphed to the Manager of the London, Chatham and Dover Railway.

There was at this moment not a hope left to Britain. The Admiralty had chains of steamers, intercommunicating with each other, and with the southeast coast, whose task was to watch and to report. And the nation now knew that on the morrow of this final-looking, sunless Wednesday was due the horror of ultimate overthrow—the going beneath the wave of the last emerging rock of the old world.

Nor had the general mass of the nation the faintest suspicion of any power in the earth which could save, or even momentarily help, it.

If a heavenly host should appear in mid-sky wrapped in flames of vengeance, then, perhaps, that surge might be stemmed. But though the people were now far from doubting the interest of the gods, their reasons were the offspring of too advanced a period of Time to await any such manifestation.

It was known that a wholly inconceivable number of floating things of every kind were massed upon the extreme northwest coast of France; and that in their passage over to England they would have one of the finest war-fleets the world had ever seen to protect them—against nothing!

And now—in this hour of world-tragedy—the British people offered to the "Eyes that regard" a good spectacle. The panic was gone. In such a place as the City of London there was, of course, no business done; but everywhere else there was business done. Shops were open; post-offices were open; the printing-press throbbed. If a man met a man in the street, one pallid lip spoke to the other pallid consciousness of the dark weather, of a business matter, of a family affair —of everything except the Chinese. The subject of the Chinese in these last days was rather looked upon as being in bad taste. The lower classes spoke of them—but, in general, with splendidly curved lip. With a sublime stoicism, with a regal disdain, Britain waited for her overthrow.

Nearly every one made a point of going about his ordinary work.

In the last resort, *the lip* remains. It is the final retort of a noble man, of a grand nation, to destiny. "The mind and spirit remain invincible. . . ."

The Meeting

What could Britain do now? She could smile.

And by this her pallid smile in that hour, she proved, in truth, her divine right to the Empire of the Earth.

Besides smiling, every man, and most boys, managed to provide themselves with some sort of weapon, sharp or blunt, dull or gleaming, which they laid quietly by.

A gentleman in Gray's Inn had for a week been training a fine specimen of the British bull-dog to fly at a Mongolian effigy set up in the gardens.

In reality, the arm of England was as strong as her soul; but she knew the strength of her soul, and did not suspect the strength of her arm.

Her arm was John Hardy.

At least he was the main muscle of it. He was as much the West as Yen How was the East.

But what is this shadow that dogs his steps?—something absurd, grotesque, yet terrible?

At eight he had sent the telegram to the railway company. At nine he drove once more from Cavendish Square, leaving a host of orders with an almost permanent committee of naval men who now attended upon him. And he had no sooner driven away, than a man in wide sombrero was asking at his door if he was at home.

In this man, Edrapol, there was not now, if there had ever been, an atom of venom against Hardy. He was merely the absurd slave of punctilio. In the view of that frivolous old brain, nothing in the world could compare in importance with the importance of an *affaire d'honneur*, a delicate point, a shade of usage. The thing first of all that a gentleman must do—in every case—whatever happened—was to settle "a delicate point."

Also, he knew the greatness of Hardy. And his vanity was prone, the moment he found himself in safety on English soil, to measure swords with him.

He knew, too, that soon the Chinese must be here also, and then ... what could be done? *Voilà une affaire manquée.* Nothing could be more annoying to a gentleman than an *affaire manquée.*

It was clear that whatever he did must be instantaneously done. The morrow would, perhaps, not "do his affair."

He took the broad hat from his long-haired white head, and he bowed largely, as old Bobbie himself informed him that Hardy was from home.

Edrapol asked whither he had gone, and the old man said:

"To Dover, sir."

Edrapol asked no more. He had brought over on his person a good sum in specie; he had also rings on his fingers worth money. He jumped into a cab, and drove in haste away.

With that noble phlegm of which we have spoken, things in England still, at this eleventh hour, ran, for the most part, their usual course. Few people were moving about, yet the trains went empty, and the show of civilization continued when its reality was like a spent heart, about to beat its final throb.

So that Edrapol found a longed-for train about half an hour after Hardy's departure; and both engines, flying simultaneously through Kent, were "express."

As for Hardy, he reached Harbour Station in his rocking train within an hour and twenty minutes from his start.

He hurried to the Cross Wall, and there had no difficulty in learning that the girl had certainly not hired any local craft, nor started from Dover that day. Nor had any craft left Dover eastward for some time.

The natural conclusion was that Ada Seward was still in Dover.

Nevertheless, Hardy spied about the harbor for some time among the steamboats, and pointed out one to a blue-jacket named Brassey, who accompanied him. Brassey was to arrange with her captain; have her fires lit and banked; and Hardy scribbled a note to South Front Barracks, signing his name with the initials P. C. N. S.; it was a request for a small three-pounder and ammunition, which he instructed Brassey to mount for'ard on the designated steamer. He himself hurried to the Royal Ship Hotel, followed by a train of watermen, policemen, and residents, eager to serve him.

The Meeting

Nothing was so certain as that, if the girl were there, in a small place like Dover, he would quickly know it. In a few minutes fifty men were dissecting the town for him, and very soon he had the whole history of her stay in Dover;

She had put up for two hours at the Lord Warden Hotel, and had then left it, taking her portmanteau in a cab. In the small period of her stay she had made herself singularly friendly with one of the chambermaids of the hotel, and confided to her the surprising secret that she was about to set out for Dunkirk. The cabman who took her away was found; and he stated that, having driven for some distance east towards St. Margaret-at-Cliffe, along the high-road, his fare had ordered him to turn down a by-road, leading directly to the shore. His surprise was immense when, about a mile from the Upper Foreland Lighthouse, which was burning all day, she again ordered him to stop and take down her trunk. He did so, laid it on the sands, and was paid. The last he saw as he drove away was the girl sitting on the box, with lonely outlook over the dim sea.

Was there no ship in the offing?

There might have been; he could not say. One could not see many yards over the sea through the dark. He was certain that there was no ship with burning lights

Here, then, was the last link: the chain ending at the girl watching the drear sea from her box on the sand.

It did not, however, need a very vivid imagination to conjecture why she sat there; and in half an hour after hearing the news, Hardy had the North Pier Signal-Light dwindling into nothingness on his port quarter; and the Downs-trotter which bore him was panting and quivering as she had not panted for many a day. He calculated that the girl had, at most, an hour's start of him.

As he passed out between the two piers, Edrapol arrived at Priory Station, and began to make inquiries for Hardy. After a time he heard the truth, but his disappointment was solaced by the information that Hardy would very likely return before morning.

At this time Ada Seward, borne in one of those safe, but rather clumsy, Havre-Antwerp boats, was fifteen miles or so on her way from the English coast.

Some months before this a singular adventure had befallen the girl.

Walking along the street, she had been accosted by a man—a Yankee, as she judged by his goat beard, his lank lounge, and his talk.

He nodded with cool confidence to her, and he said this:

"Well, young woman, I guess you are in luck's way this time, anyhow."

· In ten minutes he had left her, and leaving her, insinuated £50 in Bank of England notes in her hand. This, he explained, was only "to go on with" for a day or so.

He was not the principal, he said, but only an agent —" matter of business "—in which, to tell the God's truth, he did not stand in so badly. But he was not the principal in the deal: the principal she would see on the next evening at the hour and place which he named.

The "principal" was a large, pigtailed, silk-dressed Chinaman—a great man in his country.

All he wanted of Ada Seward was to be permitted to buy her grand houses, and carriages, and footmen, and downs, and luxuries. For this nothing, on his honor, in return, save that she should be under his eye, and obey him as a daughter. The Yankee acted as go-between, and Ada thought she would like all this.

So, away now with Pattison's, and the nursery; and shopping now all day for Ada at Peter Robinson's, the carriage waiting outside.

She changed her name, breaking with her poor, but proud, relations, who, in spite of her protestations, believed that her foot had slipped. Her brother tossed back the gold she offered him into her face.

Then came proposals from the "principal." Ada was wanted in China, where wealth, beyond all dream, awaited her. She refused.

Now first she heard the name of Yen How in the matter, and began to understand. That little doctor at whom she had scoffed. . . .

Then came pressure, threats. But apart from the pressure, and the threats, she understood now that she had sold herself into slavery. She was subjected to a most rigorous, unremitting surveillance, like an upper-class woman in China; and she had at bottom a rather touchy, independent pride of character. Add to this surveillance the pressure, the threats, and to these her uneasy consciousness of her people's displeasure, and what she did may be guessed: she collected all the trinkets about her, which now amounted to many hundreds of pounds' value, and she ran away.

It was then that she set up on her own account in the Bloomsbury flat. Already she was too much of a lady to do without a servant.

She hid herself with such absolute craft, that neither "principal," nor "agent," nor for a long time the agents of Hardy, nor her brother, could find her.

It was on learning this flight that Yen How decided that, whatever happened, none of the women of England must be killed. . . .!

Then, when the end was near, when it was certain that England was doomed, a noble throe leapt into life within this girl. She conceived the quixotic, but subjectively fine, notion of sacrificing herself for her country. On condition that England was spared, she would go to Yen.

And boldly breaking from her seclusion, she presented herself with this proposal before the "agent"; and agent and principal, in a room in Portland Street, where the principal lived now in strictest retirement, gloated over this thing.

And they two, with elaborate cautions and precautions, made two voyages to the French coast, one with the glad message in the girl's own writing, from which they returned with Yen How's "come"; and one to arrange minute preliminaries of the meeting.

And thus it happened that in order to get to France, Ada Seward sat alone on her box on the Foreland sands, and looked across the sea.

She was genuinely confident that she was "saving" something large and not very definite; and, as she stepped into the boat which quickly made its appearance at the surf, the thought in her beating, yet bold, heart was this: What a One am I !

In order to lay his eyes once more upon this girl at the earliest moment, Yen How was ready to fling to the winds, or at least postpone, a world of affairs which no head but his could surely organize. But the momentum of events overpowered him. He could not go.

He himself chose the safest-looking, tidiest, and smartest of the smaller craft of which the Outer Harbour, the Commercial Dock, and the Naval Dock were now one thickly crowded mass.

He had then been at Dunkirk two days, making the Casino des Dunes his headquarters. But when he looked abroad upon that once neatest of cities, and considered the heaped-up horror of its red streets, and the whirling drama of mixed revel and warlike preparations going forward within its walls, he knew that here, at least, his bride could not come.

Standing, however, a little back from the Sea Baths at Rosendaël, two miles away, was a lonely villa, backed by the desolate sand-dunes, and within ear-shot of the continual rumoring of the shore. Here, at eleven in the night, almost alone, restless, perambulating, expecting, was Yen How.

He had rescued himself with a sort of stealth from Dunkirk.

He was like some singer, the darling of the world, who yet is the secret victim of drink; and while the plaudits still ring through the opera-house, *he*, in the inmost recess of the green-rooms, has the tilting bottle at his lips.

By midnight the lights of Dunkirk were well in sight of the steamer which bore Ada Seward. The boat was manned by Japanese, men in whom Yen How had confidence. But she was unarmed.

She was traveling at her utmost speed, and carried only one light—a mast headlight.

This fact made her *outré*, an object of observation; it was sufficient to hint her identity; and behind her, straining every timber to catch her, came frothing a slightly faster boat.

So that when the boat ahead was perhaps not half a mile from her anchorage opposite Rosendaël, the boat behind was five hundred yards only from the boat ahead; and it was then that the former sent a guess-work shot, but a shot aimed by Hardy's own hand, into the stern-works of the other.

The Japanese boat at once shot round, and went steaming in a changed direction, rudderless. Consternation reigned on her decks: over the sea came to Hardy's ship sounds of shouted voices.

The girl, who had been lying on the red-velvet cabin-cushions, rushed on deck. And as she reached it, again she heard the boom of cannon, and screamed.

And all that happened from that moment during ten minutes was a mere horrid whirl to her; there was a scampering of men, and yells, and everywhere a rush of the sea, and a leap into a boat, and a singing in her ears, and a smell like brimstone, and the flash of a bull's-eye in her eyes.

Then she felt firmness beneath her feet, and presently she was crying, half-lying back on cushions.

Hardy, sitting near, eyed her curiously for some minutes of silence. Here was a force greater than a 100-ton gun, great as the moon and the tides; old Astarté sobbing there in a dainty West-end bonnet—the strong sex of Woman.

The presence of the girl, in his power at last filled him with a certain calm. With her, he felt, he might win.

The sobs died gradually lower. And he said:

"You feel better now?"

"Yes—thank you—sir," she answered jerkily.

Up to now she had not recognized him.

"Then I can talk to you. You understand, that it was to get *you* that I sank the other ship?"

"*Me?*" she queried, sitting up at once in wide-awake interest.

"Yes. I knew you were going to Yen How, and I

wanted at all hazards to prevent you. Whatever induced you to act in that unworthy way?"

"Which unworthy way, sir? But stop, are you——"

"Yes—we have met before. But that is not the point. Tell me, why have you been so foolish and wicked, Ada?"

"Oh, come now, this is a little too much, you know!" cried Ada. "Who are you? And what right have you to take me in this way? *I* foolish and wicked? It is absolutely untrue; and I don't think you'd be ungentlemanly enough to treat a poor girl in this way if you knew all."

"Well then, tell me all. And do not cry, because that wastes time."

"Oh, it is all very well to talk in that way, sir!" she answered saucily, though her heart misgave her at the look of the face before her. "Who are you? I am not aware by what right——"

"But you are wasting my time. John Hardy is my name, and I have the right of a man trying to serve his country. Tell me now."

"Oh, John Har——! Well, you will excuse me, won't you? I was not to know that. But was it you, then, all the time, at the music——"

"Yes. Now tell, me."

"Why I was going, you mean? Well, if it comes to that, wasn't I going for the same reason which you say —to serve my country, too?"

"Is that really so?"

"It is, sir."

"And how?"

"Well, since you seem to know about me and Yen How—didn't he give me to understand that, if I came, he would save England from the Chinese? And isn't that why I am going to him? to make him keep his army away from England?"

At this exhibition of inherent confidence in her power over Yen, this radical, unquestioning trust in the might of her sex, a smile flitted through the brain of Hardy. He said:

"Then you are not wicked, after all; but only foolish. As I have you in my hands, and as I am going to take you back to England, I will let you understand why. You are right in believing that Yen How is very much attached to you; that is so; I know it well. I believe that his attachment to you is as extraordinary in its force as the man himself is extraordinary. Well now; but can you be so simple as to think that the way to make use of this infatuation for the good of your country is to come and put yourself in his power in this fashion? Supposing he even tried to keep his armies from going over to England and killing us all, he could not permanently succeed, you know; and supposing he succeeded, you have sense enough to know, have you not, that England would be no good at all with the rest of the world full of yellow men? In that case she had better go under, too, like the rest, don't you think? You would not care to live in such a kennel, nor would I, nor any of us English. So, you see, you are throwing away yourself for nothing. But I, now, have a better card to play, I am thinking! Do you know that I have been searching everywhere for you for weeks? My idea was this: that this vast Chinese people would be no good at all when confronted with the harsh, steady, untiring frown of England and America—provided we could only get their leader well dead. That is the first thing to do. Yen How is the weak point of all that great host; and you, Ada, are the weak point of Yen How. That is why I wanted to have you safe in my hands all this time, so as to be sure that you were there. If you are in England, I have not a doubt that Yen How will come, like a fish to the bait; and if he comes, as sure as fire we'll catch him. But if I let you go over to him in this way to France, you see, don't you, how that would spoil everything?"

"I see, sir," said Ada.

"Well, now, in what we have got to do to-night you can help us: we want to let Yen How know that you are safe in England, and in my hands. He must not have any doubt about that in his mind; and as he is expecting you, I suppose, in the ship I have sunk, he will have a doubt when she does not arrive, unless we enlighten him. He will think, very likely, that you are lost with the crew of the ship; and that suspicion may be enough to keep him out of our hands. So, then, I want you to tell me where, and under what conditions, you were to meet Yen How to-night."

"I can hardly say exactly," she replied; "he is in a house by itself near the shore."

"Is he alone?"

"They told me that there was hardly any one with him."

"There is a single light just ahead of us in shore: is that the place, do you know?"

"It may be, sir; I should think it would be. I cannot say."

Hardy jumped sharply up, and called "Brassey!" in a shout that made him cough.

Brassey at once appeared—a beardless, Cockney-looking man.

"How far are we in?" asked Hardy.

"About a quarter of a mile, sir."

"No lights on board showing?"

"No, sir."

"Pick three men to go with you and me in the boat; ask if they can shoot at all, and give them the pistols; better look to yours and mine. Tell them to stop speed. And find me at once, Brassey, a pair of scissors, if you can."

On a side-table in the cabin were pens, ink, and paper. Hardy sat and wrote a few words; and almost as soon as he had finished Brassey was at his side with a pair of scissors.

Hardy at once hurried across to where Ada Seward sat; he muttered:

"If you do not mind—just one little lock...."

Before she knew, he had clipped a tendril of her light-reddish hair.

He returned now to the table, and enclosed the hair with the scribbled sheet in an envelope, which he directed: "Yen How, Europe."

The Meeting

On the sheet he had written:
"From John Hardy to Yen How.
"Hair of Miss Seward, who is in the safe keeping of John Hardy, at 11A Cavendish Square, London."

A few minutes later, wrapped to his ears in a long black ulster, he was at the tiller of a boat making for the shore.

The sea was calm and only a slow, rolling *bruit* from the breaker-line informed with its murmurous monotone the very drear and dark night.

The air was stagnant as the vapid atmosphere of some dead world. It seemed pervaded by a certain visible gloom.

In ten minutes, Hardy, with a spring, was upon Chinese territory. The three men put off again a little from land; Brassey stationed himself on the wet sand, instructed how to act in case of a preconcerted signal; alone Hardy moved forward.

He had in one hand the letter, and in the other a pistol.

Yonder, shining steadily through the murky dark, was a light, which seemed nearer than it was; half a mile along the east stretch of fine sand lay Rosendaël, but invisible, deserted. The noise of Dunkirk could not be heard, but a blurred hint of luminosity marked its situation. A stone's throw away, on the left, stood a row of five bathing-machines. The upward-tending region of sand-hill and dune behind the villa was lost in gloom.

Yet the near was not invisible. Hardy having passed the broad band of level sand, was able to make his way with tolerable precision among the knolls, and light, uneven ground. Once he collided with a low backless bench, half sunken askew in a scraggy growth of grass; once and again he stumbled into a hole of sand.

The house was very far. It stood on a slightly raised plateau of firmer ground, facing the sea; and the light seen from the sea was in an open window near the ground. The villa was white, and small; its doors and windows Gothic.

He stole stooping to the window, and looked in.

The room, lighted by a lamp, was a species of *salon*. On a chair in a corner burned a Chinese lantern.

From a window on the right side also he saw ooze a radiance from within, and with cautious tread he approached it also. The casement was latticed, and overgrown with chèvrefeuille. But he was able to observe that the room was gaudily decorated, tapestried with green and crimson silk, in the center a spread table, laden with fruit and plate of gold. A multitude of colored lanterns made it a nest of variegated glamours. And here, busy about the table, he saw two richly-dressed Chinese.

He made the tour of the house, and saw no other living thing. All was dead silence and stagnation. He came back to the front window, dropped in the letter directed to Yen How, and turned away.

His way now was downhill, and he walked faster, with less precaution, swinging freely along. He had gone on in this way for perhaps five minutes, when he stopped suddenly short, all eyes and ears. He had heard the distinct sound of footsteps near.

In two or three seconds the muzzle of a pistol was at his forehead, and the muzzle of his pistol was at the forehead of a man.

They peered closely into each other's face.

"Well, you do not fire, and I will not," said the man coolly.

He was not an Englishman—something in his intonation showed that; yet he spoke English.

He had, in fact, recognized Hardy; but Hardy did not recognize him.

"It is agreed?" the man said.

"Well."

"Drop your pistol."

"You drop yours."

"And you promise?"

"Yes."

There was a thud on the ground, and a moment after another.

"Poh! You have lost your chance," said the man.

Then Hardy knew Yen.

Even though it was a totally different Yen from the pompous pigtailed Arch-Priest, the great Apostle, who had been awaiting, with restless wanderings over the dunes, his tarrying bride. It was Yen in simple English clothes, with a hard felt hat over his bald forehead, and without *queue* behind.

The consciousness of failure, of folly, thrilled through Hardy like a pain.

He had, in truth, lost the best possible chance.

"Well," he said after a minute, "and you have lost yours too, Yen How."

"I will get you another time, boy."

"If I do not get you."

"Well, well," said Yen.

They had moved on a few steps—together. There was silence in the darkness. Already in the two men was working the strange law whose operation they were to feel for long hours that night: the law which made it next to impossible to them to tear themselves one from the other.

Yen How hit upon the same half-sunken bench upon which Hardy had stumbled. Hardy put his foot upon it, and leant his elbow on his knee at one end. At the other Yen How sat down. Below them was the undulant spread of weed-patched sand, and the vague noising of the sea.

. . . . . .

Yen How, who was smoking, took the cigar from his lips, and said:

"So you got away, after all?"

Hardy did not answer.

"*How* did you get away?" asked Yen.

"God, I suppose, let me free, that I might strangle you yet, Yen," said Hardy.

"Poh!" said Yen How.

. . . . . .

Minute after minute rolled by in a silence punctuated by the faint puffing sounds of Yen How's lips—a quarter of an hour, twenty minutes. Hardy was looking forth with wrinkled, speculative brow over the sea. Yen How said:

"Did you have anything to do with the capture of the nine ships?"

"Which nine ships?" said Hardy.

"The Japanese war-vessels."

"Go to Hell, and ask me no questions."

"I suppose it was your doing, boy."

"Perhaps."

"What have you done with them, then?"

"I have them."

"Not in Europe—come now."

"How do you know that?"

"I have searched."

"Europe is a good big place, Yen."

"Big, no. A green billiard-table, my son——"

"With pockets."

"So you have got them—in a pocket—really?"

"I may. There is no telling."

"If you had, you would not try to make me think that you had."

"Ah," said Hardy, of the two one fathom the deeper.

. . . . . .

Caught in a sort of fascination, in a feeble, flaccid species of mutual mesmerism, they could not leave each other. Intense hatred and intense love are, of course, inverse forms of the same thing, and their manifestation is the same—an instinct for contact. A stab, a kiss—these are resultant varieties of the instinct. Through a grating a dog and a cat will maintain a mutual watch, lingeringly, for hours, averse to part. Here was something of that sort—a warfare and an attraction between a whale big as an ocean, and an elephant, monstrous, four-headed, big as a continent.

And as all grand intensities are primal, elementary, and resemblant to the passions of childhood, so the talk of these great men was not altogether unlike the wrangle between two bitter, lingering schoolboys, sitting on

a bench, with lumps in their throats—fastened together, unable to part.
There were few words, and a long interval, and few words, and a long interval. So a dark hour passed.

.   .   .   .   .   .

Hardy said :
"What a beast you must be, Yen, to torture a poor boy like that! What a sad beast!"
"Poh! You do not know anything. I had worse in store for you than that, boy."
"What a damned reptile for God to make!"
"Abuse away. Your mind is not really first-class, after all. You are the slave of old, popular surface-ideas. A reptile is no worse than anything else, boy. If he is stronger than other things, he is better than them."
"Ah, well, if that were so, I should be glad, too, Yen. There is not much to choose between us, now, in that way."
"What, you are of the species, too, then?"
"Something of that sort, perhaps—if venom makes the reptile. It is your own fault. You have made me like yourself. By the Lord, I warn you, Yen How . . . !"

.   .   .   .   .   .

"Poh! it is a question of strength, not of venom. You can be as venomous as you like. But what can you do?"
"Nothing perhaps; and perhaps something."
"Suppose you had a fleet to beat me at sea. Do you know how many I am sending over? All at once? You can't dream. Twenty millions. What could you do with them? It would take you a year to shoot them all. But suppose you did; there will be some more hundreds of millions left. You cannot exclude the innumerable. What could you do with them? Be as venomous as you like, my son."
"Ten good men against a hundred million rats—I bet on the men."

"Poh! I bet on the rats."

"On the side of the men—science."

"Science. What sort of science?"

"The science of the gunmaker, of the tactician, of the——"

"Well?"

"Need I say it?"

"Yes, say it."

"Of the—chemist."

And at the word Yen How started as though pricked by a goad. He said nothing.

. . . .

"But, after all, you are a fool, Yen."

"Ah. How so?"

"Well, now, I suppose you are a learned sort of dog. You know science I dare say; you know history, and on what trajectory the world has run so far. But it seems to me—can it be that you have really never caught a glimpse of the one big, fugitive Thing?"

"And you, my son?"

"Yen! sometimes it hits me straight in the eyes in one blinding flash of lightning—a momentary flash, happily, for no staggering eyeball could bear it long."

"Ah! And what is it you see?"

"A tendency in the world—the hell of a current—a secret design, Mr. Chinaman."

"Well, suppose I have seen it too, boy, or guessed it? Why call me a fool?"

"Because this invasion of yours is not in accordance with the tendency so far; and the tendency is jolly strong!"

"You think the tendency is English in feeling; and I say it is Chinese; that's all."

"I'll swear it is not Chinese, Yen How."

"Well, I don't care. Tendency or no tendency. Poh! A tree has a tendency to grow, all the universe is trying to make it grow—but how if *I* come with a saw and cut it down, my son?"

"*If* you cut it down, yes. But if it is older than

that old sea there, and has in it the toughness of eternities, and is as wide as the girth of the earth. . . ."

A murmur of contempt came from Yen How. But his left eye glanced a moment upward at the darkened heaven.

. . . . . .

" But what is it you are doing here, my son ? How if I have you captured now ? "

" You cannot. I have help near. I could more likely capture you."

" I would not be easily captured, you know. But what is it you want here, sir ? "

" I received your present of the child's heart. I came to make you one in return. I have dropped it inside the window of the house yonder."

" Ah, what present ? "

" The present of a lock of hair."

" Ah, yes. *Is she safe ?* "

His voice dropped low, clandestine, wheedling.

" Yes, she is safe."

" On board your ship ? "

" Yes."

" I knew. I heard your cannon. You are a devil for cannon, my son. But I do not look perturbed, I think. A man like Yen How knows how to wait."

" Then wait."

" I am waiting."

" It need not be for long, Yen."

" Poh ! a day or two."

" So soon ? "

" Meanwhile, if you do not want me to strangle you, get off this soil."

" Yes—I must be going."

. . . . .

Another half-hour, and Hardy sprang suddenly upright, a lank dim figure in his ulster. It was not very far from morning, yet no sign of light.

" We shall meet again, then ? " he said.

" To-morrow, perhaps," answered Yen How.

"Or to-day."

"So true. It is morning now. Say to-day, perhaps, then, boy."

"Well, to-day. . . ."

One walked hurriedly away; and the other, sitting there in the dark, smiled above his nose.

As for Hardy, he flung himself upon the cabin-cushions of the steamer as she turned her bows westward, and for four hours slept there, Ada Seward asleep, too, on the opposite side.

CHAPTER XXXII.

"TO-DAY."

SUDDENLY, a breath, a murmur, a thrill, a word of Life, ran like an electric wave through the length and breadth of Britain.

By wondrous marvel there were once more solid war-ships in Portsmouth port—ships friendly, belonging to England, not made for England by English hands, come from nowhere! By wondrous marvel . . . by the might of the Almighty God . . . by His unspeakable favor. . . .

With this miracle was coupled by the people, without knowledge, by mere infallible intuition, the magic name of Hardy. . . .

Early on the Thursday morning the wild rumor spread, incredible, yet believed. And at once the entire nation rushed into undoubting hope, gladly casting off its gloom, smitten with new and strange assurance of its high and world-wide destiny. And all the daily private business of life now, for the first time, utterly ceased, and men stood wondering to wait and watch the throes of Time, agape as though scribbled across the sky in Sanscrit of everlasting red they beheld the signature of God.

As for doubt, with rash fate they flung it quite away. In England—once more—were ships; and in England,—once more—a Captain of ships.

At this thought a thrilling heat swept through the blood of every British being.

And there was a rumor abroad that, besides these

marvelous battleships—nine, it was said, and more—there lay suddenly assembled that Thursday morning in the inner harbor of Portsmouth, a quite unacoountable crowd of *other* ships, Atlantic greyhounds, Norddeutscher and Austrian Lloyds, Royal Naval Reserve Merchant Cruisers, prodigious four-masters, tenders, Scotch and Irish coastguard vessels, unarmored cruising ships, transports, colliers, trawlers, wooden merchantmen of every build, thronging the harbor.

A great unseen ferment and movement, a wide business of preparation, unknown to the general mass of the nation, must have been going forward for many days. But to what end the concentration of all these promiscuous crafts? Clearly, not a fighting end!

At eight, Hardy stepped upon the Dover Cross Wall; and as if to show how with the awful and momentous is mingled the grotesque, and how "something infects the world," there, before him, on the quay, stood a bowing, long-haired figure.

Hardy recognized him at once, and a sound of vexed impatience started from his lips.

Edrapol tendered his shriveled card. Hardy did not take it. He said:

"I know."

Edrapol was all bows. He said:

"I take this liberty, monsieur—sir. I find myself without a friend to make me a small service in this country. . . ."

"Well, now, is it possible?" said Hardy.

"You refer to——?"

"To your frivolity, monsieur."

Edrapol bowed.

"I am here in response to your letter, monsieur. Between gentlemen——"

"I have no *time!* Is it that you still wish to fight with me?"

"The question is explicit, monsieur—sir. Can you ask? Am I not here to make you a favor, since you were unable to present yourself with me? Such terms, between gentlemen——"

"But you know, do you not, that it is not legal to fight in that way in England?"

Such a smile smiled Edrapol!

"Monsieur——!" he said reproachfully.

"Well, come now, I will fight you," said Hardy suddenly.

Out swept Edrapol's arms, and down curled his complying back.

"But not to-day, you understand."

"To-morrow—perhaps—the deluge!"

"I cannot help that, sir You are, I take it, a great man for rules and ceremonies. Well, then, I keep you to your rules. It is not, I presume, a usual thing in your country to fight duels at a moment's notice? Well, then——"

"But, monsieur——"

"No. I have no time. I am going away to sea to-day. If I come back safe, we fight at the first moment, as I promised. Even if you choose to meet me at my landing-place, which will, I think, be Dover, we fight there. You will easily find me; and I will provide you with a second, and everything. If I return at all, I shall be here by to-morrow week—nine days. I think that is not beyond the usual interval which one takes to arrange preliminaries, so you cannot complain. I cannot stay longer. Bon jour, monsieur."

Hardy walked away, while Edrapol shrugged, looking after him. With the girl, Seward, Hardy proceeded to the Ship Hotel.

He at once wrote a letter to old Robert Mason, bidding him come for the girl, recommending her to his strict surveillance, and making certain monetary provisions for her future.

He then despatched four telegrams: one to Portsmouth, announcing his coming; one to the Admiralty; a third to a Dr. Fletcher of Harley Street, in these words: "Send at once the things promised to me on board *Hirosaki*"; the fourth to one Henrik Björnson, a Norwegian, living in Parliament Street, Westminster, in these words: "Hope you will not fail to be with me by noon."

He himself made his way without delay to Brighton, and thence onward by the coast to Portsmouth, arriving there shortly before eleven.

Looking abroad from the Hard, the Cumber, the quays of Portsea, the whole harbor seemed a mere endless tangle of masts and rigging.

By this time the four thousand gentlemen who formed Hardy's army of blue-jackets were distributed among the nine new-arrived ships of war, the rank and file partly furnishing their own former officers, and being partly officered by the remnants of the regular service.

The entire still-living crew of the *Iphigenia*—the "Hundred and Eighty"—were borne in the *Hirosaki*, flagship.

We have not spoken of the doings of this gallant cohort subsequent to their departure from Far Eastern waters.

They had found at Hong-Kong some coal-ships which they loaded, and brought forward in their wake. Again they had stopped at Singapore, and doubling the Cape, steamed by night, near by the African coast, through the Straits of Gibraltar; the garrison on the Rock, at a loss as to their identity, concluding that they must be Italian.

They were well provisioned in proportion to their number, and well coaled; so, passing south of Sardinia, they steered northward to M. Dumas' uninhabited island of Monte Christo (which is some twenty-five miles distant from the nearest land), prepared for a lengthy stay, there being two or three coves and bays affording very good anchorage.

The steam-pinnace of the *Iphigenia* carried a small quickfiring gun mounted on a pedestal for'ard; and Hardy, on leaving his men, gave instruction that any craft which might come near enough to sight the fleet should be chased by the pinnace, and, if not captured, sunk. As a matter of fact, only three small Corsican crafts were captured, and their crews retained at the island.

Hardy himself left them in the *Conrad*, and at Ile

d'Elbe contrived to make terms with the *padrone* of the Maltese *speronare* in which he reached England.

The *Conrad* he left behind, in order to serve as a despatch boat.

Here, then, during some weeks, remained the Hundred and Eighty under the lazy Italian sky, shooting goats, and looking to their ships and guns. The Japanese whom they had with them they retained till the end of their stay.

At last, with glad hurrahs, they saw the ship, flying the agreed flags, which came to recall them; and on the fifth morning were at Portsmouth.

If it was true, as Hardy maintained, that it was men and not ships which fought a battle, the ships being only the tools of the men, then the *Hirosaki* was now a great fighter. She was gallantly manned.

In addition to this, she was a wonderful tool: the largest effective-tonnaged ship that had ever been launched anywhere; the latest and most exquisite product of the Thames Ironworks and Shipbuilding Company.

But with the fleet which we may call British collected at Portsmouth the resources of Europe were not wholly exhausted. Among them, arrived during the night, were four ram-cruisers, a large corvette, two ram-monitors, and five torpedo gun-vessels from the Netherlands, the remainder of Holland's armament having been caught by the Japanese, or being with her East Indian Navy; there were also three small Norwegian torpedo-vessels; also, the first question asked by Hardy at Portsmouth was this: "No sign yet of the Spaniards?" There was none: the reason being that, as the entire home-navy of Spain left her by America lay at anchor in Lisbon harbor, together with some Portuguese, they had been attacked by a Japanese cruiser-squadron. Not one escaped without damage.

So rapid had been the course of events, that no ships from across the Atlantic had yet arrived. It was not until half-past eleven, that a great cheer was heard raving vaguely on the ships assembled in the port: and at once it spread up the harbor, re-echoing with universal acclamation. Three fast cruisers, flying the stars-and-stripes, had arrived. They brought the news that the whole American Navy was on the way—but at a distance behind which made it certain that they would be late for the battle. However, as the Portsmouth force passed down Spithead, they were joined by a force of nine Spanish sail, mostly very small, consisting of torpedo gun-vessels, all unarmored.

Thus in this new Armada, the Spaniard and the Englishman, and the American, in strange neighborhood, fought side by side.

There could be no doubt as to the day, or even the hour, of the final forward step of the yellow races. Already, at two of the previous night, it was known in London that incalculable masses of men had put off from Dunkirk, Calais, Boulogne, St. Valéry, Tréport, Dieppe, all along that coast, borne mostly in flats with single paddlewheel astern, in French-barge fashion—the most elementary form of steam motion—requiring from eighteen to twenty hours to attain the nearest point of the English coast.

The front of this floating host must, therefore, be upon British soil at some almost calculable moment during the afternoon.

They were, as a matter of fact, retarded by an event which, though normal, came upon every one with the effect of a surprise: the air, which for six days had seemed settled in a thick stagnation, at about ten in the morning—moved. A sensible breeze sprang up from the N. W., driving the sea-surface in sharply-lined ovals before it.

And at once there was a slight lightening of the murk of the atmosphere.

Near noon a brief meeting of captains took place at Government House. Hardy had little to point out, except that the battle upon which they were about to enter was with men of different, less nice, *morale* than ordinary European sailors—clever apes—islanders, yet real foreigners on board a western ship-of-war. He tossed his hand, and added : " It is true they are flushed with a consciousness of power, gentlemen, and are greatly superior in metal and numbers. But that will not weigh too much with you."

He also said that when definite orders went abroad on the impending of the contest, it was his will that his purposes should be explained by captains and commanders to every person in the fighting fleet.

He also said that they would be wasting their energies in this battle, unless one man, whom he had reasons to think would be there, were killed or captured; and he himself undertook to discover, without fail, in which ship that man was borne.

Immediately a move was made by captains towards their ships in the port, and a few minutes after twelve the signal "weigh" went up.

At the same time a great bustle of preparation was taking place within the harbor itself. Dark smoke left particles of soot on flapping sail. A host of boats flitted to and fro. Never did Gosport, Portsea, Portsmouth, Southsea, and the forts around them, and the still harbor between them, hear so widespread a rumor of rattling chains and hurrying feet, and shouted God-speeds, and ordering voices.

Cumberland and Southsea Castle Forts hooted a volley of blessings and farewells as the war-ship fleet slipped down the flood-tide. A few minutes later the nine Spaniards hove in sight.

The fleet was also augmented by the *Hero*, the *Nile*, the *Sfax*, the two gunboats taken in the battle of the Channel, patched up now, and three French composite gun-vessels captured during a Mediterranean battle.

They made up a respectable fighting-power: the nine captured ships being considerably the most powerful of the Japanese navy, and the *Hirosaki* the most powerful of ships.

Yet it was only the audacity of Hardy that would, with any hope, have led this force against, we will not say the weight, but the numbers, opposed to him; and the havoc which overtook his comparatively little fleet in the battle that followed would certainly, had his judgment been absolutely cool, have been foreknown to him—or perhaps was foreknown.

Since the year 1892 Japan had placed orders with firms all over the world for a hundred and seventeen new ships, making an aggregate of some hundred and fifteen thousand tons, half to be completed by 1902, and half by 1906. At the period of this new program, she already possessed a very respectable navy, and at the time of the outbreak of the European war, more than one quarter of the new ships were already in her hands.

Hardy therefore opposed a fleet of forty-three ships all told (only eleven being ships of a high class) to a fleet of one hundred and thirty-nine sail, including the Chinese vessels, mostly of extreme modernity, and high fighting power.

His main dependence at this time seems, as he said, to have been upon the comparative *morale* of the two crews. He commanded a fleet manned, except for the Continentals, wholly by British gentlemen and American marksmen; the enemy were imitators, acquainted with tactics recommended in books, incapable, he conceived, of originating, incapable of combating originality. He guessed, too, that small as was his force, he happened to have a superiority in one weapon—not in general a very reliable one—the torpedo.

Perhaps trusting to one or both of these things, he contrived to give the impression (though it is questionable if he was as sincere as usual) that, on starting from port, he was without suspicion that he might now fail to account for Asia as he had accounted for Europe.

The breeze freshened, but the air, though lightened, continued murky; there was some difficulty in deciphering signals; and to facilitate messages by trumpet-call, the ships moved onward in close formation, the Dutch to the extreme starboard, the Spaniards and Americans to port.

Ten miles astern spread far the great mass of merchant craft.

Alone sat Hardy in the *Hirosaki* conning-tower, her flag-captain and staff standing on the bridge. The conning-tower stood on the after-part of the forecastle-deck, very strongly armored, and communicating by a host of knobs, and an armored tube, right down to the armored deck, and every part of the ship.

In that hour, so great a travail came upon this poor, troubled soul, that he could hardly bear to live. Here was the Gethsemane of the young man. All the Care of earth burthened upon him : all the floods and the waters of Destiny passed over him. He groaned ; the forehead that rested upon his hand sweated great drops. A year ago he had thought himself a simple Hampshire sailor-lad—and see, now, with the cracking thews of Atlas he must uphold the world ! " Oh, if it be possible—if it be possible—" This old cry of passionate agony rived through all his being. That he alone should bear the whole, he—one frail back ; that *he* should be the ordained to shriek in solitary travail with the birth-pangs of the new Future that was to be, and be rent to shreds and atoms by the eruption of his monstrous offspring, this was piteous. To be a Saviour, it seems, is no light matter : the Redeemer from Hell must himself traverse the flames. At all events, the brain upon which what we call civilization now depended was near to frenzy. That his toiling back could bear the horrid mass at all proved the dazzling splendor of the boy—but he writhed. The weight was strong : his sinews creaked. Also, in that hour of his gloom, his shattered nerves represented to him the world which he upheld as a world black, draped in crape. " Oh, if it be only possible . . ." again and again, in groan on groan, he uttered his agony of spirit, longing only to die, to die. And even as he longed, he sprang up briskly, and he rang :

" Twelve knots ! "

A little S.W. of Beachy Head the fleet was joined by the fast private yacht of a gentleman who was acting as scout. He went on board the *Hirosaki*, and was conducted before Hardy.

The Japanese fleet, he said, were on the way between the Somme-mouth and the Sussex coast, but very much spread out, not apparently expecting serious opposition, and steaming at the rate of perhaps four or five knots. A vast breadth of channel was parterred for league on league with masses of barge-like craft, which, if one might conjecture, were concentrating toward the narrow part of the Strait. Their progress was very slow; but some were by now certainly not more than nine or ten miles from the Kent coast. The gentleman had passed so near to one mass as to see through his glass a distribution of some sort of green pottage in one barge, and what looked like a fight between two Chinamen in another. He had not been fired at. The boats were incredibly overcrowded. He had heard, he said with a smile, that about 70,000 men were massed upon Hastings, and that forty Maxims were in position on the sea-front.

Shortly before four a scout of the enemy directed from beyond effective range the rays of two search-lights upon the British, and at once hasted back to eastward.

By half-past, the British made out a great bank of cloud to eastward. The breeze had now freshened to a moderately stiff gale from the northwest. For the first time for a week, hurrying dark clouds above were visible athwart a gloom of twilight. The sea was curling into fore-running hollows before the British stems, like backing pages, who, with bows and graces, usher in the visitor.

John Hardy's brain, and heart, and life, was in his eyes. He glared through his glass like a famished wolf.

The bank of smoke quickly cleared; he could discern forms of ships—eight miles from him, a line abreast—and moving, it was clear, rapidly. Legion was their name. His eyes started and stared; he muttered with his lips.

He gazed for two minutes, crazily, hundred-eyed; then he started, and hissed a swift "By God!" Then he flew to the communications.

To be signalled to the fleet:

"Keep speed and formation. Use no torpedoes in combat."

To his own engine-room:

"*Full speed ahead!*"

The engines of the *Hirosaki* instantly quickened

their throb and complex turmoil. She forged forward. Her best speed was nearly nineteen knots. She was like an ugly, stout island in a hurry.

The wondering question went pervading his fleet—was he about to fight the entire navy of Japan *alone?* Was he not rushing like the demented whom the gods destroy into the very mouth of hell?

The *Hirosaki*, we have said, was undoubtedly the best engine of war that was ever devised and built. She was armored with Harveyed nickel steel, and her belt, which extended from stem to stern, was over eight feet in depth, and nine inches thick throughout engine, boiler, and magazine spaces. Now, above this belt, her side to the height of the main-deck was covered with 6-inch armor for a length of some 250 feet, enclosing two barbettes; while at each end of the belt there was a curved bulkhead fourteen inches thick between the armored and main decks; so that a quite complete citadel, 250 feet long, was formed.

Her gun-casemates, moreover, were shielded both on the inner and outer sides, so that their crews worked under protection almost ideal; while her barbettes, circular in plan, were protected with 14-inch armor, rising to a height of 4 feet above the upper-deck.

With such a tool of war something might be dared. Nearer she went, plowing in impressive, squat haste straight towards the middle of the interminable Japanese line; and while the rest of the British fleet were still beyond effective range, a sudden rain fell from the military-tops of two cruisers upon her decks.

The *Hirosaki* did not answer.

With ripped decks and annihilated boats, on she went, straining her engines, every egress from the stoke-holds closed by the devoted men who toiled like salamanders in her depths.

Within two minutes from the opening of fire, a shell from the 32-cm. gun of the *Akitsuschima* (one of the two ships at the point where Hardy aimed to break the enemy's line) had burst through the shield of the fore-barbette, killed or wounded all its crew, and disabled the turn-table.

And now a horror of wonder and consternation spread among the crew of the *Hirosaki*—at her strange silence —at her frenzied adventure.

Where was Hardy ? Was he stricken dumb ? Was he dead ? Was he dancing mad ?

An ashen-faced London barrister in one of the port casemates of the 6-inch quick-firers on the main-deck gasped in a dry-throated whisper:

"He is dead !"

And Brassey of Kiao-Chau, ashen-faced also, gasped in answer:

"Bah ! what are you talking about ?"

The engines roared, the sea whitened, the *Hirosaki* walked grandly down an arcade of flame and smoke.

She had passed through the first line of the enemy between two cruisers, the *Akitsuschima* and the *Hasidate*, which she could have sunk by a mere snarl of her broadsides. Yet she did not speak.

Before her came two more, the *Ten-rio*, and the *Takao;* and the two before and the two behind concentrated upon her their fires.

Every one looked to see her sink ; certainly, it was only a question of moments—of how many moments the fire continued from such close quarters. The outward appearance of the ship, by the time she reached the second Japanese line abreast, was one of mere ruin and havoc.

The enemy were as astounded at her conduct as her crew. But in a few instants they knew—they thought that they knew.

Twenty or twenty-two cables behind the second Japanese line came a ship of considerable size, alone— that is to say, protected by the whole præposited mass of her navy. Yet she was a ship-of-war.

As soon as the *Hirosaki* emerged from the world of coppery gloom into which she had passed, as it were, a living thing, to come forth, but for her central citadel and propelling mechanism, a dead—she turned her bows upon this ship.

The ship was the *Yoshino ;* though powerfully armed, she was one of the ships called "unarmored" ; smoking over a map in her cabin sat Yen How.

Hardy had reached him! One well-directed shell, one happy torpedo, and, beyond doubt, the yellow host will be leaderless. . . .

And now, at last, the *Hirosaki* talks; but she talks in such a sorry, effete, and slip-shod manner, that a whole crowd of Japanese captains who are already hastening to the rescue of that one precious ship, laugh in their conning-towers. Was there ever such miserable aiming? such false sight? Not one of the shots takes effect. The *Yoshino* keeps on her way untouched. The rash *Hirosaki* has run that appalling blockade of flame in vain. And to complete her ignominy, immediately upon her first feeble effort, she turns tail, and goes blundering in defeated flight to the S.E.

She was evidently the flag-ship of the British, and the fact that she had reserved her fire in her passage through the fleet, and had then singled out, and fired upon, the *Yoshino*, proved to the Japanese that the British knew in which ship Yen How was borne, and that their one and only object in fighting now was the destruction of Yen How.

The one and only object of the Japanese must therefore be the protection of that one ship, the *Yoshino*.

It was in order that they might arrive at this very conclusion, that Hardy had made his awful passage through their fleet, had abstained from firing,—and had fired upon the *Yoshino*.

It was his design that the enemy should be, above all things, anxious to protect her. And he used the *Hirosaki* for the adventure, because he knew well that no other ship at his disposal could have continued on her way forty seconds through that flaming avenue.

But the on-lookers slandered the *Hirosaki's* crew in supposing them such very sorry gunners. The same mind which had bid them fire had bid them miss. The *Yoshino* was needed.

"The *morale* of the fighters!" With the most astounding precision Hardy seems to have divined it. How much of his mind the enemy would guess, and exactly where their guessing power would cease, he appears by some divine instinct to have known infallibly. A European crew, knowing the fame of Hardy, and observing his present fatuity, might have surmised some design, all the more appallingly rough and rude in its results, in proportion to its consummate depth. The Japanese simply read the surface of his mind, and were proud of their reading.

They concluded that his main design was to destroy the person of Yen How—and it was—they were right. But his thoughts were as much beyond their thoughts as the heavens are beyond the earth.

He goes careering to the S.E., and three very swift cruisers that follow in chase he promptly sinks.

Yonder, at the front, the general battle has begun, and a sound breaks out like the sound of ten million rocks battering in rowdy degringolation down a wooden stair reaching from the moon to the earth. And see how, really, that is good for Hardy—native to the very temper of his mother's womb—the sole rough music in the universe which can make his large spirit *dance!* It would be hard now to recognize in him the gloomy, cowering, burdened wight, who, half an hour ago, groaned in the *Hirosaki* conning-tower. His exhilaration is boundless; his face is flushed. If it were possible, joy now would re-dye the hair which grief had blanched. Here is his element, his day—great *Thursday*—and he, once more, Saxon Thor, red-handed, swinger of thunderbolts, tosser of linked lightnings. The oil of gladness is on his head. He feels his arm, his soul, his ordination. He knows that he cannot fail.

He wheels :—the *Hirosaki*, left alone, is steering S.—S.W.—W.—Then W. by N. What is left of the European fleet, thirty-five craft, most of them already gravely injured, have now changed places with the Japanese, they being to the east, the Japanese to the west of them. Both sides put their helms down to re-form and change. Only a solid phalanx of twenty ships remain in guard about the *Yoshino*, which is slowly forging ahead in her old direction.

The *Hirosaki* is signaling. The old starboard half

of ships are to follow her in single file; the old port are to watch evolutions of *Hirosaki*, and follow suit on their side.

Immediately the *Hirosaki's* bows turn a little to the south of eastward. Nineteen ships follow her with bows a little to the south of eastward. Sixteen ships follow her with bows a little to the north of eastward. At the utmost speed of the craft of lowest power they steam away in these directions.

The yellow men discern that the white are flying. Or is it not rather a mere feint to get at the precious, guarded ship? Yes, that is soon evidently it! for the two files of retreating ships turn south and north, and then in wide curves westward. The Japs are after them.

Between the Europeans are intervals of not more than six cables. The crowd of Japanese come two abreast, the nearest four about a knot astern of the two hindermost Europeans. The *Hirosaki* leads now the port European limb, the *Hero* the starboard.

The two hindermost Europeans in the two limbs are the Duch corvette *Van Galen*, and the British-Japanese battleship *Fugi*; these are the only direct combatants, and are using stern-guns. In three minutes the *Van Galen* dives, and the *Fugi* cranks and stops. The British force is reduced to thirty-three.

So far not a single yellow ship has sunk. Five, in the first charge, have been disabled, the rest only seriously injured by the destruction of unprotected crews. Hitherto they are victors twice and thrice.

They gain upon the retreating squadrons. The average of their speed is greater than that of the Europeans.

Suddenly, after four knots from the start, Hardy turns, and in a short outward curve comes back eastward. The starboard limb with a short outward curve, follow suit.

And now it becomes quite clear to every one on his side that, whatever his design, he is accomplishing it at a murderous, a disastrous cost. For as the ships come back, they present a long line of broadside to a still greater length of Japanese broadside—at horribly close quarters; and in the sudden, exclamatory, almost momentary, outrage of hell-fire which burst from both sides, the ships sink fast. The Yankee aim is like Fate; the gentlemen of England acquit themselves well, with precision, with tympana that do not quite burst, with brains that do not quite faint, with hands that do not fail. In that loud squall of wrath they

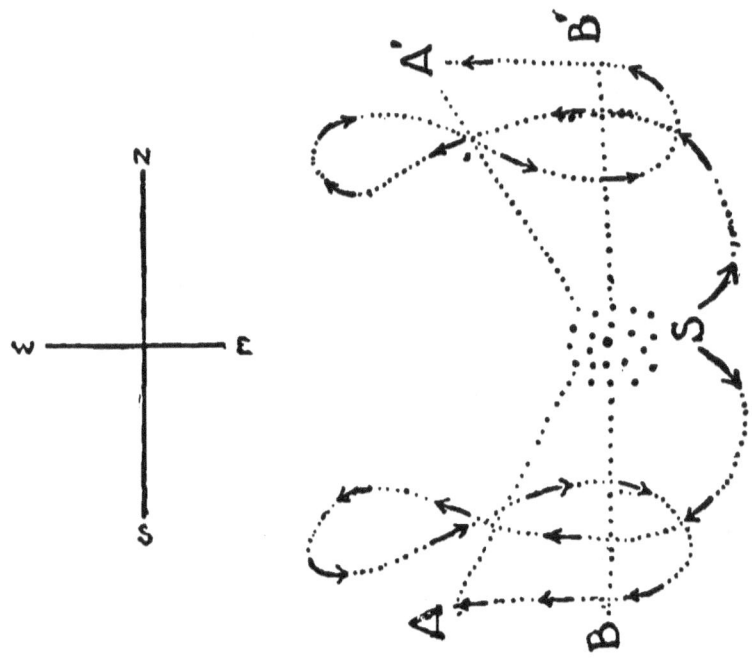

[The arrows in the diagram will show the course he took, S being the region of his start, and the dots in the central part representing the twenty ships round Yen How.]

sent twenty Japanese and Chinese ships to their graves in the two limbs; and they themselves are nine the less. The Japanese can afford the loss. Not they.

And now, in a minute—so fast do they tear along—the hostile fleets are parted. The enemy, all very near together, go on through the evolutionary curves which the British have described, and come following eastward.

They look now for a rush of the British upon the guarded ship, ready to follow. But no rush comes. The British keep on their way almost directly east.

A rush will come. But Hardy intends it to come when the Japs are in a position to intercept and cut him off. His thought, his patience, is far beyond their divination.

On he goes, leading them grandly through the mazes of that tragic, coiling minuet; and they follow, hasting gladly after him, triumphant, blind, fated.

The Pied Piper and his retinue . . . !

His ships sink one by one. He is aware of it with guilty disquiet. Will enough be left for his purpose? The falling out of each one by the wayside is to him like the taste of the second death.

The Japanese follow, not gaining ground this time, purposely keeping their distance, even increasing it, waiting for the next curve to westward, and the disastrous swift broadside.

And round again goes Hardy, wheeling outward, this time in a broader curve; and outward wheels his northern limb.

And once again clatters the sudden, exclamatory outrage of hell-fire, bursting from both sides, and Hardy comes out of it leaving behind him four, and the Japanese seven ships.

But the numerical strength of Hardy's remaining ships by no means represents his real strength. He is far weaker than he seems. Twenty-two floating craft are still visible to his eye, but craft so broken and undone, that he knows them incapable of further serious combat. Nearly ninety Japanese are as good for fight as ever.

Once more he is running westward, and the enemy, conscious now of easy victory, follow.

Westward—till his two foremost ships reach the positions marked A and A' in the diagram; and then hard to starboard races his helm. He goes driving sharp and straight with straining engines for the packed group of ships around the *Yoshino*.

This, then is " the rush "! But the Japanese ships,

their foremost being the position marked B and B', are nearer to the *Yoshino* than the British—are in the exact position in which Hardy, at the price of so much, has led them by the nose in long twining dance in order to place them.

What they will now do, he knows with certainty: they will cut him off. And, in fact, they turn sharply inward towards the precious, guarded ship, in order to intercept, and with one unanimous battery of their entire navy, finish at once his small remainders.

And thus it has suddenly happened that the whole yellow fleet is packed into a mere bundle of ships whose crews can speak to each other, whose steersmen need be cautious to avoid collision.

And when Hardy sees them so,—herded together by his harsh and baleful forethought,—like sheep driven into the penfold,—he knows that the yellow wave is dammed, and the greatest of his works is accomplished.

He could shriek aloud with cruel glee. . . .

Abroad roams his eye over the sea at his sinking and battered fleet. And as he looks he sees the foundering of the *Nile*.

And swift, with concentrated fury, the massed Japanese open fire upon his feeble residue.

At that moment the two limbs of the British are not more than three hundred yards from the front of the enemy.

And at that moment it is that an appalling, horrid, unparalleled thing is happening to the Yellow Men.

Hardy has signaled to his ships to launch among the crowding enemy every possible torpedo in his fleet.

His prohibition to use torpedoes in the combat had led his captains to expect some such final order. They were well ready.

The torpedo was, of course, the most deadly of the then instruments of war. If it exploded beneath a ship, *without fail* it destroyed her. But precisely the most deadly was also in general, the most unreliable of weapons. In general it might be counted upon to explode, not beneath an enemy's ship, but beneath a friend's, or, more likely still, beneath nothing at all. No serious tactician depended upon it.

In other words, it was not a good engine of aim at a given target, for it usually missed the target. Its course was more or less deflected by the waves—many things happened to it.

It was left to the eye of Hardy to perceive that its proper function was not one of aim at all toward a particular target, but one of loose direction toward a general mass. Under such conditions, it might be counted upon to annihilate in an instant all the assembled navies of the earth.

Prompt upon his order, the *restes* of his fleet, shattered as they were, were able to launch a ripping navy of nine more torpedoes than there were crowding Japanese and Chinese ships. The *Hirosaki* sent five: one from a bow-tube above the water-line, four submerged. All the other ships were ships with a varying number of tubes.

Three exploded in mutual collision before they reached the hostile fleet.

The rest arrived.

Men clapped and squeezed their hands upon their ears in expectant horror. The sea began to start, and rush and quake. A swift series of venomous, behemoth bangs—*quickening into ever madder swiftness*—and bawling at last into a steady brooling roar of passionate volleyed thunder that seemed to proceed from the very throat of Jehovah—rent the universal air, and split the hearing of all about that sea.

In London, men, three-eared, lifted a listing hand; far over Europe the rumor of it was heard; it was heard in Paris; it was heard in Brussels.

The British ships, shocked at each swift-recurrent detonation, jerked and started in convulsive throes, like dying fowl, upon the spasmic, kicking water—started, and leapt, and dived, and foundered. And as though in response to some vast upheaval of nature, down upon the sea swept at once a passion of wind, and a furious rain, and a black and total gloom.

Wide over the ocean the floating millions of yellow men heard the staccato of that dread tumult. And many a one imitated and repeated the sound with his lips.

Pop, pop, pop, they went; and pop, pop, pop, they went.

CHAPTER XXXIII.

THE "CRIME" OF HARDY.

It is not our business here to defend what has been called by leisured persons, sitting secure in their studies, the "crime" of Hardy.

Napoleon, taking the "Laws of Heaven" into his own hands, poisoned at Acre a number of his sick soldiers to save them from the hands of a cruel enemy. This, too, raised a cry, and was called "crime."

Another of that genus took upon himself to break the old Sabbath, and this raised a cry; but he did not mind.

Personally, we believe that the Great Man has, naturally and properly, these powers; that what he does is right; that the King can do no wrong.

Having cleared the sea of hostile war-ships in that world-tragedy in the Channel, Hardy found himself confronted with the problem of an army which was approaching a long line of English coast—not far off—an army which was not so much an army as a locust host.

What was he to do with them?

He could not set about and shoot them, for that, supposing he had had a large fleet, would have taken him a year, as Yen How said. Moreover, he had next to nothing to shoot them with.

Possibly he might, by spreading out his vast merchant fleet, armed with small guns, along the southeast coast, have kept them off till they starved; and this was supposed by his captains to be the course he would adopt.

But twenty million putrefying, derelict Chinese in barges floating at random in the Channel fair-way for the next year or two does not seem to have been after his mind. And to starve them on the open sea . . . even his pitiless heart revolted from that.

Or, they might have been driven back to France; or, seeing that they could not land on England, they might have returned to France on their own initiative. But Hardy did not wish them to return to France, thinking that there were already there a sufficient number of millions to engage the energies of his country for many a long day to come.

And so it happened that with the next morning's light —for at last something resembling a sun was seen, in spite of a furious gale of wind now blowing from the northwest—a strange, new spectacle, somewhere rather south of the latitude of Harwich, was seen— an immense multitude of ships covering the entire circle of sea, crawling painfully northward, each one trailing behind her a long line of barges crowded with men.

Hardy had the twenty millions in tow.

Not one had landed. To this diversion from their purpose they had made practically no resistance. If a Chinaman fired at the tug which came to secure his barge, the barge was promptly sunk by way of stern example. Most were unarmed with fire-arms.

For many hours during the afternoon and night of the battle thay toiled by the aid of search-lights, the ships having rendezvous at the N. Foreland, where, at about midnight, they congregated.

And now began the long, toilsome voyage northward.

What made the sufferings of both whites and Chinese worse, was the fact that, from the first bleak sunrise to the last, a heavy wet sea was running in the direction of the gale, and the creaking and laboring ships continually drenched their length in spray shipped over the dipping bows. A monotonous, light rain fell from the dark-gray and hurrying sky; and wide over the heaving, stale sea-water rolled down stretches of foaming sea-spue, as though the sea, sea-sick of itself, spumed the vomit of its bitter old unrest adown its own weary bosom. Through the cordage skirled in many tones the gale ; and salt was in the weird sagas that it skirled, and salt on the drenched decks, and salt in the wet sea, and the world was made of winds and brine.

Ever and again, a ship staggered through every timber, and stopped, tugged from behind by a backward swing of her ponderous following. Then on, crawling, again.

Here the tail led the dog.

Ever and again, pop would go a stout hawser, and away would go drifting to the S. E. the lessening scream of a barge-load of Chinamen.

Northward, northward, in vast funereal procession. And far yonder in the van of all—the *Hirosaki*, shattered-looking, butting, bulkily at the billows, as one who has seen worse things,—and come through them. In her cabin, which is crowded with wounded men, sits Hardy ; and near him, in long colloquy, a man named Henrick Björnson, a Norwegian sea-captain, who can shout broken English. What Hardy's deaf ears cannot make out, the man writes.

Northward crawls the unspeakable procession. It crosses the latitude of Hull, of Edinburgh ; it approaches the Norway coast ; it is at Bergen, at Christiansund. Always it crawls northward, and the *Hirosaki*, like the Pied Piper, leads. . . .

On the Tuesday foreday, the *Hirosaki*, in latitude 67° 48', slackened speed, and, while the dawning was still gray and ineffably bleak, the stragglers of the fleet came in.

Hardy had reached the grave-side now—the side of the one grave which Europe offered him for the burial of his dead.

Here and now a very great stress and sound of stormy winds was abroad, struggling for the held-on hat, blowing long ribbons of rope, and rolling before it billows of the sea.

The *Hirosaki* trumpeted a semicular formation, and

this for about an hour, from ship to ship, went trumpeted, till it reached the outermost rings of ships ten miles away. And in another hour and a half the vastest curve of ships, stretching northeast and southwest, that had ever been seen by an eye—the horns looking like tiny toys to the center, and invisible to each other—lay assembled, slowly steaming, or sailing close-hauled.

The morning lightened, but with ever a slow, and drear, and raw melancholy. It was the morning of an execution.

Hardy, with the flaps of an oilskin hat about his ears, in oilskins to his feet, stood clinging to a roping aft, facing the strong blast that loaded his breast with spasms of violence, and struggled for the ends of his flapping and quarreling skirts. And near him, in oilskins, stood a tall, broad-bearded man, the sea-captain Björnson.

Björnson touched him.

Hardy said:

"Well?"

Björnson took out his watch, held it before Hardy's eyes, put his mouth to Hardy's ears, and shouted:

"*It is time!*"

Hardy said:

"All right."

Already in the look of the water round, there was something horribly *outré*. It seemed as if the sea was getting calm—too calm for the wind that blew. It acquired a certain pallid oiliness in its heave.

Hardy called his trumpeter; he said:

"Tell the captain of the *Umbria* that I want a hundred and fifty Chinamen taken on board his ship—at once."

And down the wind went his command to the neighboring ship.

And in ten minutes this other:

"Ships to cast off barges, and follow flag-ship in same formation, west by south."

At once the *Hirosaki* put her bow in this direction.

The other ships, as their hawsers astern tightened on their new course, slipped them. A thousand hawsers slapped the sea.

The ships moved on. The barges remained.

But not stationary. They, too, moved—slowly—glidingly—right in the teeth of the wind—northward—all of them, over many a mile.

The barges fell into long strings, and patches, and colonies, like trailing sea-weed, always, as they glided, retaining their fixed relative positions.

The men in the barges saw surely that they moved. But what moved them? The crude early-morning blast blew upon their most woful, sallow faces.

Their rate of motion, from moment to moment, quickened. . . .

There was something now detestably baleful in the aspect of the water. The great waves had died to a glassy, heaving smoothness. Only, here and there in irregular patches over the surface, broke out stretches of vapid foam, or ghastly bubbles. And the ocean went gadding, gadding northward.

This is the first mood of the Maelstrom. . . .

Then a wonder happened: A string of barges shot suddenly askew, and went wildly hasting in a long curve to the east; and another string shot askew in a western curve; and in not more than a minute a hundred thousand barges were flightily ranging in curves of every shape and direction over the sea, flying a while—then slowly stopping—then flying off in new curves again.

Suddenly, all this motion ceased. The sea settled into a lake-like stillness, except for patches of bursting, simmering bubbles on its face.

But with the suddenness of the thunder-clap came a change. The surface rapidly assumed a morose hue of the deepest blue, a blue which was liker black. And at once it began to heave itself up into waves, mountain-high, which danced like the Merrymen in a swinging, oscillatory, up-and-down jig, as if buoyed up by some great submarine power which dandled, and tossed, and danced them. And down the steep sides of these cones of water poured the barges of the clinging, staring, screaming men.

But now again, suddenly, the mood is changed—and a Voice goes forth over the waters, a doleful sound of the sea. The high dancing waves die down, and immediately an awful wide change is taking place—a rapid, intense reorganization of the whole sea-surface—a breathless hurry and scurry of preparation for some unspeakable drama of the deep. There are tracts of black and choppy sea tumbling in roaring haste one way, and tracts tumbling like herds of ten thousand bellowing bisons another, as if flying across to take sides in some impending agony. And all at once the whole is over : and every wave, and eddy, and barge, and flake of froth slips into the sweep of one mighty, bawling, racing whirlpool.

Within the writhing uppermost ridge of this vast circumference, invisible under a fierce white wrath of shrieking spray, fly with a thousand wings the barges of the yellow men, fly on even keel, fly uplifted, spurned from the polish ebony of the dizzy basin of water. And as they fly, the storm smothers their gasping breaths, and lifts their hair. And as their speed intensifies to the droning sleep of the spinning-top, their queues stiffen and rise horizontal like darting serpents ; and twenty million straight and fluttering pigtails, keeping ever their distances, race in narrowing whorls towards a bottomless, staggering abyss, that yawns, six furlongs broad, within the central space.

Six miles away, his glass at his eyes, stands John Hardy, musing. . . .

. . . .

Opposite Christiansund, the *Hirosaki* and the *Umbria* were very near together ; and here a change of crew took place ; the entire crew of the *Umbria* transhipping into the *Hirosaki*, and one hundred and thirty of the *Hirosaki's* crew going over into the *Umbria*.

These hundred and thirty consisted exclusively of "Hundred-and-Eighty" men of Kiao-Chau fame.

It was a mysterious proceeding, incomprehensible to *Umbria* men, but readily comprehensible to some of the "Hundred and Eighty." These had sworn an oath.

On board the *Umbria* were a hundred and fifty Chinese.

Murray (he of the Diary) took over with him to the *Umbria* a small packet which he had received from Hardy's hand—which Hardy, in his turn, had received from a Dr. Fletcher of Harley Street.

The packet contained some hypodermic syringes, and three vials, containing a thick dark-gray liquid. . . .

The *Hirosaki* then continued on her southward way; but the *Umbria* put in at Christiansund.

There, on the strand near the town, shortly before morning, they landed two of the hundred and fifty Chinamen. In the right forearm of each of these two men was a tiny needleprick; and as they went walking toward the town, an ink-black spot appeared on the cheek of each, and a black froth ridged their lips. . . .

The *Umbria* then continued her voyage, which lasted two weeks. She stopped at Copenhagen, at Königsberg, at Stockholm, at St. Petersburg. And wherever she stopped, she landed two Chinamen with black spots on their cheeks, and a black froth at their lips. . . .

She continued her voyage. She stopped at Amsterdam, at Boulogne, at Bordeaux, at Genoa, at Constantinople, at Odessa, at seventy-five European ports. At each she left two Chinamen with needle-pricks in their forearms.

· · · · · · · ·

"Well, well, Brassey," said Hardy in the *Hirosaki* cabin, his arm flung spasmodically round the neck of Brassey, who had remained with him, "well, well, boy. I was once—I was once—different from this——"

His arm dropped heavily. Then suddenly, he pushed Brassey violently on the breast.

"Go away—go away—sir," he cried.

And in an instant his arm dropped heavily again, his chin on his breast.

He was no longer sane. His hand was thicker than itself with brother's blood. His final hour of darkness and tragedy was hasting to meet his life. All his sky was an ink of clouds. Now again he tarried, cowering, in Gethsemane.

He no longer slept. Now he roamed the cabin like a wild man: now he sat still and languid, his head on his hands, his eyes having in them the senility of old people's. Every five minutes he bent double in paroxysms of moist coughing. Always the sailor, Brassey, was by him.

The *Hirosaki* arrived at Dover on the Friday evening at seven. A red brand of fever was then on Hardy's brow.

He was taken through the crowd in a close carriage to the Lord Warden Hotel. The news was flashed abroad that he had arrived, and all the bells of England gladly lilted and welcomed his coming. Hardy could not hear them.

For him was neither joy nor sleep. Doctors were summoned, but Hardy would not see them.

He threw himself on a bed; but rose again and paced the chamber in shirt and trousers and socks to a late hour.

At eleven there was a ring. Brassey, who was in an ante-room received a card at the door from a servant, but said there was to be no admittance of any sort that night.

Hardy appeared suddenly at the inner door of the ante-room; he said:

"What is it?"

Brassey handed him the card, and Hardy looked at it.

"Ha! ha! ha!" he laughed at once. "My friend Edrapol! Ha! ha! ha! Edrapol, my old friend!"

He had wholly forgotten Edrapol.

. . . .

Behind the ruins of St. Mary's Church, northeast of the town, at two that morning—they fought.

The "Crime" of Hardy

Here the strong, prone will of Hardy had asserted itself. He had insisted, and could not be withstood by Brassey. Edrapol's second was a sailor from the *Hirosaki*, Hardy's was Brassey; and the weapons used were *Hirosaki* swords of Japanese design.

A full moon shone. Yonder on the footpath leading from the East Cliffs waits a carriage, which has been coachmanned by Brassey.

It is a barbarous duel. There is no doctor there. Positively only four men are in the secret.

They take places, sword in hand, stripped to their shirts. The seconds take their places too. There are two Admiral Colomb ship-lanterns.

This is a duel without venom on either side. In one mind there is the mere prone desperation of an hour of tragic gloom; in the other a mere coxcombish pleasure at finding once more a sword in his hand, and an antagonist before him.

Only two hearts throb as though they must burst the imprisoning bosom—the hearts of the seconds. The hearts of the principals are cool, though Hardy's body burns with fever.

The moment comes. Hardy coughs; Edrapol waits. Then the swords lift and cross.

And now ensues a three minutes' contest between the most exquisite conceivable science on the one side, and the shrewdest, quickest wit on the other.

Briskly ply the complex, gleaming steels, with feint and thrust and parry, in tierce and quarte and staccado, stab and hew—to the infinite surprise of Edrapol, who finds here a man that can fight, and is glad.

He braces himself to the matter, Edrapol. He rises *à la hauteur* of his antagonist. But rise as he may, the fame of great Edrapol is henceforth stained, and his sleeve—with a thin trickle of blood.

He flushes somewhat, Edrapol. It is necessary, then to *couper court?* He rises to a still greater height. Among the long white hairs of the famous man plays the night wind.

Then there is the sudden "Ah———," and the limp failure, and the strong contrast of red on white, and the sword clattering to the ground. The steel of Edrapol is in Hardy's bosom.

. . . . . .

The next morning Britain learned with woe and terror that he was wounded. He lay at the Lord Warden Hotel, and was unconscious ; but as to the wound, it was not dangerous. So ran the bulletins.

But by the next night he was tossing in acute hyperpyrexia, and was delirious. Miss Isabel Jay had hurried to his side in almost crazy scare, and about his apartment waited two royal ladies. In one of the anterooms of the suite sat old Mason, stricken to death, swaying his decrepit body from side to side.

Half-hourly bulletins were issued by the royal physicians.

At one time during the second night, Hardy seems to have gone back in imagination to the period of his tortures, uttering fearful screams, and exhibiting signs of the most abject terror. But toward morning, he became calmer under the influence of opiates.

About noon, Miss Jay's hand being then firmly gripped in his, he said quite coolly:

"A good strong coffin of Harveyed nickel steel dropped into the middle of the Channel. . . ."

And there stopped. Nor spoke again till some three hours afterwards, when, lifting up his right arm, he cried in a loud voice:

"By the Lord, I warn you, Yen How . . . !"

After this the delirium appeared to leave him. He sank into a quiet sleep, which, however, was made ominous by a throat-rattle, and the venous transparency of his far-sunken eyelids.

The nation waited on in a bitterness of suspense, humbling before the Almighty in anguished prayer for his life, *but* for his life. . . .

But at seven in the evening the end came. Hardy suddenly woke from his feeble slumber, jerked his body upright on the bed, as if an answer to some official summons and roll-call, screamed a sharp "*Here!*" and gasped, and died.

His Calvary was not heroic—without "vigor and rigor."

That the great man of England should perish by the hand of an impossible, very-foreign professional duellist, here was the very irony of Destiny. But so it was.

CHAPTER XXXIV

THE BLACK SPOT

WITH the death of Hardy the minuter detail of our chronicle must end.

The results of his malignest act of enmity against the yellow race—results far surpassing in horror and vastness those of any of his other acts—he did not live to witness.

It is certain that he could never have expected so widespread a result from the distribution of the injected Chinamen about the European coasts, for the simple reason that he did not know of Yen How's inauguration of the Yellow Gods at Paris, which inauguration was the chief cause of the universality on the Continent of the new Black Death.

As soon as an idol-less Chinaman was griped by the malady, or even saw the black spot on a neighbor's cheek, his first instinct was to rush toward the one place of hope—the temple at Paris. And as he rushed, he went spreading far and wide that winged plague, that more putrid Cholera, dissipating it among thousands, who, in their turn, rushed to infect wide millions. Within three weeks Europe was a rotting charnel-house.

But there came a check to the spread of the malady. It was effected partly by the bullet, and partly by fire. From every army headquarters troops were drafted abroad by the Japanese generals, with the mission of shooting down every plague-infected person. Entire towns were surrounded by armies, and then burned with all they contained. Over Europe these great holocausts mixed the solemn flares of their funeral fires with the running shrieks of massacred millions. China had turned her glutted sword upon herself; and on the earth was heard the wails, and seen the smoke, of Tophet.

Yet in the course of some five months the plague was over, the flames died down, the massacres ceased; and still the white races found themselves confronted with the long, enormous task of clearing out of Europe over a hundred million yellow men.

The work was only made possible by the fact that, immediately on taking possession of a country, each Chinese army of occupation had, as we have explained, split itself up, become demobilized, and filled the towns and villages like ordinary settlers, after slaughtering those of the inhabitants whom they found there.

But in each of the old European countries a nucleus of the great nomad hosts had been ordained by the forethought of Yen How to retain their organization; and these, provided with headquarters, staffs, and garrisons, remained as standing armies, using the military centers and apparatus of the nations they had displaced. In Russia there remained three million yellow soldiers; in Germany and Austria, four; in France, two; in Italy, one; and Scandinavia some thousands. These ten millions would, but for the plague, have numbered seventeen millions.

And it was with these ten that the two English armies withdrawn from France and Germany at the moment of the irruption, together with the white races of the New World and Australia, had to do.

The United States had no army worth mentioning; alone of nations she had, however, that spirit of intelligent audacity which, by a species of swift magic, can turn her every citizen, not merely into a soldier, but into a general. And now she was roused: a wave of ineffable indignation, of high enthusiasm, of tender brotherhood, passed over the land. Into all the centers of enlistment, thousands upon thousands of volunteers poured each day. Before the end of the plague, three army corps of 100,000 men each had been shipped from

New York, Boston, and Philadelphia in detachments of twenty or thirty thousand raw levies, bringing vast supplies of field-stores, horses, ammunition, and clothing. The New World was coming back to save the Old. So far off and unguessable are the meanings of Destiny.

The six millions of Canada and the six of Australia sent out each a hundred thousand of their sons; and the fleets of the states of South America, forgetting their mutual jealousies, conveyed an army of mixed races, numbering eighty thousand, to the shores of Britain. England became the rendezvous of the white world.

Still, at the beginning of the four campaigns, all these contributions provided an army of less than a million, with which to confront ten millions of yellow men.

The ten millions, however, were divided into five war-hosts. To fight their combination would have been impossible; to destroy them in detail not so hopeless.

The great brain which could have welded, and wielded, and led them, by sure, infallible commonsense, to certain victory, was dead.

The main white army fought in Germany: it consisted of the British forces withdrawn from France and Germany, and was led by Kaiser Wilhelm. (Wilhelm, having refused to leave the Fatherland on the Chinese irruption, had been seized by the members of a conspiracy initiated by Count Caprivi; the gallant man had been taken *bound* to a ship, and brought over to England. To him was given the command of the most seasoned division of the invading armies.)

The French division was led by Lord Wolseley in person, with General Miles as second in command; it consisted solely of the small standing army and the new levies from the United States; Australians and Canadians combined followed Lord Roberts to Cronstadt; and the Latin races of South America were led by Sir Evelyn Wood into the Bay of Naples.

The same general system of tactics was adopted by

each of these armies—the tactics of Fabius: ill-armed, unskilled, and inchoate, as were the hosts with which they fought, those hosts were still overwhelming in number, desperate in temper. The idea of the white men was to wear them out by galling sorties and swift retreats; to demoralize and undermine them by strategic subtleties, harassing attacks, and untiring maneuvering.

The campaigns, accordingly, were long-drawn. The setting sun of the century was already on the point of disappearance when, simultaneously, in Lombardy and at Moscow, the last armed mob of yellow men in those countries scattered to the winds.

But through all that space of plain from Waterloo to Quatre Bras, the conflict between the small army, now an army of veterans, and the large army, now not so large, was still at issue. And in the flat-lands round Stralsund, Wilhelm, with his English, was hard put to it to maintain a footing.

It was here that the great crowning event of that world-drama of the yellow deluge transacted itself, on the 25th of August, 1900.

It was toward four in the afternoon: a dull, hot day, which made the outposts on both sides rely rather upon their ears than seek to penetrate with the eyes the marsh-mists that enveloped the plain.

The Kaiser, in harmony with long-tried tactics, had organized that morning a Reconnaissance Corps, specially drafted from the wings of his army, for the purpose of hurling it in a well-timed sally upon the advance lines of the Chinese. The division consisted of the Seaforths, the 1st Royal Dragoons, the Royal Irish Regiment, and other troops of the first class; cavalry and infantry being supported by nine batteries of Horse Gunners. The corps rested till the afternoon on the seaward slopes, somewhat toward the left of the line of fortifications. The rank, chill mist thickened from hour to hour.

The division consisted of not more than 20,000 infantry and 5,000 sabers, a body not too unwieldy for agile movement and ready retreat, yet large enough to leave motionless behind it ten times its number of pigtails.

Soon after four it went moving rapidly over the plain. It was commanded by Lieutenant-General Henderson of the Buffs.

The Chinese army, at this time, was not without discipline of a kind; it had seen fire, and stood it, and returned it with effect. It had become a genuine instrument of war.

The alarm that the white men were upon their center was no sooner given than the advance ranks put themselves in a position to receive the onset of the English; and when a hot fire from all arms came pouring into their midst, they only wavered slightly; by the time the white infantry had come into moderately close conflict with the front ranks, a battery commanding their advance from a rising ground near by was plowing them with shrapnel.

And a few minutes afterwards, a rally in the yellow front ranks was effected by three of their vast regiments hurrying up from the main body.

A colonel of the 2d Life Guards, clearly perceiving now that the advance had been too rash, that retreat, in spite of the mist, must mean mere havoc to the whole corps, pointed frantically at the battery, shrieking above the din, "Guards! those guns must be taken!" And, with sabers waving, the regiment went careering for the guns.

Before they reached the foot of the hill, they were mown down almost to a man.

The Reconnaissance Corps, now inextricably involved with the enemy, seemed cut off from hope. But a dragoon, who had been despatched to warn headquarters of the position of affairs, met two regiments of infantry hurrying up at the double, and soon learned that fighting orders had been passed all along the British lines. Wilhelm had resolved upon a decisive blow there and then.

The *motif* of this mad-looking step lay in a despatch which he had just received by sea from Lord Wolseley. By a supreme stroke of tactics, originating from his

The Black Spot

second in command, the Commander-in-Chief's Texas rangers and Colorado bushmen had accomplished at Waterloo an appalling rout of the enemy, leaving seven hundred thousand dead on the field. The Belgium-Germany railway lines were in his hand: he was on the point of setting out to augment the forces round Stralsund.

Wilhelm thereupon made a calculation of rates and distances, and partly in the hope of relieving the intangled Reconnaissance Corps, with rash faith in his lucky star, and éager once more to whirl his own saber in the air, he resolved, late and dark as it was, to give instant battle.

It was like the attack of an eagle upon an elephant. With splendid suddenness his whole army hurled itself forward. The onset was dashing, impassioned, gallant, but desperate. The Chinese front lay along a length of ten miles, and precisely because every attack, at every point, made by the British was successful, therefore their destruction was the more certain. Everywhere they were surrounded. While the battle was still desperately raging, night fell.

Already there lay on the plain, of the British 20,000 dead, and of the yellow men 300,000.

At eight the whirl and uproar of battle was still unabated; and the heart of the Kaiser misgave him, as he looked from a mound through a night-glass at the wheeling scrimmage in which the 1st Dragoons were desperately seeking to extricate themselves from the trampled death, and the furious tornado of life, around them. From far away through the night there came to him an occasional unanimous scream of ten thousand parching throats—sure sign of some finished victory of the yellow man.

But either he had calculated well, or the tendencies of the world were on his side.

Away back, nearly as far as Franzburg, a party of wild horsemen, with knees jammed into the ribs of horses without saddles, come scampering through a brigade of astounded yellow men, which stood awaiting fighting orders. They are white men come pelting from nowhere, born far where the sun sets: the farthest East and the farthest West have met.

And, presently, the wide storm of clattering, spattering hooves come thundering in overwhelming torrents, in thousands and hundreds of thousands, in heaped-up, ever-succeeding accumulation, like rivers of rushing sound. Their impetuosity cannot be checked, because the wind cannot be checked; and they attack in the rear; and each of them is a general.

And now the eyes of Wilhelm, noting wide confusion from afar, lighten; and strange raving rumors and growths of sound come to his ears from out of the distant dark. And within fifteen minutes, the millions of the yellow men, hurried inward from front and rear, are no more an army, but an astounded rout, flying from nothing upon death, caught in error and delusion, bewildered, blind, and panic-struck. They cast away their weapons in a horror of haste, they trample themselves to death in purposeless fury. Never on the earth was half such an extravagance of carnage in similar space, such an excess and waste of slaughter, such a *banalité* of death, such a frenzy of *mêlée*. The white men, drunk with blood, become mere beasts of prey, chopping at flesh in feeble, exhausted ecstasy. The night grows old, and still they hunt, they track; they slip in moving lagoons of gore, and fall, and faint; and die trampled, careless; or rise, and hunt, and hack. The battle degenerates into a debauch of hell. . . .

And with the morning light the plain of Stralsund, viewed from the summits of the low hills, is like a saffron ocean of stagnant putridity, whereon twist and coil, feeding on the ancient slime, myriads of jet-black snakes. Here in Armageddon—the last great agony of struggle between the white man and the yellow: the Act is over.

But only the Fourth Act. The earth remains; Spring, and the joy of life, and the intensities of the pulse, will return. Let us look a moment, four months later, at a great Assembly in the Albert Hall at London. It is on what, properly speaking, is the third day of a new century—the 3d of January, 1901.

Far up the tiers of galleries human heads throng indistinctly, incalculable as leaves in Valombrosa. The great circle of the hall is gay with drooping flags; the platform is draped with them: the flags of two nations, which yet, by a mystery of Destiny, are forever one.

About the building the people of the two nations throng all the streets, knowing that this day is a Hegira of the world, such as has not yet been. And orators emerge above that sea of heads, and there are huzzas, and wide tendencies and motions, precisely as when through the innumerable forest the breezes run tittering in torrents of rumors.

But within, on the platform, the President of the American States is sitting, and beside him the Prime Minister of England stands speaking: and sometimes, so solemn and world-wide is felt to be the occasion, that the spoken words have in them something of the strain of prophecy:

"This reshipment, then," he says, "of the remnants of the yellow men to their natural home being now well on the way toward completion, we are faced by the task of rehabilitating and administering that portion of the earth, which, since authentic history, has played the greatest part in its events. Once more to us of these modern days comes forth the command: Go forth and replenish the earth, and be ye fruitful, and multiply. Happily, the task before us is made far less complex by the extraordinary event of which our eyes have been the witness. In the complexity of the nations, who, before that event, contended for the possession of the earth, there had come to be a certain madness, an impossibility of solution, a Babel of purposes. Never on any eternal basis could Peace—the first essential to that predicted ten-thousand-years of Man's upward march—have been established. Now our way—most marvelously, if you will think of it—has been made plain before us. One all-dominant race has been so clearly marked out by Destiny to renew and administer the earth, that no impulse to contradict the fact will arise in any other: a race divided, indeed, into two portions, yet so essentially one, as to resemble not so much two brothers, as two arms of the same body. If the configuration of the map of the world has shown it to be convenient to hand over to the Western branch of that race the administration of the continent of Asia, while the Eastern exercises its special sway over Europe and Africa, it is not that any bargaining has been found necessary between us, as though the left arm should envy the right. Rather has our thought been of the immense difficulties which, whatever convention be made, must now necessarily lie in both our paths. Yet not to that near and arduous future, but to the farther and fairer time which, surely now, lies ahead, let us all look. The centuries are not ended—the years of Destiny will unfold themselves. The Apostle John, being in the Spirit on the Lord's Day, predicted that Time shall Be No More; I, standing before you on the threshold of this late new Era, predict that Time shall Be. I foresee that the relative positions of the Suns shall change; and the Sword of Orion shall curve into a Pruning-hook, and between the Virgin and the Lion there shall grow hoar —a *rapprochement*. Viewed from this mood, the race of man seems but to have begun its course; yet not so immature is its history but that it has had space to exhibit, if never before, then now, the fact of some Secret which informs it, and some Wind which wafts it. It moves—it moves! The dreams of the poets were not extravagant enough; see, the world overtakes them, and surpasses them! to-day, already we see the strange accomplishment of that vision of yesterday:

"When the war-drums throbbed no longer, and the battle-flags were furled
In the Parliament of Man, the Federation of the World. . . ."

THE END.

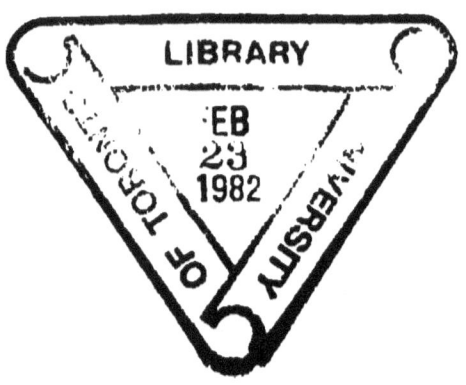

**PLEASE DO NOT REMOVE
CARDS OR SLIPS FROM THIS POCKET**

UNIVERSITY OF TORONTO LIBRARY

PR   Shiel, M. P (Matthew Phipps)
6037   The yellow danger
H57Y38
1899

www.ingramcontent.com/pod-product-compliance
Lightning Source LLC
Chambersburg PA
CBHW030341230426
43664CB00007BA/488